AF230795

# Language, Crime and Courts

in Contemporary Africa and Beyond

**EDITORS**

Russell H. Kaschula

Monwabisi K. Ralarala

Georgina Heydon

*Language, Crime and Courts in Contemporary Africa and Beyond*

Published by African Sun Media under the SUN PReSS imprint
Place of publication: Stellenbosch, South Africa



First edition 2023

ISBN 978-1-991260-18-5
ISBN 978-1-991260-19-2  (e-book)
https://doi.org/10.52779/9781991260192

Set in Warnock Pro Light 10/14.5

Typesetting and production by African Sun Media
Cover design by African Sun Media Create

SUN PReSS is an imprint of African Sun Media. Scholarly, professional and reference works are published under this imprint in print and electronic formats.

This publication can be ordered from:
orders@africansunmedia.co.za
Takealot: bit.ly/2monsfl
Google Books: bit.ly/2k1Uilm
africansunmedia.store.it.si *(e-books)*
Amazon: amzn.to/2ktL.pkL

Visit africansunmedia.co.za for more information.

# CONTENTS



## Part I | Language and the justice system



## Part II | Language and gender-based violence

## Part III | Language and crime

# LIST OF TABLES

# LIST OF FIGURES

# SERIES FOREWORD

*Series Editors*

Monwabisi K. Ralarala (SA)

Russell H. Kaschula (SA)

Georgina Heydon (Australia)

**Studies in Forensic and Legal Linguistics in Africa and Beyond (SF&LLA)** is an exciting book series on forensic linguistics, and language and the law. The role of language in the legal process, in establishing a just society, cannot be overemphasised, particularly in a multilingual and multicultural African context. Through case studies, as well as through empirical research, the intention of the series is therefore to explore issues of relevance in forensic linguistics and in language and the law. This series distinguishes itself by encompassing specific disciplines in the domains of humanities and social sciences. A research programme of this nature is highly interdisciplinary, involving scholars from the fields of linguistics, interpreting and translating languages, migration, psychology, criminology, policing and the law. The peculiarity of the series is its foregrounding of African linguistic and legal contexts within the broader framework of worldwide research that resonates with the African experience. These volumes not only strive for contemporary relevance, but also share research findings with the potential to effect positive change in people's lives. The purpose of the series is to discuss various theoretical frameworks and methodological choices, along with their applicability in a variety of contexts. In this way, the series will provide a global audience with a unique analysis of the benefits gained through these studies, as well as the challenges encountered. To this end, we wish to encourage scholars with a keen interest in this field to submit book proposals for consideration in the series.

## Published

1. *New frontiers in forensic linguistics: Themes and perspectives in language and law in Africa and beyond* (2019)

2. *A handbook on legal language and the quest for linguistic equality in South Africa and beyond* (2021)

3. *Language and the law: Global perspectives in forensic linguistics from Africa and beyond* (2022)

# ACKNOWLEDGEMENTS

The editors of this volume would like to express their genuine gratitude to anonymous peer reviewers who took the time to engage profoundly and meticulously with the review process. Their thoughtful contribution and helpful recommendations are acknowledged. Of note is that all the chapters between the covers of this book have been subjected to the required process of anonymous peer review.

From time to time, we have enlisted the research assistance of our postgraduate students, Ms Andrea Shireen Barnes and Ms Buhle Sondwana, whose enquiring minds and willingness to form part of this community of practice has kept us going. We owe much of the smooth completion of this book to their project administration capabilities.

Finally, we wish to express our appreciation to Dr Jenny Wright who served as a critical reader for this volume. Her thorough grounding in editing has served well in ensuring additional quality control for this work.

This work is based on the research supported by the National Heritage Council (NHC). Opinions, findings, conclusions and recommendations expressed in this publication are those of the editors and authors, and the NHC accepts no liability in this regard.

# ABOUT THE EDITORS

**Russell H. Kaschula** is a Professor in the Department of African Language Studies at the University of the Western Cape, where he is the Postgraduate Coordinator. He also holds the Chair in Forensic Linguistics and Multilingualism. He has published widely in the field of Applied Language Studies. His recent books include *Languages, identities and intercultural communication in South Africa and beyond* (winner of the 2022 UWC Book Award), published by Routledge in New York and London; and he has co-edited the *Handbook on legal languages* as well as *Language and the law: Global perspectives in forensic linguistics from Africa and beyond,* published by African Sun Media. He is one of the founders of the Handbook of Language Planning for Africa Series (HLPA) published by BRILL (Netherlands). The first book, dealing with the SADC region, was published in July 2022. He has a particular interest in language and crime, literary geography, as well as sociolinguistics more generally. He serves as Secretary to the newly formed African Association of Forensic and Legal Linguists (AAFLL); he is also a member of the International Advisory Board to the *International Journal for the Semiotics of Law.*

**Monwabisi Knowledge Ralarala** is a Professor and the Dean of the Faculty of Arts and Humanities at the University of the Western Cape. Apart from being a Canon Collins Educational and Legal Assistance Trust alumnus, Monwabisi Ralarala is the 2017 recipient of the Neville Alexander Award for the Promotion of Multilingualism. His research interests are quite diverse but follow three lines: language rights and multilingualism in higher education; forensic linguistics, and translation studies. He has also published articles and book chapters, mainly in forensic linguistics, translation studies and language policy in higher education. His co-authored and co-edited books include these: *African language and language practice research in the 21st century: Interdisciplinary themes and perspectives* (2017, CASAS); *New frontiers in forensic linguistics: Themes and perspectives in language and law in Africa and beyond* (2019, African Sun Media); *Knowledge beyond colour lines: Towards repurposing knowledge generation in South African higher education* (2021, UWC Press); *A handbook on legal languages and the quest for linguistic equality in South Africa and beyond* (2021, African Sun Media), and *Language and the law: Global perspectives in forensic linguistics from Africa and beyond* (2022, African Sun Media). He is the founder and Chief Series Editor of Studies in Forensic and Legal Linguistics in Africa and Beyond (SF&LLA), as well as the International Advisory Board Member for the *International Journal for the Semiotics of Law.* He serves as Chairperson to the newly formed African Association of Forensic and Legal Linguists (AAFLL).

**Georgina Heydon** is a Professor in Criminology and Justice Studies at the Royal Melbourne Institute of Technology, Australia. Her research analyses the language of police interviewing and other forms of evidential language in the justice system in Australia, as well as in Mozambique (with Dr Eliseu Mabasso) and in Indonesia (with Dr R. Dian Muniroh). Prof. Heydon is a past President of the International Association of Forensic and Legal Linguistics and, as a forensic linguist, she provides expert evidence on authorship identification and commercial trademark cases. Her current research focuses on the reporting of sexual assault. She is also working with Aboriginal community organisations towards developing a methodology for research field interviews that combines cognitive interviewing and traditional yarning methods.

# FOREWORD

Let me begin with a 'faction', a blend of fact and fiction. It draws on factual material presented by Sister Makoni (2013). It is the story of X, an adult isiNdebele-speaking female, married, and with minimal education. Steeped as X is in her cultural traditions, she uses *isihlonipho sabafazi* in addressing her male in-laws as well as in more formal, public settings. *Isihlonipho* is a gynocentric variety of isiNdebele and, indeed, of other isiNguni languages. The name by which this gynolect is called translates literally as 'language of respect'. A hallmark of *isihlonipho* is indirection and deference. X is reluctantly in court to seek justice.

She has been raped.

She is under cross-examination by counsel to her assailant. The trial language is isiNdebele. Although the defence counsel is also female, and knows *isihlonipho*, she is in court in a different identity, in a professional lawyerly capacity. She is poised to exploit the indirection and other expressive restrictions that *isihlonipho* places on its users to cast doubts on X's credibility and to secure her client's acquittal. She knows the courtroom is packed with X's husband, in-laws, other family, church members, among others. She also knows that, in courtrooms, trial discourse in (whatever language) values straight and precise utterances delivered in a manner constructed by the court as confident, which may mean: sustained eye contact, upright bodily pose, a specific tone of voice and pace of delivery; no hesitation, nor pauses, except when passed off as necessary for providing an expected, well thought-through, accurate response. In short, the language of trial discourse is everything *isihlonipho* is not.

In the following faction, an exchange translated into English, we see the defence attorney putting her strategy to work. The vagueness and the shyness associated with the use of *isihlonipho* can be gleaned from the expressions and actions in bold.

> **Defence attorney**: So, after he tripped you, what happened?
>
> **X**: He **uncovered the girl**.
>
> **Attorney**: What girl?
>
> **X**: **(Quiet, avoids eye contact, begins to sob)**
>
> **Attorney**: Anyway, let's continue. What happened next?
>
> **X**: He gave her ... **a wheel**.
>
> **Attorney**: Wheel? Are you referring to his penis, yes or no? And did you take it, yes or no?

> **X**: (looks down, after a few long moments, answers): He had a knife and he pushed his pipe into the cake.
>
> **Attorney**: Now, there was also a cake, apparently. What time was the cake baked or rather, what time was this cake eaten with a pipe?
>
> **X**: I don't know. I think it//…
>
> **Attorney**: //you think? You don't know?
>
> **X**: My shadow was not showing in front of me.
>
> **Attorney**: You do know a lot of things: the other girl, a wheel, a pipe, a knife, a cake, shadow, all of which you have shared with a comportment that makes you very believable. I have no further questions, my Lord.

Yes, X's attorney will have the opportunity for redirect examination. Yes, X's attorney might have objected to certain questions. Yes, a sympathetic trial judge may, within limits of what an adversarial proceeding allows for, have intervened to protect a vulnerable witness by alerting the defence attorney to X's aversion to explicit descriptions. Yet there is no mistaking how the defence attorney's concluding tongue-in-cheek remark exploits the verbal constraints, and accompanying non-verbal semiotics of *isihlonipho*, to attack X's competence and credibility as a witness, a witness to her own defilement.

Through a decolonial and Southern epistemologies lens, this exchange raises a concern for legal jurisprudence and for forensic linguistics in Africa, especially in light of Elder Ngugi wa Thiong'o's (1998:90) view, as cited by Sister Makoni, that "[l]awyering is really an exercise in words and definitions. Even the slightest nuance in a word or sentence can be crucial in determining the outcome of a case. Yet the victim is completely outside the linguistic universe of the justice system".

The question arises as to what justice is dispensed in an African temple of justice, where law of evidence and procedure:

- is in part at least characterised by its colonial heritage;
- is not primarily informed by local circumstances in its application of principles related to burden of proof, relevance, admissibility, competence and credibility of witnesses;
- reflects a culture of language use with provincial origins that is today passed off as universal.

In many post-colonies in Africa and elsewhere in the Global South, common law, civil law and procedural law, reflect the cultural script of their colonial heritage. Cultural scripts are "different unwritten rules about how to behave, how to speak, and also how to think and how to feel", which are inferred from the words and expressions used in languages of specific groups (Wierzbicka, 2006:92). Indeed, some of the earlier work on contrastive rhetoric and semiotics pointed out differences across cultures in such aspects of discourse as linearity vs circularity, directness vs indirectness, responsibility for unpacking the contents of a message residing with the author/speaker vs reader/listener, the role of oculesics in communication, etc.

Legal culture, the law of evidence and procedure in this instance, equally bears the imprint of this cultural script irrespective of whether a trial is conducted in English or in isiNdebele. This culture "strongly reflects a number of values that Wierzbicka identifies as core Anglo values" (McCaul 2011:14), including the "emphasis on distinguishing what one knows from what one thinks" (Wierzbicka, 2006:37). Plaintiff X is thus indeed left "completely outside the linguistic universe of [a] justice system" that considers witnesses as less believable because their testimonies:

- are not linear and direct,
- are not offered with eyes fixed on the interlocutor,
- do not unpack for the court, and in a manner that is effortless, all the sordid and obscene details of an event,
- do not place events recounted within a monochronic orientation to time,
- do not get the import of the distinction between 'I think' and 'I know'.

The foregoing provides a snapshot of the challenges that the scholarship of forensic linguistics in Africa, in collaboration with decolonial legal jurisprudence, is called upon to address. As an applied linguistics discipline and profession, forensic linguistics elucidates and uses knowledge from principled language study to generate evidence that supports, perhaps even impedes, fact-finding in a range of contexts, and especially in the dispensation of justice by law enforcement and/or the court system. Posers for decolonial activists in forensic linguistics and legal jurisprudence may include the following:

- To which extent does the discourse of courtroom trial and the jurisprudence on evidence and procedure reflect a cultural script that is indexical of patriarchy and values of European (Roman, Dutch, English) society?
- To which extent are judicial officers aware of how language interfaces with culture to engender unfair prejudice, specifically through interpretations of a set of related concepts, such as burden of proof, relevance, admissibility, and the probative value of testimonial evidence?

It is against this backdrop of a need for critical engagement with jurisprudence that this volume is to be appreciated. The editors and contributors are to be congratulated for offering a range of perspectives from the Global South that detail how language is central to the preoccupations of the justice system. The insights in this and other volumes in the series managed by the editors bid fair to provide a basis for thinking about pathways to decolonise sources of the law and to enhance semiotic access to the law and to justice. This will no doubt also gladden the heart of Elder Roger Shuy (author of Chapter 1 of this book), whose involvement as linguistics expert in the Cullen Davis murder trial in 1978 is widely acknowledged as signalling the birth of forensic linguistics (Baugh, 2022).

**Professor Bassey E. Antia**

*Department of Linguistics*
*University of the Western Cape, South Africa*

# References

Baugh, J. 2022. Linguistics for legal purposes. In: S. Makoni, S. Madany-Saá, B.E. Antia & R. Lomeu Gomes (eds.). *Decolonial voices, language and race*. Bristol: Multilingual Matters. 84-97.

Makoni, B. 2014. Feminizing linguistic human rights: Use of *isihlonipho sabafazi* in the courtroom and intra-group linguistic differences. *Journal of Multicultural Discourses*, 9:1, 27-43.

McCaul, K. 2011. Understanding courtroom communication through cultural scripts. In: Anne Wagner & Le Cheng (eds.). *Exploring courtroom discourse: The language of power and control*. Surrey: Ashgate Publishing. 11-28.

Thiong'o, Ngugi wa. 1998. *Penpoints, gunpoints, and dreams: Towards a critical theory of the arts and the state in Africa*. Oxford: Oxford University Press.

Wierzbicka, A. 2006. *English: Meaning and culture*. Oxford: University Press.

# INTRODUCTION

*Russell H. Kaschula*
*Monwabisi K. Ralarala*
*Georgina Heydon*

In 2019, the first volume in this series introduced readers to the state of forensic linguistics in Southern Africa at that time. Previously, during an inaugural conference on forensic linguistics held on 7 June 2018, in Cape Town, scholars from across the main disciplines of linguistics, interpreting and translating, and law, shared their insights into various aspects of language used in legal or judicial contexts. This was a landmark event in several ways: it was the first such meeting in Southern Africa; it led directly to the publication of the edited collection, *New frontiers in forensic linguistics: Themes and perspectives in language and law in Africa and beyond* (Ralarala, Kaschula & Heydon, 2019), which launched the current book series; and it marked the beginning of a closer relationship between forensic linguistic scholars in sub-Saharan Africa and the global forensic linguistic community. Since that conference, African scholars in language and the law have continued their thoughtful engagement with this field, making further contributions in a range of journals and, of course, through this book series. In 2022, the African Association of Forensic and Legal Linguists (AAFLL) was formed at the 23rd Biennial International Conference of the African Languages Association of Southern Africa (ALASA) held at the University of the Western Cape. A forensic linguistics workshop was also held at this conference.

With these developments, coupled with the launch of Volumes II and III: *A handbook on legal language and the quest for linguistic equality in South Africa and beyond* (Docrat, Kaschula & Ralarala, 2021), and *Language and the law: Global perspectives in forensic linguistics from Africa and beyond* (Ralarala, Kaschula & Heydon, 2022), we can safely say that there is a concerted effort, not only to grow the discipline on the continent, but also to meet the growing interest and demand for advanced training in scientific linguistic analysis of language and its application, use and relevance to legal matters.

It is worth noting that the field of forensic linguistics is still developing in many parts of the world, including sub-Saharan Africa; and further research, such as that presented in this volume, is needed to understand fully the extent and potential of its applications in the region. In particular, it is possible to identify several contentious aspects of forensic linguistics that have motivated many scholars and professionals in Africa and elsewhere to push for further development within the field:

- Reliability of linguistic analysis: The results of linguistic analysis may sometimes be subjective and open to interpretation, leading to questions about the reliability and validity of linguistic evidence in legal proceedings.
- Expert witness credibility: There may be disputes over the qualifications and credibility of linguistic experts in legal proceedings, with questions raised about their impartiality and expertise.
- Admissibility of linguistic evidence: There may be debates over the admissibility of linguistic evidence in court, particularly when it is used to support or undermine witness testimony or other forms of evidence.
- Language proficiency and interpretation: In multilingual contexts like South Africa, there may be challenges in ensuring that all parties to legal proceedings have a sufficient level of proficiency in the language used in court and in written legal documents. There may also be disputes over the interpretation of language evidence, particularly where different languages are used.
- Bias and discrimination: There may be concerns about implicit bias and discrimination in the analysis and interpretation of language evidence in legal proceedings, particularly in cases involving minority language communities.

These contested aspects of forensic linguistics highlight the importance of careful and transparent application of linguistic analysis in legal proceedings to ensure fairness and impartiality.

The research represented in this volume, and in the series as a whole, is intended to provide critical analyses and findings that can underpin the development of language policies, practice guides and other resources that support a fair and accessible legal system. However, this will also require well-developed teaching and research programmes, so it is our intention that this volume will continue to support the growth of forensic linguistics in Southern African universities and nurture the next generation of scholars dedicated to forensic and legal linguistics. This aim will be supported by the newly formed African Association of Forensic and Legal Linguists (AAFLL), which will help to coordinate the study of forensic linguistics in Africa. A proposal for an African journal of forensic and legal linguistics is being considered as part of this suite of initiatives.

Thus, this book series, Studies in Forensic and Legal Linguistics in Africa and Beyond, Volumes I, II, III and IV continues to play an important role in bringing African forensic linguistic scholarship to a wider audience, while simultaneously promoting the field amongst academic and legal institutions in Africa.

# Outline and summary of chapters

The book comprises three interconnected themes:

Part I:  Language and the justice system;
Part II:  Language and gender-based violence (GBV); and
Part III:  Language and crime.

## *Part I: Language and the justice system*

Chapter 1 in this section is titled 'The constants and variables of forensic linguistics'. This chapter is the work of Roger Shuy, one of the leading authors on the topic of language and crime. For this reason, the chapter serves as the first chapter of the book. The role of forensic linguists in the legal arena is to consult with retaining lawyers or the court. Sometimes the linguist serves as an expert witness who writes reports and testifies at hearings and trials. The chapter points out that, since most criminal and civil law cases contain language evidence, it is altogether appropriate for experts to analyse this language in the same way that medical, accounting and engineering experts analyse the evidence in those fields.

The chapter further highlights that linguistics is a science that the legal community is gradually coming to recognise as useful and often crucial to the process of reaching justice, a process that includes examining the language of police interrogations, the language evidence in a case, and the language used by law enforcement, witnesses, lawyers and judges during the various stages of the legal process. The courts now recognise forensic linguistics in many jurisdictions of the world, including England, Wales, America, Australia, Germany and, increasingly, in Africa. Meanwhile, jurisdictions in other parts of the world are beginning to recognise the usefulness of linguistic analysis of legal evidence. This chapter provides an overview of the linguistic analysis of legal evidence in various contexts. It therefore provides a 'parting shot' to the book, given the role of guns and weapons in relation to crimes committed globally.

Chapter 2, written by Wellman Kondowe and George Mtanga, is titled 'Interruptions as linguistic whistles: An examination of judges' language in Malawian courtroom discourse'. This chapter investigates the role of interruptions in the administration and delivery of justice in the law court using data from Malawi's 2019 presidential elections case. Data was downloaded from websites in MP3 and MP4 formats and transcribed manually. The authors applied Wanying (2011) and Murata's (1994) taxonomies of interruptions as analytical frameworks. Drawing on the discourse of the panel of five judges who presided over the trial, the chapter reports that judges interrupted disputants to perform their judicial role as administrators of justice. The chapter demonstrates how judges need interruptions to manage the conduct of trials, request more information, seek clarity, and control and monitor disputants' behaviour. The concept of interruptions as linguistic whistles introduced in this chapter is meant to emphasise that interruptions are important linguistic tools in adversarial systems, and their use must be encouraged for the mutual benefit of the disputing parties. This chapter therefore argues that interruptions should be treated as an integral part of the courtroom conversation culture. The chapter concludes that linguistic phenomena that support the realisation of positive communicative goals need to be encouraged. From the perspective of Africa, where research on interruptions is still lean, the findings of this chapter are especially relevant.

In the following chapter, Chapter 3, Paul Svongoro and Monwabisi Ralarala discuss 'Zimbabwe's constitutional safeguards for persons with communication disabilities: Implications for access to justice'. This chapter examines access to justice for persons with communication disabilities (PWCDs) in Zimbabwe's justice system. Specifically, the study examines: (i) whether Zimbabwe's constitutional and statutory provisions promote or impede access to justice for PWCDs; (ii) whether those provisions are fully implemented in practice; and (iii) where possible, how the justice delivery system should transform to reduce identifiable barriers to justice for PWCDs. The study employed a qualitative research design. First, data collected from Zimbabwe's constitutional and statutory provisions were submitted to document analysis to ascertain the guarantees for PWCDs; these were then compared with regional and international provisions regarding PWCDs' rights. Secondly, data was collected during observation of open-court proceedings involving PWCDs. Observation focused on identifying barriers that could impede full participation of PWCDs in the trial process. Researchers also identified any court accommodations to assist PWCDs to participate actively in proceedings. The collected data was analysed within the framework of transformative equality, which aims to address inequalities and injustices and targets certain structures and systems (including the court system). The chapter establishes that, although Zimbabwe's legal documents make vital provisions for PWCDs' rights and access to justice, many subtle barriers to access still exist. The chapter therefore concludes that, contrary to principles of transformative equality, Zimbabwe's constitutional and statutory provisions regarding PWCDs' access to justice exist on paper but with little practical application, impeding access to justice for many of those persons.

## *Part II: Language and gender-based violence (GBV)*

Chapter 4 is titled 'The immoral complainants: A critical discourse analysis of appeal decisions on cases of marital rape'. The chapter is written by Brazilian colleagues, Débora de Carvalho Figueiredo, Ana Luiza Soares Barcelos, and Luiza Ferreira da Costa. The chapter aims to analyse the reasoning used in appeal processes regarding marital rape in the judicial system in the state of Santa Catarina, Brazil. Its purpose is to analyse critically the judicial discourse (along with responses from the defence attorneys and the judges), given that this discourse expresses the legal view on women's rights and on the meaning of consent; and recognising that this judicial discourse represents the view of the state itself on the issue of sexual violence within the context of a marriage. A critical analysis of judicial discourse on this subject is relevant as the judicial responses define how reliable the system is for those seeking justice for matters associated with marital sexual violence. Contemporary statistics show that only 10% of cases involving rape in Brazil are reported to the police, while as much as 58.5% of the Brazilian population believes that female behaviour is a contributing factor in incidents of rape.

In Chapter 5, Ndikaru Wa Teresia analyses language evidence challenges and administration of justice for victims of domestic violence during the Covid-19 pandemic in Kenya. The outbreak of this pandemic saw in its wake the perpetration of various crimes, including increasing incidents of domestic violence largely affecting women and children trapped at home through lockdown and curfew restrictions intended to limit the spread of the pandemic. Domestic violence increased; and it is argued in this chapter that the avenues for victims seeking legal redress were increasingly restricted, particularly with the scaling down of court procedures. This chapter examines the language of victims' accounts of their difficulties in seeking for, and/or accessing justice in the Kenyan justice system. Victim accounts include testimonies about domestic violence published in both print and electronic media between March 2020 and October 2021. These testimonies, analysed using discourse analysis, showed, firstly, that the legal structures for seeking redress for domestic violence during the pandemic were compromised; secondly, challenges experienced in seeking justice preceded the pandemic; thirdly, legal channels were not considered an option due to cultural perceptions associated with domestic violence; fourthly, recognition that domestic violence is like any other crime was lacking; and, lastly, health services provision, so critical in administering justice to victims, was minimal or absent. These factors contributed to the difficulties experienced by victims of domestic violence in accessing justice.

Chapter 6 is co-authored by Russell Kaschula and Zakeera Docrat. The chapter provides a sociolinguistic analysis of loaded language during cross-examination in South African criminal trials. Adopting a case-based approach, the chapter seeks to analyse how language and the law interact on issues of taboo, euphemism and ribald language usage, or what could be referred to as 'loaded terminology', in South Africa's criminal justice system. The chapter refers to selected case law as examples. The authors concentrate on the case of *State* v *Omotoso* (2018) to observe how, in courtroom discourse, loaded terms are dealt with by those participating, including witnesses giving evidence, and interpreters. In many instances, it may be found that there are cultural and linguistic vacuums when it comes to using terminology related to sex and sexuality, for example, or even politics, when such terms are interpreted into English, the language of record in South African courts. In this chapter, the authors explore the notion of linguistic equivalence between languages such as English and isiXhosa against a sociolinguistic backdrop.

In Chapter 7, Patricia Muraguri and Emmanuel Satia discuss the ranking of descriptors referring to complainants in a Tanzanian court of appeal. These rankings are based on perceived victimhood and the descriptors provide a case of written opinions. The chapter examines terms used in written judgments to refer to persons who have experienced sexual assault. These terms are referred to as 'descriptors', since they describe how a complainant's experience is conceptualized by the court. The researchers conducted a qualitative analysis of the Tanzanian Court of Appeal's written judicial opinions which are published online. The study draws on the concept of a hierarchy of victimization proposed by Carrabine et al. (2009). Descriptors used for those who experienced sexual assault were collected and analysed to determine how descriptors used in different cases are graded hierarchically, based on perceived victimhood. The descriptor choice may reflect an assessment of the truthfulness of the accusations levelled against the accused and the perceived credibility of the women who have been sexually assaulted; this perception may either lead to the recipient of the alleged assault being regarded as innocent or blameworthy. Study findings revealed that, in the hierarchy of victimisation, the descriptor 'victim' occupies the highest position, followed by 'complainant'; thereafter 'prosecutrix' and 'alleged victim'/'alleged prosecutrix' follow; 'liar' and proper names appear at the lowest levels. The lower level descriptors are mainly used where it is perceived that sexual assault charges are fabricated, while descriptors at higher levels reflect a belief that charges brought against the appellant are justified.

Chapter 8, by Emmanuel Satia and Joyce Wambura deals with female genital mutilation in Kenya. This chapter examines the role of language in normalising and legitimating violence against women among the Kuria. It specifically analyses the use of lexical items, metaphors and rhetorical devices in the female genital mutilation (FGM) songs of the Kuria people and critically examines how the linguistic choices are used to discriminate against groups of women by positioning them as subordinate to others. Anchored by critical discourse analysis theories, the chapter analyses linguistic choices that have been purposively selected and used to describe circumcised and uncircumcised women in different, biased ways. Using Fairclough's Textually Oriented Discourse Analysis procedure, these linguistic choices are critically scrutinised, revealing that language is used in a subtle way to embody violence-related ideological assumptions that, with time, are taken to be commonsensical, expectable and anticipatable – even good – but which contribute to sustaining existing unequal power relations generally and perpetuating violence against women. The ultimate goal of the chapter is to challenge the existing retrogressive and discriminative practices and suggest ways of ending the violence.

Chapter 9, 'Fuelling the fear factory: A rhetorical criticism of selected South African television news reports on violence against women and children', is written by Sisanda Nkoala. This qualitative study undertakes a rhetorical criticism of selected South African television news reports on violent crimes against women and children, focusing on the yearly campaign, 16 Days of Activism for No Violence against Women and Children. Drawing on Kenneth Burke's notion of language as symbolic action and Pumla Gqola's concept of the 'Female Fear Factory', the central question the study sought to answer is: How did selected South African television news broadcasts, aired during the campaign, use language as symbolic action to depict the crimes? The data collected was acquired from 32 English-language prime time SABC 3 and eTV news bulletins aired from 25 November to 10 December 2020. The study found that news reports were inclined to use language that empowered men as agents, while women were depicted as subjects who are acted upon, as though they were not human. The reports also tended to use passive language in relation to the role of men as perpetrators of abuse, thus invisibilising their complicity in crimes.

## Part III: Language and crime

Chapter 10 in this section on language and crime is by Gilbert Francis Odhiambo and Daniel Ochieng Orwenjo. The chapter is titled 'Terrorism threat notes as criminal speech acts: A corpus-based approach'. The threat of terrorism is real the world over. Terrorist communication that precedes attacks is in the form of threats. This chapter generally sought to analyse the linguistic features of terrorism threat notes, focusing on conceptualising terrorist threat notes as illegal speech acts (Tiersma & Solan, 2012). This was achieved by adopting a corpus-based approach to data collection, whereby selected terrorism threat notes were retrieved from the websites of four terrorist organisations, al-Qaeda, al-Shabaab, The Islamic State (ISIS) and Boko Haram. A stratified purposive sampling technique was used to obtain written, audio and audio-visual texts. Applying Speech Act Theory (SAT) (Austin, 1962; Searle, 1969, 1976), the chapter analyses terrorism threat notes in terms of the nature of terrorism threats and the categories of speech acts therein. In terms of the act of threatening, the chapter reports that the threats in most terrorism texts analysed are indirectly realised as they are frequently expressed as promises; and most threat notes are statements that are understood to be expressing threats explicitly and implicitly.

Chapter 11, written by Rosette Sifa Vuninga, is titled '"Everyone is doing it": The complex relationship between criminal and anti-criminal networks in Bukavu, Democratic Republic of Congo'. The chapter explores criminal networks in Bukavu, the capital city of the South Kivu province in the eastern region of the Democratic Republic of the Congo (DRC). The chapter exposes that, in the post-Mobutu Sese Seko era, while these networks have not just increased exponentially, they have evolved in terms of their modus operandi. The triple alliance between the community, civil society and the state is at the centre of understanding both the nature and the modus operandi of these networks, their changing dynamics and, particularly, why they persist. The chapter analyses recent trends in crime and anti-crime networks in Bukavu. The chapter argues that *débrouillez-vous* and *auto-prise en charge* are at the centre of understanding the complex relationship that exists between criminal and anti-criminal networks in Bukavu. Since the Congo conflict in the post-Mobutu era, these (*débrouillez-vous* and *auto-prise en charge*) have respectively evoked the notion of (a) relying on the informal economy, and (b) relying on oneself (rather than on the State's security forces like the police and military) in the fight against crime and insecurities. The chapter links crime to the notion of human survival at all costs and the normalisation of such criminal behaviour. The chapter also conducts an analysis of terms such as 'crime' and 'gang' to show how the meaning of such terms goes beyond the notion of unlawfulness.

In Chapter 12, the final chapter in the book, Colin Michell explores author determination in 'Determining the author(s) of a defamation website: Who framed Graeme Joffe?' This chapter is personal in nature: it refers to a time when Michell was approached by a legal associate of a well-known South African sports journalist, Graeme Joffe, who had been the subject of a defamatory website set up to discredit him due to his investigative journalism into corruption in South African sporting administration. Michell's work was to ascertain the identities of the website authors. As three potential authors had been identified by Mr Joffe, samples of the known writings of these three potential authors were gleaned from their publicly accessible Twitter accounts. Using a forensic stylistic approach, the writing used in the defamatory website was compared with that of the samples. It was found that non-standard punctuation usage was the most distinctive style marker, with two unique punctuation constructions pointing to one potential author. However, the differences in linguistic styles in the defamatory website, along with the time lapses between the different sections, pointed to the possibility of multiple authorship. Finally, however, by using an adapted version of the Scientific Working Group for Forensic Document Examination (SWGDOC) scale, it was determined that one author of the three had most likely authored the defamatory website.

## Concluding remarks

Appropriately, the book begins with a wide-ranging chapter espousing Western theory and empirical data, while showing forensic linguists in practice. This opening chapter is written by well-known author, Roger Shuy. In general terms though, the book attempts to draw together Africa and the West.

Crime is a given in any society – there will always be those who seek to benefit from criminal activities. This book is an attempt to grapple with issues of crime, language, and access to justice.

The book speaks clearly to globally accepted Sustainable Development Goal (SDG) number sixteen, which calls for access to justice, as well as effective delivery of justice alongside the building of efficient and effective judicial institutions. The chapters in this book grapple with the challenges espoused in this SDG and others dealing, for example, with gender equity.

The book will appeal to criminologists, all role players within the courtroom context, sociolinguists and applied language studies, anyone interested in language and the law, as well as forensic linguists.

# PART I

## Language and the justice system

# THE CONSTANTS AND VARIABLES OF FORENSIC LINGUISTICS

*Roger W. Shuy*

## Introduction

The role of forensic linguists in the legal arena is to consult with retaining lawyers or the court. Sometimes the linguist serves as an expert witness who writes reports and testifies at hearings and trials. Since most criminal and civil law cases contain language evidence, it is altogether appropriate for experts to analyse this language in the same way that medical, accounting and engineering experts analyse evidence in those fields.

Linguistics is a science that the legal community is gradually recognising as useful and often crucial to the process of achieving justice by examining the language of police interrogations, the evidential language in a case, as well as the language used by law enforcement, witnesses, lawyers and judges during the various stages of the legal process. The courts now recognise forensic linguistics in many jurisdictions of the world, including England, Wales, America, Australia, and Germany. Meanwhile, jurisdictions in other parts of the world are beginning to recognise the usefulness of the linguistic analysis of legal evidence.

To be relevant and effective, forensic linguists must be able to define, hear and use language clearly and stay within the boundaries of their 'constants', meaning the theory, research and tools that constitute their competence. Failure to do so can lead to disastrous results.

It can be difficult for linguists to apply their competence effectively to fields that have rules, procedures, tools, and ideologies that are different from those of linguistics (referred to here as 'variables'). Success in applying forensic linguistics in the legal context depends on the linguists' ability to achieve a balance between their far more familiar 'constants' and the newer and lesser-known 'variables' placed before them by the lawyers and judges who can benefit from this work.

This chapter first highlights the important constants that forensic linguists offer to the legal community. They are constants because they comprise the toolkits that linguists bring to legal cases. Any effort to go beyond these constants can lead to ineffectiveness and possible failure. The chapter then highlights the important variables created by the legal arena that the forensic linguist must recognise and accommodate as they apply their field in the legal arena. It is prudent for forensic linguists to be fully aware of these in their efforts to impact the legal community. Overlooking these variables can be disastrous, not only for the case but also for the linguist's reputation and future in the field.

When linguists apply their analyses to any other field, they face this same problem. A venerated principle of learning is that teachers accommodate their students by beginning with the learners' current knowledge. Linguists have made their most useful contributions to the field of language learning, teaching, and testing when their contributions have fit into the variables posed by the target field's existing knowledge, ideologies, and frameworks. Similarly, forensic linguists can make their most useful contributions to law cases by being relevant to the framework, ideology and knowledge of the legal field that creates the variables in the context for which the linguists use their constants. The published literature on linguistic constants is growing rapidly and those provided here are intended to be representative rather than comprehensive.

## The constants

First and foremost, forensic linguists are well-trained linguists who use a set of tools growing out of accepted linguistic theory, research, and practice. This set of tools includes phonetics, morphology, syntax, semantics, pragmatics, speech acts, sociolinguistics, speech events and discourse analysis. These define the forensic linguist's constants.

Phonetics is the study of the speech sounds of a language system. Competent forensic linguists use this tool to analyse the language evidence in law cases. Phonetics is used in trademark disputes to determine the similarities and differences in trade names, and it is particularly useful in determining the accuracy of government transcripts of interviews and conversations. For example, in one bribery case, the government's transcript of a conversation that took place in a noisy restaurant showed one suspect saying to another suspect, "I would take a bribe, wouldn't you?" Careful analysis of this conversation revealed that he actually said, "I wouldn't take a bribe, would you?" (Shuy, 2013). The government transcriber transported the negative of 'would' from the first to the second clause, and missed where the pause was placed. This phonetic error made the difference between the speaker's guilt or innocence.

Syntax is the study of the rules that govern the way words are combined to make sentences and to determine how phrases and clauses branch and are processed. Syntactic variation can help determine the possible identity of unknown writers and speakers, as well as the conveyed meaning of the language evidence in cases of bribery and contract disputes, and the language evidence of confession statements. In a murder case, the police offered into evidence the written confession of a 12-year-old murder suspect. The linguist compared the syntax in that confession with samples of the syntax of the arresting officer, after which the officer had to admit that he wrote the written confession and then convinced the barely literate boy to sign it.

Semantics is the study of word meaning. Many words convey several meanings that are often determined by the grammatical and social contexts. For example, the conjunction 'or' is often assumed to convey alternatives between two different elements, as in 'soup or salad'; but 'or' can also convey that these two elements are the same, as in 'wild animals are free or unfettered'. This same conjunction can also refer to indefinites with two separate different elements, as in, 'I exercise two or three times a week'. Contracts and insurance policies sometimes fight over conjunctions like 'or'. Contract disputes wrangle over the important difference between an employee who has been 'dismissed' versus one whose 'contract has not been renewed', an important issue in the hiring process.

Sociolinguistics is the study of variation in a language. This includes known language variation based on a person's geographical location, race, gender, age, education, and sometimes even occupation and religion. This tool is especially valuable in assessing anonymous messages by a speaker or writer.

Pragmatics differs from semantic analysis that deals only with meaning, without reference to its users or the communicative functions of sentences. Pragmatics is the study of language choices and constraints from the perspective of its users during social interactions, including the effects of that language on other participants, based on their existing knowledge of the real world. Pragmatics includes how speakers use and understand speech acts, which are the functional ways people get things done with language, such as advising, threatening, opining, thanking, and warning, among others. Utterances have two kinds of meaning: propositional and illocutionary (the effect of an utterance or text on a listener or reader). Pragmatic analysis is useful when examining the evidence in criminal cases, such as perjury and bribery, as well as in civil cases of discrimination and scrutinising product warning labels.

Discourse analysis is the study of language units larger than sentences, such as topics, responses, entire conversations, lectures, sermons, or interviews. The scope of discourse analysis ranges from smaller units, such as adjacency pairs, and address forms to larger units, such as topic framing and identifying the speech event in which the topics are framed.

Linguistics experts' knowledge and skills of other fields are neither appropriate nor relevant for their analyses, reports and testimony in law cases. In fact, linguists can get into trouble when their analyses fall outside the established four corners of linguistics and their analyses invade the territory of other disciplines in which they are not experts. For example, they must avoid including anything in their reports and testimony that is more appropriately reported by experts in psychology, criminology, sociology, and other disciplines. Those experts deal with important factors relating to their fields, while forensic linguists must deal only with the constants that are applicable to the language evidence. Little can be more embarrassing than having analyses, reports and testimony rejected by courts because they fall outside of the expert's area of competence and expertise.

This chapter first describes the constants used by forensic linguists as they consult with retaining attorneys or judges on various types of criminal and civil cases and then points out some of the variables that forensic linguists must accommodate.

## The linguistic constants

The forensic linguist's target area of law includes both criminal and civil cases. Depending on the charges, however, some cases can be tried as either criminal or civil cases. One such area is determining the possible identity of unknown authors and unknown speakers. This area of forensic linguistics is considered here before cases that are clearly designated criminal or civil.

### ■ Constants in analysing unknown authors

Perhaps the most frequently recognised use of forensic linguists is in cases in which the majority of known evidence resides in a document of unknown origin. These cases usually involve comparisons of the writings of unknown authorship with samples of writings of known authorship, with the goal to determine similarities and differences that can suggest single authors (McMenamin, 1993, 2002). In these cases, linguists can use virtually all their constant tools, the most common of which are phonetics, syntax, semantics, sociolinguistics, pragmatics, and discourse analysis.

After using past research findings about language features that are known to characterise individual groups of writers, forensic linguists can pose competing hypotheses of a same or different author, which are based on the language indicators that best support those hypotheses. Note, however, that it is not within the province of linguistic analysis to claim with certainty that any one person was the actual author. One reason for this is that, since the number of potential linguistic markers is much larger than any single sample can provide, the sample evidence may be too limited to include the most diagnostic features. Many of the writer's habitual uses of known sociolinguistic, grammatical, lexical, and discourse features may not be present in the writing sample. Another problem is that the potential identifiable features are social group variables rather than markers of an individual writer.

In authorship cases, therefore, forensic linguists are limited to opining about which of two hypotheses is most consistent. Here a legal variable comes into play. Expert witnesses are not permitted to reach case-binding conclusions, a task that is the sole responsibility of juries or judges. Even when linguistic experts strongly opine that their analysis demonstrates a convincing match of the authors of the unknown and known documents, saying this in court falls outside the variable imposed by the legal system. All that the linguists can present is based on their linguistic constants derived from their comparisons of the similarities or differences in the language evidence.

■  *Constants in analysing unknown speakers*

Although analysis of the recorded voices of unknown speakers provides more linguistic evidence than samples of writing, the linguist's constants remain present. First, the linguistic expert must be qualified to use the most current knowledge and techniques to analyse speech. Knowledge of the constants of phonetics and sociolinguistics are helpful, but today's legal context often requires additional expertise in acoustic analysis that uses appropriate electronic equipment (Schilling & Marsters, 2015).

Speaker identification analysis is also used to addresses questions about native languages of refugees seeking asylum in new countries when they are being questioned by law enforcement officials (Patrick, Schmid & Zwann, 2019). As in authorship analysis, the same legal variables apply. Linguistic analysis of possible speakers must not invade the province of the jury or judge by concluding that the unknown speaker can be positively identified.

## The linguistic constants in criminal cases

Forensic linguists have been retained in criminal cases of bribery, perjury, solicitation, sex crimes, threats, and police interviewing practices. Although crimes of terrorism and treason have increased nationally and internationally in recent years, forensic linguists have so far been only sparsely retained.

■  *Constants in analysing police interviews*

Investigations of crimes usually begin when the police interview suspects and witnesses. The purported purpose of such interviews is to gather evidence (Gudjonsson, 1993). During these interviews, many law enforcement officers also try very hard to obtain a confession. In some jurisdictions, suspects are first advised of their civil rights to remain silent and have a lawyer present, referred to in the United States as 'the Miranda warning' and in other jurisdictions as 'the police caution'. Regardless of whether a particular jurisdiction has such rules, the police interview provides rich material for the forensic linguist to analyse. The linguist's questions are whether the interviewer used conversational strategies that are fair to the interviewee, including clarity of the officer's questions and ambiguity of the respondent's answers (Ainsworth, 2008; Fraser, 2003; Haworth, 2018). The primary constant of a linguist is to include the tools of phonetics, syntax, semantics, discourse analysis, pragmatics and speech acts, as well as determining whether an interview is consistently conducted as a fact-finding interview, speech event, or turns into an accusatory speech event that falls within the proper domain of the prosecutor but not the police interviewer.

### ■ *Constants in analysing evidence of bribery*

Although laws about bribery may vary among jurisdictions, the general principles are similar. Persons are guilty of bribery if they offer, confer, solicit, agree or accept something of value in a *quid pro quo* consideration for the other participant's illegal action, decision or recommendation. The evidence of bribery is usually spoken language that is covertly recorded by law enforcement after a person has been suspected of willingness to participate in a bribery speech event. Since forensic linguists should provide the same analysis for the prosecution or defence, they can be used by either side of the case.

Bribery case evidence is commonly gathered during recordings covertly made by law enforcement agents. The linguist's first useful task is to identify the speech event that characterises all or part of the recorded conversation. Is it a genuine bribery speech event in which the language of the participants clearly indicates that they mutually agree that they are talking about bribery; or does the speech event start as a legal speech event that camouflages the agent's subsequent efforts to make it look a bribery speech event? Some undercover agents do not make this clear and allow their oral exchanges to appear to be legal business transactions, campaign contributions, or some other outwardly legal exchange (Shuy, 2013).

As forensic linguists analyse bribery evidence, they determine the clarity or confusion of the speech event by calling on their tools of discourse analysis by identifying the topics introduced and responded to by the participants and by carefully noting whether the topics indicate legal or illegal intentions. They also point out ambiguities created by lexical choices and syntax created by pronoun and deictic references. Since voluntariness is an important guide, the linguist examines whether the government agent used the speech acts of urging, advising, or otherwise coercing the suspect to agree to give or accept a bribe.

## ■ *Constants in analysing evidence of perjury*

Laws about perjury vary among legal jurisdictions, but in most cases persons under oath can be charged with perjury when they intentionally give false testimony that is material to the point of the inquiry. 'Material' means that certain false statements, whether they are unintentional memory lapses, do not constitute perjury.

Since language is the medium through which perjury is discovered, the linguist's constants can provide useful tools to help judge whether speakers make false statements. For example, a prosecutor's language can reveal how they ask questions that lead witnesses to give purportedly false answers. The sociolinguistic context can also play an important role. Many witnesses have never been in a speech event that is anything like the frightening experience of a courtroom where their responses are severely limited to answering specific questions that do not permit them to describe the language and social context that is missing or distorted by the questions (Shuy, 2011). For example, police and prosecutors tend to ask far more questions that require 'yes' or 'no' answers. These questions eliminate important information that might have been clarified if the questions were open-ended, such as, 'What happened next?', in which case the respondent could explain the context. As linguists analyse the verbal exchanges, they call on their constants of phonetics, morphology, syntax, pragmatics, speech acts, sociolinguistics, and discourse analysis.

## ■ *Constants in analysing evidence of solicitation*

The crimes of soliciting murder, obtaining sexual favours, and purchasing or selling illegal materials are called inchoate crimes, meaning that, even though a criminal act has not yet been committed, there is sufficient evidence of an intent to do so. Such evidence is usually based on covertly recorded conversations or, less commonly, on written evidence that the suspect thought was private and confidential.

Forensic linguists retained by either the prosecution or the defence can call on their linguistic constant of speech act analysis to determine whether the language evidence contains felicitously made speech acts of agreeing, offering, promising or denying. Linguists also must know about any legal constraints in the jurisdiction where the cases are brought. In some jurisdictions, the legal doctrine of voluntariness obtains (Shuy, 2014). Voluntariness refers to an action carried out by design or intention, unconstrained by inference and not impelled by outside influence. Such outside influence can also apply to accused persons who are juveniles, mentally impaired, or under the influence of alcohol or drugs. It likewise applies to police interviewers who exert undue pressure on subjects who are not inclined to confess crimes, as well as to undercover agents who use this tactic on suspects.

■ *Constants in analysing evidence of sex crimes*

Recent years have brought an increasing amount of linguistic research about crimes of rape (Cotterill, 2007; Matoesian, 1993, 2001), sexual misconduct in the workplace, solicitation of sex, adult-on-child sexual misconduct, and cases of unacceptable touching and fondling without intercourse (Shuy, 2012). Many accusations of sex crimes are not brought until long after the event has occurred, producing problems with the accuracy of the accuser's memory. To avoid this problem, some law enforcement agencies have used the technique called 'confrontation calls' in which either the victim or the police telephone accused persons in an effort to get them to admit, confess, or at least apologise for the crime. If the call meets this goal, the evidence can be convincing.

Linguists who use their constants to analyse confrontation calls can use speech act analysis effectively. Were admission statements made felicitously about the suspect's guilt, or were they admissions of something other than the actual crime? If the caller receives an apology from the suspect, was it a felicitous apology for that crime, or did the suspect apologise for something else? Also, in the forensic linguist's tool kit is analysis of vagueness and ambiguity, often created by unclear pronoun and deictic referencing. In addition, the prosecution commonly produces a written transcript of the covertly recorded conversations. One of the forensic linguist's important contributions to all law cases includes their phonetic skills to help determine the accuracy of government transcripts (Fraser, 2003; Heydon, 2005).

■ *Constants in analysing evidence of threats*

Although persons may feel they have been threatened when they receive oral or written messages, such feelings are usually insufficient to bring successful legal charges. In contrast, if the message says, 'I will kill you if you don't resign your position', it contains a *quid pro quo* threat of the sender's personal intention to intimidate and produce fear that is sufficient to bring legal action against the sender (Fraser, 1998). If the message says only, 'We have placed a bomb in your building', the receiver can be intimidated despite the lack of a personal *quid pro quo*. However, not all purported threats are that clear and direct. Some can be indirect or conditional, in which case the language in which they are couched becomes the legal question. For example, if the sender writes, 'You are a terrible boss and I know where you live', the receiver can be justified in inferring danger of being stalked or perhaps even killed.

In cases of threatening, the forensic linguist's most useful constant tool is speech act analysis. Direct speech acts of threatening can be distinguished from the speech acts of complaining, warning, or advising, none of which reach the level of threat and therefore can fail in trials where the sender is accused of the crime of threatening (Shuy, 1993).

## *The linguistic constants in civil cases*

Forensic linguists have been retained in many civil case disputes over trademarks, product liability, discrimination, contracts, defamation, and plagiarism.

■ *Constants in analysing evidence in trademark disputes*

Individual jurisdiction trademark laws vary somewhat but a central issue is whether consumers will be confused about the source, identity, and origin of a trade name. The underlying questions are whether the names sound alike, look alike and mean the same. Five categories of marks are commonly recognised: generic, descriptive, suggestive, arbitrary, and fanciful (McCarthy, 1994). The weakest marks are generic and descriptive. The stronger marks are suggestive, arbitrary, and fanciful. Since these all are language-related categories, forensic linguists can use their constant tools of phonetics, syntax, semantics, pragmatics, and speech acts to assist retaining lawyers with their cases (Butters, 2008; Shuy, 2002).

A second trademark question is whether the name defames social groups in a society, as illustrated by the dispute about the name of a professional football team once called the Washington Redskins. In disputes such as this, forensic linguists can call on their constants of sociolinguistics, semantics and pragmatics.

■ *Constants in analysing evidence of product liability*

Many jurisdictions have statutes based on laws about negligence and breach of warranty, making manufacturers liable if their products can cause injuries to purchasers. A common way to avoid liability is for the manufacturer to provide their products with readable, visible and clear warnings about the potential danger these products pose to the health of consumers if they choose to purchase and use them. Failure to provide such warnings can lead to lawsuits against the manufacturer (Dumas, 1990). Since warning labels appear as written language, this provides an area in which forensic linguists have been used.

To address product liability cases, forensic linguists can use several useful constants, especially speech acts, syntax, semantics, and discourse analysis to determine whether these required warnings are written in such a way that they attract the attention of readers and provide acceptable warnings. Discourse analysis can show how warning labels are not optimally sequenced and framed. Syntax analysis can point out where modal verbs like 'could' and 'may' are used to ameliorate the negative effect of the dangers. Semantic and pragmatic analysis can point out where readers must infer any dangers that are not clearly stated. Speech act analysis indicates whether the required warnings are couched as advice rather than as felicitous warnings. Forensic linguists can also point out where warning labels describe the seriousness of a product's possible danger without clearly associating this danger with the product itself (Shuy, 2008).

■ *Constants in analysing evidence of discrimination*

This area of law is not consistently present in some countries. In the United States, the Civil Rights Act forbids discrimination in employment based on age, race, nationality, religion, handicap, the right to vote, housing opportunities, education, and extension of credit. Forensic linguists in jurisdictions having such laws or any or all of these discriminatory practices can make good use of their linguistic constants of semantics, pragmatics, speech acts and discourse analysis to review the language of employment interviews, references, application forms and public speeches made by employers. The evidence of discrimination is commonly found in written documents, although sometimes it exists in the form of electronically recorded oral language (Baugh, 2003, 2018).

■ *Constants in analysing evidence in contract disputes*

Although lawyers are usually very good at preparing documents such as employee contracts, insurance policies, laws and wills, their vocabulary, grammatical references and discourse sequences are sometimes vague and ambiguous enough to result in legal battles about what these contracts meant or were intended to mean (Shuy, 2008; Tiersma, 1999). Forensic linguists who are retained in such cases can call on their constants of syntax, discourse structure, pragmatics and speech acts to unravel ambiguities and vagueness.

■ *Constants in analysing evidence of defamation*

Slander is defamation through speech, while libel is defamation through writing. Both have language regulations that prohibit the use of any language that lowers a person's reputation in the eyes of the community or deters third parties from dealing with them. In some jurisdictions, such as in Germany, insults and malicious gossip are considered defamatory (Kniffka, 2007).

Forensic linguists who consult on defamation cases call upon important constants in their toolkits, including pragmatics, speech acts, syntactic referencing, and discourse analysis (Shuy, 2010). When people who feel that they have been defamed bring lawsuits against the person who said or wrote what they consider defamatory, their cases are based on subjective feelings. A common defence is that the critical passages are couched as opinions rather than assertions. Linguists have shown that objective analysis of the illocutionary force of the actual language evidence is superior to the receivers' subjective feelings (Tiersma, 1987).

When forensic linguists are retained in defamation cases, they can make good use of their constant tools. Speech act analysis can determine whether the language was couched as an opinion or an assertion. Semantic analysis can help determine whether the offending language was malicious. Discourse analysis can identify how the topics and framing of the purported defamatory statements can provide clues about whether defamation was present.

■  *Constants in analysing evidence of plagiarism*

Forensic linguists are sometimes asked to analyse the language evidence of persons accused of borrowing, copying, or otherwise plagiarising the work of others. Two common contexts of such disputes are writings of students in the school setting and commercial copyright battles in the courtroom. One difference is that school plagiarism is usually considered a moral issue in which those found guilty receive penalties ranging from a failing grade to expulsion from school. In cases where students contract a third party to write their papers, this can be considered a criminal act. In commercial copyright infringement cases, the guilty parties generally receive monetary penalties, removal of their publications from the public domain, and are sometimes required to make a public apology.

Although adjudication of these two types of plagiarism is remarkably different, the forensic linguist's analysis is much the same in both. The quantity and quality of the alleged plagiarism can be difficult to measure but long identical passages can be easy to spot while shorter passages are not as easy to consider plagiarised. Grammatical substitutions of singular nouns for plural ones, lexical substitutions of words like 'harm' for 'damage', and phrasal modifications, can be obvious signs of copying from the original. However, forensic linguists also have other constants in their toolkits that are seldom considered, such as the similarity of the use of speech acts and the sequencing of discourse topics (Shuy, 2008).

# The variables created by the legal context

Forensic linguists must not only adhere to the constants of their field but also must adjust to the variables imposed by the target areas of law that are quite different from those in the linguist's familiar academic context. Some of the important differences of which the forensic linguist must be aware are the variables of the relevant laws, the communication restrictions in the courtroom, the ways to work with retaining attorneys, the ways to teach audiences of lawyers, judges and juries, the rules of confidentiality about the evidence analysed, the very practical matters of getting paid for the work, and the ethical issue of taking credit for any successes. These variables are discussed here in the sequence in which they tend to occur in the forensic linguist's practice.

## *Variables of the law*

All applied linguists begin with the known constants of their field and tactfully accommodate them to the target areas, such as education, medical communication, law and others. In this case, forensic linguists must first acknowledge and consider the statutes, ideologies and procedures of the legal community. Perhaps the most important variable is for linguists to be sure that their analysis of the evidence accommodates and fits within the four corners of the relevant laws. In the absence of such awareness, their work can risk being considered irrelevant and ignored.

Some forensic linguists have legal training, but most do not. Those without it can rely on their retaining lawyers to help them with the legal requirements relating to their reports and testimony, but it is still prudent for experts to learn as much as possible about the statutes and legal procedures. Forensic linguists' analyses of the language in legal disputes may be appropriate in one jurisdiction but less so in another legal context. For example, German defamation law is considerably different to that in other Western jurisdictions because a country's statutes define insulting language as defamation, while in other nations it does not (Kniffka, 2007).

Criminal cases in which Sharia Law favours the husband in divorce cases may require similar adjustments in forensic linguists' analysis of language evidence. In multilingual jurisdictions, earlier remnants of French, Dutch, German or Afrikaans codes can also provide features for forensic linguists to accommodate. Even in national jurisdictions such as the United States, where the major language is English, there are many variables caused by differences in state laws. In addition, local courts may interpret laws differently.

Some legal variables in Africa exist because so many languages have been declared official languages of the court. Note that, since 1996, there are several official languages in South Africa, including Afrikaans, English, isiNdebele, Sesotho sa Leboa, Sesotho, siSwati, Xitsonga, Setswana, isiXhosa and isiZulu. Controversially, English is the only language of record in the courts. In some jurisdictions, however, participants at trial may speak three or more languages with the same interpreter being used for all three (Moeketsi, 1999). This puts pressure on court interpreters to convey accurately the syntax, speech acts, pragmatics, and discourse structures of the speakers' language evidence. Although the language evidence in such cases may be in the original language of the speakers, the way it is interpreted at trial can pose problems for the forensic linguist who always must be alert that this original language evidence is preserved, even though it may have been altered by interpreters.

■ *Variables in communicating with retaining lawyers*

Forensic linguists may think it only natural for their retaining lawyers to communicate regularly and adequately with the experts they retain. Many do, but this is not always the case. Since lawyers are busy with their own briefs and witnesses, they may be working simultaneously on other cases and so their time for experts can be limited. This means that linguists must make a strong effort to be sure that they and their lawyers agree about the expert's task. Personal meetings are necessary, not only to get the feel of each other's style but also to teach the lawyer what the linguistic analysis is and how and where it will fit best in the trial. Frequent telephone calls and electronic messaging can also help. The mutual roles of teaching and learning are important for the proposed reports and testimony to be successful.

■ *Variables in communicating in court*

After forensic linguists and their retaining lawyers have agreed on what the linguist will have to say about the language evidence, the next task is to communicate this adequately to the court, either in their written reports, courtroom testimony, or both. The required medium varies among jurisdictions, often depending on whether it is a civil or a criminal case. In some jurisdictions like the United States, for example, most civil cases require experts to write a report first, which is then shared with the opposition lawyer, who subsequently 'deposes' the expert in a formal procedure that is much like a trial, except that its major purpose is to allow the opposing lawyer to review the experts' qualifications and methods used in their analyses. Depositions enable opposing lawyers to decide whether they need to retain their own forensic linguist to rebut experts.

The linguist can use some technical language, provided it is clearly explained. Opposing lawyers can request clarification if they do not understand. Experts should answer only the questions asked and not volunteer any information that is not requested. Forensic linguists can find depositions emotionally trying because no judge is present to control the exchanges. The retaining lawyer is allowed to be present, however, and can make objections for the record when necessary. Depositions are recorded by a court reporter, after which they become part of the entire trial findings. Linguists must be certain that what they say at trial does not contradict what they said during their depositions.

Experts are not commonly deposed in criminal cases, although judges can hold pre-liminary hearings about the evidence (called 'evidentiary hearings') in which forensic linguists may be required to give testimony about their qualifications and the general principles guiding their analyses. In some international jurisdictions, experts in criminal cases are required to provide only written reports rather than oral testimony at trial. It is prudent for forensic linguists to know exactly what the court case will require them to do.

If the forensic linguist testifies at trial, the previous well-organised plan with the retaining attorney should be followed as closely as possible, after which the opposing lawyer can cross-examine the expert. Cross-examinations can be emotionally draining experiences because opposing lawyers try hard to find inconsistencies and errors. Some experts say that cross-examinations are similar to their nerve-wracking PhD oral exams. No matter how satisfying forensic linguistics work can be, cross-examination is not for the weak of heart.

Experts cannot be advocates, nor should they be. It is important for forensic linguists to know that they should never try to opine about the guilt or innocence of their lawyers' clients. It is the lawyer's job, not the forensic linguist's, to be the client's advocate. No matter how sympathetic experts may be about the lawyer's client, their only role is to analyse the language evidence from a neutral and dispassionate position in a stance that remains outside the confines of the role of the triers of the facts. Unfortunately, it is far too easy for experts to identify as teammates of their retaining lawyers and join sides with their clients. Experts also cannot opine about the legal conclusiveness of their analyses. Only the triers of the facts can and must do this. Linguists present their analyses objectively and then stop.

Some jurisdictions require experts in criminal cases not meet or talk with their retaining lawyer's clients. This rule is followed less rigorously in civil cases. Whether a local jurisdiction follows this constraint, it preserves the expert's objectivity not to see or meet these clients before the trial begins, and not to communicate with them during the proceedings. The only exception to this is when the case requires forensic linguists to interview the lawyer's clients to determine and test their language competence. Even then, however, the dialogue must pertain to the language alone.

■  *Variables in teaching*

As noted earlier, most forensic linguists are experts in their field where their major work is in the classroom. Now the task is to teach a very different audience – lawyers, judges, and juries.

The first job is to teach lawyers about the relevance of linguistics to the evidence in their criminal and civil cases. Next, is to teach them about the specific linguistic tools that are relevant to their cases. This may be the easy part of teaching because the lawyers know that they have a problem, or they would not have retained a linguist. Many retaining lawyers have used experts before and are open to learning how linguistic analysis can help them.

A more challenging teaching role is to teach judges that linguistic analysis is relevant to the cases over which they preside. In the past, many judges have been slow to understand how linguists can assist their cases. Some of them rule that, since the participants in the trial all speak the same language, there is no need for an expert to explain it to them. Other judges have ruled that a linguistics expert's technical explanations will only confuse the jury. In a healthy movement to combat purported 'junk science' experts, some United States judges invoke the Daubert rule, which sets up stringent requirements for expert witness testimony. Expert witnesses must be sure to accommodate this ruling. To be accepted as experts, forensic linguists must teach judges that linguistics is a science; and, like all sciences, it follows the requirements of accepted theory, extensive research, and widespread practice. In some jurisdictions, forensic linguists proposed as expert witnesses are first interviewed in court with what is called a *voir dire*. Success in convincing the judge that the proposed testimony fits the requirements of an expert requires experts to explain clearly the science underlying their testimony.

After being retained, completing the analysis, and being accepted by the judge, the forensic linguist's important task in jury trials is to communicate effectively while teaching these triers of the facts, who comprise a very different audience. Linguistics is a subject most jurors are not likely to know, making the task difficult for experts who are more accustomed to teaching college students. Nevertheless, a long-held principle of teaching is that you start with the students at their point of understanding. This principle is equally relevant to juries who are not linguistics students. It is important to explain and illustrate linguistic terms and concepts in simplified ways. For example, they can explain speech acts, such as 'the way people get things done with language', then give appropriate examples of denying, apologising, warning or threatening. When it seems necessary to clarify syntax analysis, the linguist can use concepts and terms that the jurors may vaguely recall from their own grammar school education. Other linguistics terms and concepts can be taught similarly. If doing this makes the points clear, it should not be thought of as an abandonment of current linguistic theory. The experts should turn their eyes toward lawyers as they ask their questions, but they should focus on the jury whenever possible they answer, because the jurors are the ones being taught. Noticing how they react can be a clue as to whether the point being made needs clarification.

■  *Variables of conducting a business*

Very few forensic linguists are engaged in legal consulting as their full-time occupation. It becomes a business sideline quite different from their regular employment. They now face the variables of how to conduct this part-time work, how to deal with require-ments of confidentiality, and how to conduct a very different process of being paid for their efforts.

To get a consultancy business started, forensic linguists first must be retained by lawyers or the court. The best way for them to be retained is to possess already the necessary qualifications and status that will attract lawyers to ask for their help. This is not unlike the dating ritual of young ladies waiting for a nice young man to invite them to a dance. Lawyers who recognise the possibilities of linguistic assistance take the first step by retaining the most promising experts.

So how can the forensic linguists become attractive enough to get hired? Many lawyers usually do not retain beginners. Instead, they choose experts that they perceive to possess the best qualifications and experience. This important qualification usually means holding the highest academic degree. The requirement of experience does not mean that the expert has worked on previous law cases, but rather that they have achieved some status in their field, usually through their publications and public presentations. Unfortunately for novice forensic linguists, lawyers tend to hire experts who have been retained in the past and whose analyses have been shown to have been helpful in other law cases.

Experience has shown that hanging up a shingle that says, 'Forensic linguist for hire' and advertising in a local newspaper have not been effective. Offering to do some free work for a human rights organisation or a local lawyer can be a more useful way to get started and this also can be a first step toward bolstering an attractive resume.

Another business variable concerns the linguists' ability to publish articles and books based on their analyses. Some civil cases require experts to sign confidentiality statements that are in force during the legal process and even after the case concludes. In such instances, the experts are asked to sign these statements before they begin their work. If forensic linguists are not bound by confidentiality requirements, many jurisdictions such as those of the United States permit experts to write about the case once it becomes a public record. This applies to journalists too. However, to avoid potential legal problems of their own, before writing articles or books about the cases on which they work, it is important for linguistic experts to know the specific confidentiality requirements that apply.

Being paid for the work is still another variable that the linguist faces. Most of them hold full-time positions as college or university professors, where they are considered experts in their fields. Linguists do this work on the side as independent contractors. This means that it is prudent to be clear from the beginning about how to get paid for their work, a sensitive subject that requires patience, conscience, and tact.

In civil cases, lawyers' clients may be corporations involved in disputes about trademarks, contracts, product warning labels, and discrimination. Corporations can be expected to afford experts. In such cases, forensic linguists might expect to be paid at rates similar to those of experts in other fields, such as in medicine, accounting and engineering. However, since forensic linguistics is relatively new when compared to other specialisations, it may be prudent to expect their fees to be somewhat lower.

In many criminal cases, the lawyer's clients may not be able to afford experts. This suggests that forensic linguists should have variable fees that depend on individual clients' circumstances and, in some cases, the expert's willingness to alter or even forgo fees altogether. Even experienced forensic linguists sometimes work *pro bono* based on their humanitarian goal of promoting justice for deserving fellow human beings. Occasionally working for no pay has the advantage of enabling their resume to attract future lawyers to use their services.

## Conclusions

There are many benefits that accrue from forensic linguistic work. Perhaps the greatest is the opportunity to participate in the pursuit of justice. But forensic linguists must learn to step carefully into the less familiar reality of the legal world. Perhaps most important, is that they must not confuse the procedures, ideologies and rules of academic discourse to present and strongly defend a valued position to a field with very different discourse rules, procedures and ideology imposed by the legal context and in which the linguist's only role is to analyse the language evidence objectively and dispassionately. This means that it is crucial for forensic linguists to stay within their constants, the four corners of linguistics, while carefully adjusting to the variables presented by the target legal context. Failing to do this can have disastrous consequences for the effectiveness of forensic linguists' contributions and can negatively impact judges and lawyers.

Forensic linguists work with retaining lawyers, judges and juries, a task that is quite different from working with linguistics students and colleagues. Teaching three different audiences (lawyers, judges and juries) at virtually the same time, requires finely honed personal and pedagogical skills. The forensic linguists who wish to continue this work also must learn about managing a consulting business.

Many criminal and civil law cases contain language evidence that can be considered at the margins, meaning language passages where it is possible for juries, lawyers, and judges to interpret meanings in more than one way. In such cases, triers of the facts that are charged with reaching a verdict have no other choice but to infer the meanings conveyed in the language evidence. This is especially true with ambiguous language.

In cases that include spoken language evidence, forensic linguists should be well equipped to clarify phonetic distinctions that may be central to a case. This skill is especially important in transcripts of spoken language that are produced by the government.

When grammatical or semantic ambiguities exist, listeners often have to infer what the speakers must have meant and what those who were listening must have understood. Grammatical ambiguity often involves unclear references to people, events or things. Each language has its own potential problems but, in English, a common confusion comes from unclear pronoun references such as 'they', 'them' and 'their', and 'you', 'your' and 'yours'. Although there is no way that anyone can reach into the minds of speakers to know with certainty what they intended to say, forensic linguists can rely on their constants to provide important clues to this.

Pragmatics and speech act constants are most helpful in cases containing large amounts of continuous discourse, such as written contracts or recorded interactions. The first thing to identify is the speech event and then determine how the communication is consistent with it or varies from it (Shuy, 2013). Unless the participants' language indicates that they are in the same announced speech event, their responses can be misinterpreted. The well-trained forensic linguist can point out how such distorted perceptions occur.

Likewise, forensic linguists' sociolinguistic constants can help determine the possible identity of unknown speakers or writers; and their expertise in discourse analysis can identify the flow of topics that can help find clues to the intentions of speakers. Their analyses of discourse framing help to reveal much the same thing (Shuy, 2010).

Forensic linguists must not only adhere strictly to their constants but as noted earlier, they must also adjust their work to the variables provided by the legal setting in which they participate. Whatever personal beliefs or feelings forensic linguists may hold about a case are completely irrelevant, because experts are not advocates. That is the job of lawyers. Nor can experts take any credit for winning cases. It is lawyers who win or lose cases.

Regardless of which side of the case forensic linguists are retained, their analyses, reports, and testimony should be objectively the same. Based on current experience, however, it appears that criminal defence lawyers have been far more likely to retain linguistic experts than prosecutors. This suggests that, so far at least, forensic linguists have not yet convinced prosecutors that their cases can be enhanced by linguistic analysis of the language evidence. This is one of the next goals for forensic linguistics for expanding its usefulness in the legal arena.

# References


Ainsworth, J. 2008. "You have the right to remain silent … But only if you ask for it just so": The role of linguistic ideology in American police interrogation law. *International Journal of Speech, Language and the Law*, 15(1):1-22. https://doi.org/10.1558/ijsll.v15i1.1

Baugh, J. 2003. Linguistic profiling. In: S. Makoni, G. Smitherman, A. Ball & A. Spears (eds.). *Black linguistics.* London: Routledge. 155-168.

Baugh, J. 2018. *Linguistics in the pursuit of justice.* New York: Cambridge University Press. https://doi.org/10.1017/9781316597750

Butters, R. 2008. Trademarks and other proprietary terms. In: J. Gibbons & T. Turrell (eds.). *Dimensions of forensic linguistics.* Amsterdam: John Benjamins. 231-249. https://doi.org/10.1075/aals.5.16but

Cotterill, J. 2007. *The language of sexual crime.* Houndmills: Palgrave. https://doi.org/10.1057/9780230592780

Dumas, B. 1990. Adequacy of cigarette package warnings: An analysis of the adequacy of Federally mandated cigarette package warnings. In: J. Levi & A.J. Walker (eds.). *Language in the judicial process.* New York: Plenum Press. 309-352. https://doi.org/10.1007/978-1-4899-3719-3_11

Fraser, B. 1998. Threatening revisited. *Forensic Linguistics*, 23:113-133. https://doi.org/10.1558/sll.1998.5.2.159

Fraser, H. 2003. Issues of transcription: Factors affecting the reliability of transcripts as evidence in legal cases. *Forensic Linguistics*, 10:203-226. https://doi.org/10.1558/sll.2003.10.2.203

Gudjonsson, G. 1993. *The psychology of interrogation, confessions, and testimony.* New York: John Wiley and Sons.

Haworth, K. 2018. Tapes, transcripts and trials: The routine contamination of police interview evidence. *The International Journal of Evidence & Proof*, 22(4):428-450. https://doi.org/10.1177/1365712718798656

Heydon, G. 2005. *The language of police interviewing: A critical analysis.* Houndmills, Basingstoke: Palgrave. https://doi.org/10.1057/9780230502932

Kniffka, H. 2007. *Working in language and law: A German perspective.* Houndmills, Basingstoke: Palgrave Macmillan. https://doi.org/10.1057/9780230590045

Matoesian, G. 1993. *Reproducing rape: Domination through talk in the courtroom.* Chicago: Chicago University Press.

Matoesian, G. 2001. *Law and the language of identity.* New York: Oxford University Press.

McCarthy, T. 1994. *McCarthy on trademarks and unfair competition.* 4th Edition. Toronto: Thomson Reuters.

McMenamin, G. 1993. *Forensic stylistics.* Amsterdam: Elsevier.

McMenamin, G. 2002. *Forensic linguistics: Advances in forensic stylistics.* Boca Raton: CRC Press. https://doi.org/10.1201/9781420041170.ch9

Moeketsi, R. 1999. *Discourse in a multilingual and multicultural courtroom: A court interpreter's guide.* Pretoria: J.L. van Schaik.

Patrick, P., Schmid, M. & Zwann, K. (eds.). 2019. *Language analysis for the determination of origin: Current perspectives and new directions.* Berlin: Springer. https://doi.org/10.1007/978-3-319-79003-9

Schilling, N. & Marsters, A. 2015. Unmasking identity: Speaker profiling for linguistic purposes. *Annual Review of Applied Linguistics*, 35:195-214. https://doi.org/10.1017/S0267190514000282

Shuy, R. 1993. *Language crimes: The use and abuse of language evidence in the courtroom.* Cambridge, MA: Blackwell.

Shuy, R. 2002. *Linguistic battles in trademark disputes.* New York: Palgrave Macmillan.

Shuy, R. 2008. *Fighting over words.* New York: Oxford University Press. https://doi.org/10.1093/acprof:oso/9780195328837.001.0001

Shuy, R. 2010. *The language of defamation cases.* New York: Oxford University Press. https://doi.org/10.1093/acprof:oso/9780195391329.001.0001

Shuy, R. 2011. *The language of perjury cases.* New York: Oxford University Press. https://doi.org/10.1093/acprof:oso/9780199795383.001.0001

Shuy, R. 2012. *The language of sexual misconduct cases.* New York: Oxford University Press. https://doi.org/10.1093/acprof:oso/9780199926961.001.0001

Shuy, R. 2013. *The language of bribery cases.* New York: Oxford University Press. https://doi.org/10.1093/acprof:oso/9780199945139.001.0001

Shuy, R. 2014. *The language of murder cases.* New York: Oxford University Press. https://doi.org/10.1093/acprof:oso/9780199354832.001.0001

Tiersma, P. 1987. The language of defamation. *Texas Law Review,* 66(2):314-322.

Tiersma, P. 1999. *Legal language.* Chicago: Chicago University Press.

# INTERRUPTIONS AS LINGUISTIC WHISTLES

## An examination of judges' language in Malawi courtroom discourse

*Wellman Kondowe*
*George Mtanga*

## Introduction

Since the introduction of forensic linguistics as a branch of linguistics in the 1970s, the field has grown in both scope and methodological orientations. Forensic linguistics is dedicated to investigating the language of law. While the study of the language of the law was previously considered an irrelevant endeavour that diverted attention from more serious scholarly studies in law, today law itself has been characterised as having a special discourse that has direct implications for people's lives. The fields of linguistics and law are, thus, inseparable because law is strongly based on, and is practised using, language. The present chapter contributes to the growing debates on studies of legal language by examining the language of judges, and it introduces a new concept of interruptions as linguistic whistles.

On an everyday basis, we enter into different conversational contracts with different participants for different reasons. For such communication to be orderly and successful, Sacks, Schegloff and Jefferson (1978) recommend that only one speaker should talk at a time; and the one holding the floor should be the one to decide who talks next. This model prescribes a convention that governs the conduct of how language users can achieve maximum communication. However, just like the Politeness Theory of Brown and Levinson (1987), such models idealise communication and give the impression that participants are always orderly and templatic when using language, while in reality, they are not. For instance, communication that happens in court is prominently goal-orientated, constrained, procedural and highly rule-governed, with disputants having their own clearly defined goals from the very beginning (Liao, 2004). Prosecutors, claimants, and defence lawyers are parties with conflicting interests. This creates a very hostile communication environment where judges act as judicial referees, guardians of the procedures, and administrators of justice (Bogoch, 2000). However, modern scholars have not taken a keen interest in studying how judges use language to manage this role of judges being referees and administrators of justice.

## Judges as referees, and interruptions as linguistic whistles

In her study, *Judges as language referees for Caribbean English vernacular speakers: How do they score?*, Brown-Blake (2019) provides a comprehensive discussion of the process and approaches of evaluation used by judicial officers in determining the linguistic proficiency of courtroom speakers. The study further provides some tools that judges and magistrates can use when weighing the disputants' narratives. Illuminations shared in her research provide a primary foundation for this chapter. The concept of 'linguistic whistles' introduced in this chapter supports the notion that judges are judicial referees who are empowered by the law to oversee justice in legal systems. Since court battles are contested orally, for judges to execute their duties ably, they also need oral linguistic tools, such as interruptions, just as referees need whistles to control the behaviours of the competing game players. The set-up in most games is that there are (at least) two parties, with each contesting for victory. This set-up is similar to that of a typical courtroom interaction. Despite many studies reporting negatively on the role of interruptions in communication, this chapter argues that judges need interruptions in their toolbox to control and monitor the behaviours of disputants, as these interruptions play a vital role in the administration of justice, when used by judges.

By definition, interruption entails a deep intrusion into the utterance of the current speaker. It generally occurs when two persons talk simultaneously and where the second speaker invades the syntactic structure of the first speaker (Zimmerman & West, 1996; Liao, 2009a). The current study has paid special attention to a civil trial referred to as *Chilima & Anor.* v *Mutharika & Anor.* (also known as Constitutional Reference 1 of 2019), which took place at the High Court of Malawi, Lilongwe District Registry. The case was certified as a constitutional matter by the Honourable Chief Justice Andrew Nyirenda. (For convenience, this chapter shall refer to the case as 'the 2019 Malawi Presidential Elections case'.) The matter started in August 2019 and concluded in February 2020. The case was chosen because it presents unique scenarios appropriate for the study. Another basis for selection was the manner in which the case attracted widespread public opinion and interest.

## The status of studies on the language of law in Malawi

Despite forensic linguistics being a fast growing and promising field of study, it has not enjoyed much scholarly attention in Malawi. While the field is new in most African countries, the situation in Malawi is gloomy compared to other African countries like Kenya, Zimbabwe, South Africa and Nigeria, where there has been a tremendous growth of research on the subject. The Malawian situation is perhaps not so surprising because currently, it is largely Mzuzu University that, since 2015, has been offering courses in forensic linguistics to undergraduate students. The University of Malawi also has some courses offered within the Bachelor of Arts in Law Enforcement and Leadership programme. However, there is less than a handful of studies that can be pointed out: Kishindo (2001): *A study on the use of African languages in courts*; Kondowe, Liao and Ngwira (2022): *A study on insincerity*; Kondowe (2022): *The principle of believability*; and Kondowe: *Lawyers' questioning strategies*. This study is, therefore, an effort to add to that lean body of studies on courtroom discourse in Malawi by introducing new perspectives to the study of interruptions and the language of judges in general. The introduction of a master's programme in forensic linguistics (named 'Law Enforcement Discourse') at Mzuzu University is a blessing and we expect a boost in research output on language and the law.

## The 2019 Malawi Presidential Elections case

The 2019 elections trial is the first in the history of Malawi in which presidential elections were legally challenged and contested in a court of law with a full hearing (Kondowe, 2022). The claimants were the opposition candidates, Dr Saulos Klaus Chilima, who came third, and Dr Lazarus McCarthy Chakwera, who came second. The two, referred to as 'the first petitioner' and 'the second petitioner' respectively, went to court to argue that the elections were full of irregularities, thereby rendering untrustworthy the result that Arthur Peter Mutharika was duly elected as President of the Republic of Malawi. Respondents to the case were Arthur Peter Mutharika and the Electoral Commission. The trial was contested over six months and, finally, the High Court nullified the election results. The outcome of this case attracted both local and international attention as it is unusual for courts to annul presidential elections, let alone oust a president who has already been sworn in (Kondowe, 2022). Malawi became the second African country to nullify a presidential election, after Kenya in 2017. Table 2.1 shows the composition of the disputants' teams in the trial:

**TABLE 2.1**  Composition of the disputants in the trial

| Disputants | Lawyers | Witnesses | Total |
|---|---|---|---|
| Petitioners | 13 | 10 | 23 |
| Respondents | 13 | 45 | 58 |
| TOTAL | 26 | 55 | 81 |

Data from this case was chosen because the trial brought together a panel of five judges who could have been identified separately in isolated cases. Despite being a legal requirement that an election petition be presided over by no fewer than three judges, such cases are extremely rare in Malawi: the majority of cases in Malawi are tried by a single judge. Therefore, having this data to work on alone has made it very useful for this chapter. The names of the judges were Honourable Justice H. Potani; Honourable Justice I. Kamanga; Honourable Justice D. Madise; Honourable Justice M. Tembo, and Honourable Justice R. Kapindu. Furthermore, as Table 2.1 shows, the trial had 81 participants, a comparatively large number, and an indication that it was a high-level case compared to many other lawsuits.

The entire trial was represented by 26 lawyers, excluding the *Amici Cariae* lawyers for Malawi Law Society (MLS) and Women Lawyers Association (WLA) because of their neutral participation. The disputing teams had 13 lawyers each, with 13 representing the petitioners and 13 representing the respondents. There were about 10 witnesses for petitioners, and about 45 witnesses for both respondents. The entire hearing process lasted over six months. Scenarios of this nature are uncommon in most court cases in Malawi where, ordinarily, most lawsuits are represented by no more than two lawyers; and they do not have such an overwhelming number of witnesses. It is therefore expected that the more the judges, lawyers and witnesses a trial has, and the longer the duration, the more instances of interruptions are to be expected. Throughout the entire hearing period, the nation witnessed heightened tension due to an increased number of interruptions and trapping modes of questioning employed by the disputants' lawyers. However, the role that interruptions played in the general outcome of a trial remains unclear, partly because of the paucity of data on the language of judges that is biased towards the role interruptions play in the legal process.

## Literature review and theoretical underpinnings

Several researchers have studied courtroom discourse by looking at different language behaviours during the trial process, such as questioning procedures, speech acts, turn taking and turn allocation, interpretation, address terms, language and power as well as interruptions (Mead, 1985; Kishindo, 2001; Gibbons, 2003; Liao, 2021). Bogoch (2000) notes that courtroom studies conducted so far seem to have two basic orientations: on the one hand, there are studies that focus on the ordered nature of courtroom interaction and the legal objectives; and, on the other hand, there are studies that analyse the specific features of courtroom discourse in relation to the broader social structure. Scholars have come to realise that discourse studies can lead to a better understanding of how legal processes and behaviours are constituted and sustained (Bogoch, 2000).

It has been a common observation that communication in the courtroom is significantly different from that in non-institutionalised settings. First, courtroom discourse is highly sequenced and organised: emphasis is placed on turn taking, with principles involving changes of speakers (based on their legal roles), shifts from one speaker to the next, order and length of a turn, and conversation as a whole (Liao, 2009b). Second, courtroom talk is highly institutionalised, strongly goal-orientated with unique question–answer interaction, rigid procedures, and high-stakes for the claimants, prosecution, and defendants; and there are interruptions that greatly deviate from those in ordinary settings (Hu, 2018; Liao, 2009b). While constraints also exist in other institutional settings, in court, the constraints are explicit and ultimately enforceable through, among others, the use of interruptions.

Interruption is a speech performance that happens when a person starts to talk while the current speaker is talking; and, finally, the current speaker gives up the floor (Brown & Levinson, 1987). Shi (2021) categorises two kinds of interruption: intrusive and cooperative. Intrusive interruption entails floor taking, topic changing, and disagreement interruption, whereas cooperative interruption involves agreement, clarification and tangentialisation (Murata, 1994; Shi, 2021). Lu and Huang (2006) also classify two types of interruptions: successful and unsuccessful interruptions.

Different scholars have examined number, patterns, causes, distribution, and functions of interruptions in various courtroom data (Liao, 2009a; Sun, 2017; Hu, 2018; Widodo et al., 2019; Loughland, 2019; Liao, 2021). Examining Chinese criminal courtrooms, Liao (2009b) discovered that judges interrupted as a form of control and often stopped defendants from explaining themselves. In his study, Shi (2021) similarly reports that power and social status affect the frequency and effectiveness of interruptions. Thus, the prosecutor, being in a powerful position, controls the whole trial process, makes active interruptions, and controls the discourse through his or her power.

Hu (2018) discovered that judges and prosecutors interrupt more frequently than defence lawyers and defendants. Interruption as a manifestation of domination and power in China is also reflected in a study by Zhao and Gants (2003). Loughland (2019) presents findings of an empirical study of interruption behaviour during oral argument in the High Court of Australia. In this study, it was discovered that interruption reflected gendered and power dynamics, where male advocates interrupted female judges more than they interrupted male judges. Widodo et al. (2019) studied patterns of interruption as a form of communication in the Central Jakarta District Court in Indonesia. They discovered that interruptions were made by both the prosecution and legal advisors, mostly to reject information submitted by the opposing party.

It is evident that most scholars look at interruption as a barrier to successful and harmonious communication. It has been widely reported that interruptions manifest power imbalances, gender inequalities, domination, and control of the discourse. Such studies have examined interruptions as an undesirable aspect of courtroom communication. Even so, not much has been done to focus comprehensively on interruptions made by judges. The language of judges has been studied in passing but not as the entire focus of those studies. One of the most influential studies on the language of judges is by Solan (1993): *The language of judges.* In this publication, Solan provides a grammatical description of the language of the judges. Among other aspects, his work focuses on the use of pronouns and the linguistic markers of precision. In the face of other scholars like Tracy and Hodge (2018), interruptions made by judges could be regarded as moves that enact and endanger procedural justice.

The courtroom institution is highly constrained, power marked, goal orientated, and rule governed, where disputants try to win their side of the story. It is misleading to attribute the interruptions that judges make exclusively to the judges' exercise of their power, dominance, and control, when these judges are the ones who speak the least in the entire trial process. This chapter argues that judges do not speak or interrupt to show domination, but rather to perform their judicial role as referees and administrators of justice. This is a marked departure from the previous approaches to the study of courtroom interruptions made by judges.

## Frameworks of analysis

The framework of analysis will follow Murata (1994) and Wanying's (2011) taxonomies of interruption. In his examination of three different interactions of native speakers of English, native speakers of Japanese, and Japanese speakers of English, Murata (1994) developed two classifications of interruption, namely, Intrusive Interruption (II) and Cooperative Interruption (CI). Murata defines Cooperative Interruption as those interruptions where a speaker joins the turn of the current speaker in order to supply a word or a phrase for which the current speaker is searching, or even completes it for him or her. The new speaker neither changes the topic nor trespasses, but rather encourages the current speaker to continue to talk by showing his or her own interest, revealing listenership and participation (Murata, 1994). Co-operating with the speaker in making the conversation flow by supplying a word that the speaker is trying to find shows interest and participation in the conversation.

CI is further subdivided into three categories. The first category is Agreement Interruption. As the name suggests, AI occurs when the interrupter often makes the same point of message as the interruptee to promote the harmonious development of the talking (Murata, 1994; Shi, 2021). The new speaker interrupts with agreement words and confirms part of the information in the conversation. AI has mutual benefits, as it enables interlocutors to clarify the truth of the statement and clearly understand the facts of the topic under discussion.

The second type is Clarification Interruption. This type of interruption is meant to seek further clarification of part of the conversation. Where the speaker is not clear enough during the process of stating facts, he or she may be interrupted to provide a more detailed explanation or restatement of the facts. This type of interruption mostly occurs in the form of a question (Shi, 2021).

Finally, there is Tangentialisation Interruption, which is meant to follow up the next turn of conversation to express something with which participants in the conversation agree (Murata, 1994; Shi, 2022). In some cases, participants fail to express themselves fully in the courtroom conversation, or they fail to state facts clearly because of nervousness, so they need help to supplement information.

In Wanying's (2011) taxonomy, interruptions are categorised as follows: first, there are Avoiding Digression (AD) interruptions, which are said to occur once an interrupter takes the floor when the current speaker is saying something contrary to what is being discussed; second, there are Summarising Points (SP) interruptions where the interruption may happen to the current speaker as someone takes over the floor and summarises what has been said (Wanying, 2011); third, there are Preventing Emotion (PE) interruptions in which the current speaker is interrupted to stop him or her from speaking with emotion (Wanying, 2011); and, finally, there are Requiring Information (RI) interruptions, which happen when the interrupter wants to get more information from the one holding the floor.

Even though the two taxonomies were developed from data gathered during ordinary conversations, we find some cases of courtroom discourse to mirror similar frameworks. As seen from the data, the functions played by these types of interruption in the taxonomies in ordinary conversation are different from the role they play in courtrooms, especially if they are used by judges. Furthermore, the data clearly shows that these interruptions are not equally distributed in the language of judges. Due to legal requirements, judges have specific preferences for a type of interruption over other types to achieve certain judicial functions.

## The data

The study used data from the court trial of the 2019 Malawi Presidential Elections case, which was concluded in 2020. This trial attracted the interest of the nation and beyond. The proceedings were recorded live and uploaded to the internet by various media stations. The recordings used in this study were downloaded from the online Zodiak Radio and YouTube. The entire case took over 50 days, but the chapter has used data from the following specific days: Day 1 (Part A & B); Day 2 (Part A & B); Day 12

(Part A & B); Day 17; Day 26 (Part A & B); Day 43; Day 44; Day 45 (Part A & B); Day 49, and Day 50 (Part A & B). It was noted that all the selected days included sufficient sections where judges spoke. The recordings were downloaded as MP3 and MP4 files and transcribed manually. The transcription was done using standard orthography rather than phonetically. All instances of judges' interruptions were marked with symbols "//" during transcription.

## Results and discussion

Results of the findings are shown in two tables. Table 2.2 presents instances of interruptions as distributed amongst trial participants. Table 2.3 shows instances where judges interrupted other trial participants.

**TABLE 2.2**  Interruption distribution among the interrupters

| Interrupter | Judges | Petitioners | Respondents | Others | Total |
|---|---|---|---|---|---|
| Day 1 | 23 | 15 | 11 | 3 | 52 |
| Day 2 | 17 | 10 | 4 | 0 | 31 |
| Day 12 | 32 | 12 | 9 | 0 | 53 |
| Day 17 | 27 | 19 | 13 | 1 | 60 |
| Day 26 | 24 | 17 | 11 | 0 | 52 |
| Day 43 | 35 | 6 | 12 | 2 | 55 |
| Day 44 | 13 | 4 | 6 | 0 | 23 |
| Day 45 | 13 | 2 | 7 | 1 | 23 |
| Day 49 | 9 | 3 | 5 | 0 | 17 |
| Day 50 | 48 | 7 | 15 | 0 | 70 |
| Total | 241 | 95 | 93 | 7 | 436 |
| Percentage | 54.4 | 24.4 | 20.9 | 1.6 | 100% |

**TABLE 2.3**  Judges interrupting others (total number: 241)

| Interruptee | Petitioners | Respondent | Others |
|---|---|---|---|
| Number | 136 | 102 | 3 |
| Percentage | 56.4 | 42.3 | 1.3 |

As indicated in Tables 2.2 and 2.3, the average distribution of interruptions in the 2019 Malawi Presidential Elections case shows that judges interrupted other participants most often (n=241, 54.4%), distantly followed by petitioners (n=95, 24.4%), with respondents following closely (n=93, 20.9%).

**TABLE 2.4**   Types of interruptions made by judges (total number: 241)

| Type of interruption | Frequency | Percentage |
| --- | --- | --- |
| Requiring Information (RI) | 108 | 45 |
| Avoiding Digression (AD) | 83 | 34 |
| Summarising Points (SP) | 31 | 13 |
| Preventing Emotion (PE) | 19 | 7.9 |

Findings in Table 2.4 show that Requiring Information (RI) interruptions were used most often in the trial, accounting for 45% of all interruptions that judges made. These were followed by Avoiding Digression (AD) interruptions, which constituted 34% of all interruptions. Summarising Points (SP) interruptions occurred 13% of the time, and Preventing Emotion (PE) interruptions were less frequent, with a 7.9% occurrence.

## Types of interruptions made by the judges

As indicated in Table 2.4, Requiring Information interruptions topped the list, followed by Avoiding Digression, Summarising Points, then Preventing Emotion interruptions (preventing emotional outbursts).

### *Requiring Information interruption*

A Requiring Information (RI) interruption is similar to Clarification Interruption in Murata's (1994) taxonomy. These forms of interruption seek further explanation and more detailed explanation of what has been said. They mostly appear in the form of questions.

In legal battles, where two versions of a story are contested orally, the judge takes up the role of judicial referee who tries to gather the facts as presented in the two versions of the disputants. Interruptions are, therefore, linguistic 'whistles' that judges use to check the correctness of the facts. The dominance of RI interruptions is, therefore, not surprising because judges need to use them to request more information from the disputants. In the Malawian judicial system, judges and other participants utilise these types of interruptions as linguistic whistles in scenarios where they feel the information that has been provided is insufficient. They are also deployed to elicit clarity. According to Grice (1975), participants in a conversational contract must abide by the maxim of quantity by providing enough information, as it is required. Therefore, it can be said that RI interruptions made by judges are caused by participants who violate the maxim of quantity (see Example 1).

**Example 1:**

| Attorney General | Would you want to speak on their behalf? |
|---|---|
| Honourable Chilima | I wouldn't. |
| Attorney General | Do you know if they challenged some results? |
| Honourable Chilima | Not on this one// |
| Justice Kamanga | //May I ask the witness to clarify what does he mean when he said not on this one? Can you give more information? |

In Example 1, the judge (Justice Kamanga) observes that the petitioner's witness, Honourable Chilima, does not provide enough information on the question asked by the Attorney General. What the witness is referring to by saying, "Not on this one", violates the maxim of quantity. The judge, as a judicial referee, makes an RI and clarification interruption to ask the witness to provide more information. In this case, apart from eliciting more information, the RI interruption is also employed by judges to seek clarification on information given by the disputants. This kind of interruption by a judge shows that they are following very closely what the disputants are arguing upon. This is highly significant because judges are determiners of justice, and they base their judgment on what disputants say during a trial. That is why some interruptions by the judges are meant to seek clarification on what has been said, as seen in Example 2. In the example, the judge is seeking clarity from the counsel for the first respondent, Counsel Mhango, where some information seems not to have been addressed.

**Example 2:**

| Counsel Mhango | [...] that will be all what I wanted to make// |
|---|---|
| Justice Tembo | //What about the last point that the senior counsel made that the witness made a statement attributing to Mr Mukhondya? Can you also address that? |

## *Avoiding Digression interruption*

An Avoiding Digression (AD) interruption was the second most commonly used type of interruption in the data. It is clear that, as the facts and opinions were being presented, the court interlocutors, especially the respondents and the petitioners, tended to digress by bringing something unrelated into the topic. In most cases, this is done to hide some information or try to confuse the court to their own advantage. When a digression is observed, the judges interrupt to address it. These interruptions can be considered provoked by parties violating the conversational maxim of relation. As Hu (2018) notes, judges, being courtroom time controllers, are constantly under severe time pressure to see to it that the trial is concluded as soon as possible. In the Presidential Elections case, the situation was even more pressing as there was growing demand from the local and international audiences to hear the outcome of the trial as the nation was at a political standstill. The judges could not, therefore, entertain time wastage through participants' unnecessary digressions. Therefore, when lawyers and witnesses deviated from the central topic or indulged in trifles and unnecessary details, there was no hesitation from the judges but to interrupt.

**Example 3:**

| Counsel Mhango | My lady my lords, before the court makes determination on the Attorney General's application, we as the part of the first respondent, we had similar sentiment and I want to seek your guidance my lords and my lady that probably you should allow us to make remarks before you make your determinations and I would like to ask my colleague counsel David Kanyenda to address the court briefly on// |
|---|---|
| Justice Potani | //Proceed please to the point. We don't have enough time. |

In Example 3, Justice Potani interrupts Counsel Mhango by reminding him that Counsel Kanyenda's remarks should be in line with what is being discussed and should avoid digression. In many instances in the data, these kinds of directives were seen, where judges interrupted to control digression by respondents' and petitioners' lawyers and endeavour to get them to stick to facts.

**Example 4:**

| Attorney General | Maybe before I continue and conclude let me indicate that I'm noting my lawyers indicating that we might have been served with the first petitioner's materials. The first petitioners paged bundle// |
|---|---|
| Justice Tembo | //Maybe AG you can just confer with him so that we have to move forward as of now that's not important. |
| Attorney General | Any way, my lady my lords. Let me retrieve that statement regarding the first petitioner materials. |

**Example 5:**

| Counsel Kanyenda | Before I plunge into my oral application let me furnish this court with// |
|---|---|
| Justice Tembo | //You are taking a lot of time, if you can tell us, what is the application all about? |

**Example 6:**

| Daud Sulemani | I am waiting for Mr Kadzuwa to do the operations. |
|---|---|
| Counsel Mhango | My lady my lords, I think this is working on the wrong direction, that was the court order that it will be operated by somebody from their side// |
| Justice Potani | //Mr Chisi the court has ordered you to be there, I order you to do what I instructed to do, nothing else ... you are the director of the ICT. |

**Example 7:**

| | |
|---|---|
| Attorney General | Would you want to speak on their behalf? |
| Honourable Chilima | I wouldn't. |
| Attorney General | Do you know if they challenged some results? |
| Honourable Chilima | Not on this one// |
| Justice Kamanga | //May I ask the witness to clarify what does he mean when he said not on this one? Can you be as clear as possible. |

**Example 8:**

| | |
|---|---|
| Attorney General | I think if I will react ... I don't understand that in terms of the Law. |
| Justice Kamanga | May I intervene Chair? |
| Justice Potani | Yes, please. |
| Justice Kamanga | Let the witness answer the question// |
| Justice Tembo | //In fact the witness has already answered the question, let's proceed. |

In Examples 4 and 5, the judge interrupted the respondents and petitioners for trying to give too much or too little information; in Example 6, the interruption took place when the judge accused the respondent of not telling the truth; in Examples 7 and 8, the judges are making AD interruptions to control repetition, redundancy, and vagueness. The judges wanted participants to state facts, clearly and quickly so that justice could be delivered in good time.

## *Preventing Emotion interruption*

The data indicates that the judges used PE interruption sparsely in the 2019 Presidential Elections case. According to Sarangi and Slembrouk (1992), PE interruption is caused by the parties' violation of the maxim of quality. Witnesses who have insufficient evidence may sometimes exert emotional influence on the court or the opposite parties for the purpose of winning sympathy and enhancing persuasion. To do so, parties may show grievance or difficulties in court, complain tearfully, exaggerate the truth, and offer inaccurate information. In such cases, judges use PE interruptions to prevent or discourage their emotional exertion.

**Example 9:**

| | |
|---|---|
| Counsel Msisha | *The duplicate which is found on page 542, is it signed by all monitors?* |
| Honourable Phiri | *My lady my lords, yes I confirm.* |
| Counsel Msisha | *Can you show the court where the signatures are?* |
| Honourable Phiri | *My lady my lords where it says signatures, PEOPLE SIGN DIFFERENTLY; SOME PUT JUST NAMES//* |
| Justice Tembo | *//Honourable, don't raise your voice. Could you just respond to the question correctly?* |
| Honourable Phiri | *My lady my lord, yes there are no signatures.* |

In this example, Honourable Phiri failed to answer the question and resorted to raising his voice, which could be an indication of frustration. This utterance violates maxims of quality and manner. The judge interrupted and prevented Honourable Phiri's further emotional expression, thereby obliging him to answer the question. There are, however, few occurrences of such interruptions in the data, possibly because of several factors: first, the trial process was dominated by lawyers and learned witnesses who were aware of the courtroom culture and procedures, and most participants were in full control and avoided a display of personal emotions; secondly, the nature of the case was different from ordinary cases insomuch as emotions are usually not directly involved during an election petition case, because the evidence in such cases is mostly by way of sworn statements.

## *Summarising Points interruption*

Summarising Point (SP) interruptions are similar to Tangentialisation Interruptions in Murata's (1994) framework. These interruptions express something with which participants in the conversation agree. Where a witness is failing to express himself or herself freely due to different factors, such as nervousness, a judge can interrupt to give guidance on what kind of information they need, or the point or issue on which a party needs to address them. It is a conversational rule that speakers be brief, clear, and orderly. However, due to nervousness in court or poor language ability, some witnesses hardly make their utterance to the point, thereby unintentionally violating the maxim of manner. In such a case, the court would interrupt and help parties summarise the main points from their wordy utterance.

**Example 10:**

| Attorney General | Would you want to speak on their behalf? |
|---|---|
| Honourable Chilima | I wouldn't. |
| Attorney General | Do you know if they challenged some results? |
| Honourable Chilima | Not on this one// |
| Justice Kamanga | //May ask the witness to clarify what does he mean when he said not on this one? Can you be as clear as possible. |

SP interruptions are also very rare in the language of judges, as seen in the data. These interruptions can be done ably by the witness lawyers who might need to supplement or support their witnesses' narrations. Judges, as judicial referees, are not supposed to take sides in a trial. Hence, SP could characterise the interruptions by lawyers, unlike those made by the judges.

## Power of the judges and its linguistic implication

As Gibbons (2003) notes, it is an undisputed fact that the legal system is one of the most powerful institutions in societies and that judges are the sole custodians of those powers. Politicians make laws, but it is the courts (judges) that interpret and decide how to interpret them. To do their work, judges must have their authority recognised; and maintaining that authority is a legitimate occupation (Gibbons, 2003). Both non-verbal and verbal semiotics of the court give prominence of power to the judge. For instance, the courtroom sitting arrangement is orientated towards the judge; the rising wooden bench is used by the judge; the judge dresses in expensive gowns, and the judge is addressed and referred to by terms such as 'Justice', 'His Lordship', and 'Her Ladyship'. These are all manifestations that judges are empowered by law to perform certain legal actions and are referees and administrators of justice (Gibbons, 2003; Tracy & Hodge, 2018).

Since, in adversarial systems, truth is contested orally in court, judges need special linguistic tools for mediation. It should not be surprising, therefore, that the average distribution of interruptions in the 2019 Malawian Presidential Elections case shows that it was judges who most often interrupted other participants (n=241, 54.4%); distantly followed by the petitioners (n=95, 24.4%), with respondents coming (closely) last (n=93, 20.9%). The distribution of interruptions in the trial reflects the distribution of discourse space enjoyed by each court participant and the degree to which they were engaged during the trial. However, even though some previous studies report similar findings of judges being the dominant interrupter (Zhao & Gants, 2003; Liao & Sun, 2017; Hu, 2018; Loughland, 2019), findings of this chapter justify why, in the mediation of justice, interruptions are essential and why judges cannot work without them. They are a critical court management tool that enables the judge to control the tempo of the proceedings, without which so many things could go wrong.

The data presented in this chapter has shown dominance of Requiring Information interruption, which judges use to gather and check correctness of facts, as presented in the disputants' versions of their stories. We have also observed that Avoiding Digression interruptions are used with the next highest frequency. These forms of interruptions are used not only to manage the conduct of the trial, but also to monitor disputants who tend to digress from questions and the topic at hand. Digressions delay the trial process unnecessarily. Judges are always faced with the dilemma of striking a balance between accomplishing procedural substantive justice by ensuring that all relevant information is before the court, and the amount of time allocated to each trial. A good judge must be able to unlock these complicated decisions by balancing the number of lawsuits they are able to hear, while at the same time delivering procedural substantiative justice to the disputants (Tracy & Hodge, 2018). It is evident that judge-directed questioning usually resolves cases more quickly than a trial-like adversarial style, like the one practised in Malawi, which may make judges appear to be treating parties differently.

Judges in Malawi courtroom discourse rarely speak because they are the ultimate mediators of a dispute, and they must be seen to be neutral. Impartiality is a legal requirement provided for under Section 9 of the Malawian Constitution, which prescribes the mandate of the judiciary. Therefore, if a judge speaks, they do so to give directions, for example, "Mark it as Exhibit 1, 2" or "Ask the question". They can also speak to allocate turns to other participants by nominating who is to speak next, for instance, "Yes Counsel Y", or to encourage the current holder of the flow to continue, for example, "Counsel X, proceed". Judges in a Malawi courtroom also speak to control the court, using discourse such as, "Case adjourned until the State will be ready with other witnesses". Therefore, finding more interruptions made by the judges in the data means that there was more interaction between them and both the petitioners and the respondents. Interruptions by judges tend to be both procedural and substantive in nature because judges play a dual role, both as administrators of procedures and inquirers of facts. While lawyers argue in a trial by eliciting evidence from witnesses, the overall determination of a case in the Malawian justice system lies with the judicial officer.

We are fully aware that some interruptions made by judges can be damaging, intrusive, and blocking to disputants and witnesses. Such interruptions have the potential to hinder justice. This discussion does not in any way intend to encourage such forms of interruption. It is a legal requirement that everyone has the right to be heard. However, the right to be heard does not empower disputants to digress from central issues and provide too much information that does not match the facts being contested. Judges, therefore, employ different interruption strategies as a way of refereeing the proceedings to ensure they are conducted in a fair and controlled manner.

## Conclusions

The chapter reports on findings on the positive role interruptions play in the justice system by drawing data from the 2019 Malawi Presidential Elections case. This was a very convenient case that brought together a quorum of five judges to oversee the much-contested Presidential elections in Malawi and one of the famous lawsuits in the region.

Interruption is a common strategy used in interactive discourse, such as that of court-room discourse. Different from interruptions experienced in our ordinary daily con-versations, those used in court are related to parties' rights and interests, and they perform a very important judicial role in the administration of justice. Findings of this chapter agree with previous research that judges interrupt more in a courtroom trial than any other courtroom interlocutor. However, this study differs from prior studies, which examined interruptions as an undesirable aspect of courtroom communication. Instead, this chapter has explored how interruptions should be viewed as an essential aspect in the mediation of justice and why judges cannot work without them. The higher occurrence of judges interrupting disputants shows that judges use interruptions as linguistic 'whistles' – tools that they need as judicial 'referees'. As shown, judges need interruptions to control the conduct of a trial, monitor the behaviour of disputants and their legal practitioners, ask for more facts or information, seek clarity, and control the emotions of witnesses.

This study does not give a licence to judicial officers to abuse their powers and use interruption for purposes of blocking, intimidating or silencing witnesses and disputants. Interruptions, as linguistic whistles, are important tools in an adversarial system, and must be encouraged to enhance cooperation for the mutual benefit of disputants. Linguistic phenomena that support the realisation of positive communicative goals need to be supported and encouraged.

This chapter has both practical and theoretical implications. Practically, findings of this chapter can be a valuable resource for judicial officers, as they may illustrate how best to utilise interruptions as linguistic whistles to achieve positive judicial functions in the delivery of justice. The chapter also shows how much power judges have, and how they should avoid abuse of such power but rather using interruptions in such a way that they can promote justice delivery. Theoretically, the tools drawn from the two taxonomies can be argued by some to be templates into which the study has simply fit its data. However, it should be noted that the taxonomies were formulated using data from ordinary conversations. Using courtroom data has, therefore, helped to test which of the tools are applicable to forensic settings. Furthermore, not all tools available in the two taxonomies can be utilised equally by court participants. For instance, lawyers for claimants, petitioners, or defence may not use interruptions when questioning witnesses for the same purposes that judges do. The tools in the two taxonomies need to be modified when a researcher is working with different forms of data.

## Acknowledgements

A special word of gratitude to Honourable Justice Dorothy nyaKaunda Kamanga, Justice of Appeal, Malawi Supreme Court of Appeal; and to Justice Gladys Assima Gondwe, High Court of Malawi, Mzuzu District Registry, for reviewing the first drafts of this chapter and for providing very substantive feedback.

## References

Bogoch, B. 2000. *Discourse dilemmas and courtroom control: The talk of trial judges. Law and Social Enquiry: Journal of the American Bar Foundation*, 25(1):227-247. https://doi.org/10.1111/j.1747-4469.2000.tb00155.x

Brown-Blake, C. 2019. Judges as language referees for Caribbean English vernacular speakers: How do they score? In: M.K. Ralarala, R.H. Kaschula & G. Heydon (eds.). *New frontiers in forensic linguistics: Themes and perspectives in language and law in Africa and beyond.* Stellenbosch: African Sun Media. 149-173.

Brown, P. & Levinson, S. 1987. *Politeness: Some universals in language use.* Cambridge: Cambridge University Press. https://doi.org/10.1017/CBO9780511813085

Gibbons, J. 2003. *Forensic linguistics: An introduction to language in the justice system.* Malden, MA: Blackwell.

Grice, H.P. 1975. Logic and conversation. In: P. Cole & J.L. Morgan (eds.). *Syntax and semantics, 3: Speech acts.* New York, NY: Academic Press. https://doi.org/10.1163/9789004368811_003

Hu, P. 2018. An investigation of interruption in courtroom discourse. *International Journal of Legal Discourse*, 3(2):213-234. https://doi.org/10.1515/ijld-2018-2009

Kishindo, P. 2001. Language and the law in Malawi: A case for the use of indigenous languages in the legal system. *Language Matters: Studies in the Languages of Africa*, 32(1):1-27. https://doi.org/10.1080/10228190108566170

Kondowe, W. 2022. Towards the principle of believability: A new sociopragmatic model in forensic settings. In: M.K. Ralarala, R.H. Kaschula & G. Heydon (eds.). *Language and the law: Global perspectives in forensic linguistics from Africa and beyond.* Stellenbosch: African Sun Media. 261-278. https://doi.org/10.52779/9781991201836/13

Kondowe, W., Liao, M. & Ngwira, F.F. 2022. A study of intentional insincerity in Malawian criminal justice: Witnesses' discursive strategies. In: M.K. Ralarara, R.H. Kaschula & G. Heydon (eds.). *Language and the law: Global perspectives in forensic linguistics from Africa and beyond.* Stellenbosch: African Sun Media. 241-260. https://doi.org/10.52779/9781991201836/12

Kondowe, W. Insincerity in lawyers' questioning strategies in Malawian criminal courtroom discourse. *Text & Talk: An Interdisciplinary Journal of Language, Discourse & Communication Studies* (In press).

Liao, M. 2009a. *Courtroom questions and their interaction*. Beijing: Law Press.

Liao, M. 2009b. A study of interruption in Chinese criminal courtroom discourse. *Text & Talk*, 29(2):175-199. https://doi.org/10.1515/TEXT.2009.008

Liao, M. & Sun, Y. 2017. Cooperation in Chinese courtroom discourse. In: J. Giltrow & D. Stein (eds.). *The pragmatic turn in law: Inference and interpretation in legal discourse*. Boston: De Gruyter. 57-87. https://doi.org/10.1515/9781501504723-003

Loughland, A. 2019. Female judges interrupted: A study of interruption behaviour during oral argument in the High Court of Australia. *Melbourne University Law Review*, 43(2):1-30. (Advance copy.)

Lu, P. & Huang, C. 2006. Interruption in Mandarin mother-child conversation. *Concentric: Studies in Linguistics*, 32(2):1-31.

Malawi Government. 2018. Malawi's Constitution of 1994 with Amendments through 2017. Zomba: Government Printer.

Mead, R. 1985. *Courtroom discourse*. Birmingham: University of Birmingham Printing Section.

Murata, K. 1994. Intrusive or cooperative: A cross cultural study of interruption. *Journal of Pragmatics*, 21:385-400. https://doi.org/10.1016/0378-2166(94)90011-6

Sacks, H., Schegloff, E. & Jefferson, G. 1978. A simplest systematics for the organisation of turn-taking for conversation. In: J. Schenkein (ed.). *Studies in the organisation of conversational interaction*. New York: Academic Press.

Sarangi, S.K. & Slembrouk, S. 1992. Non-cooperation in communication: A reassessment of Gricean Pragmatics. *Journal of Pragmatics*, 17:117-154. https://doi.org/10.1016/0378-2166(92)90037-C

Shi, J. 2021. Analysis of the type of interruption in courtroom conversation. *British Journal of English Linguistics*, 9(3):39-48.

Solan, L. 1993. *The language of judges*. Chicago: The University of Chicago Press. https://doi.org/10.7208/chicago/9780226767895.001.0001

Sun, H. 2017. The cause of the interruption of limitation in Chinese civil law: Bringing a lawsuit. Advances in Social Science, Education and Humanities Research, volume 123. *2nd International Conference on Education, Sports, Arts and Management Engineering (ICESAME, 2017)*. 627-630. https://doi.org/10.2991/icesame-17.2017.135

Tracy, K. & Hodge, D. 2018. Judge discourse moves that enact and endanger procedural justice. *Discourse & Society*, 29(1):63-85. https://doi.org/10.1177/0957926517726112

Wanying, L. 2011. *Discourse and power in courtroom*. Beijing: China Social Science Press.

Widodo, A., Hidayat, D.R., Venus, A. & Suseno, S. 2019. The pattern of interruption in Indonesia court room. *International Journal of Recent Technology and Engineering (IJRTE)*, 8(2S):506-512.

Zhao, X. & Gantz, W. 2003. Disruptive and cooperative interruption in prime-time television fiction: The role of gender, status, and topic. *Journal of Communication*, 53:347-362. https://doi.org/10.1111/j.1460-2466.2003.tb02595.x

Zimmerman, D.H. & West, C. 1996. Sex roles, interruptions, and silences in conversation. In: S. Rajendra (ed.). *Towards a critical sociolinguistics*. John Benjamins Publishing Company. 211-125. https://doi.org/10.1075/cilt.125.12zim

# ZIMBABWE'S CONSTITUTIONAL SAFEGUARDS FOR PERSONS WITH COMMUNICATION DISABILITIES

## Implications for access to justice


*Paul Svongoro*
*Monwabisi K. Ralarala*


## Introduction

Although the Constitution of Zimbabwe (GoZ, 2013) makes worthwhile guarantees for persons with communication and other disabilities, persons living with disabilities, their families and members of the public generally believe that persons with communication and other disabilities still find it difficult to access and participate effectively in the country's criminal justice system. While reasons for this commonly-held perception differ, some attribute this perceived inaccessibility to procedural barriers related to situations when persons with communication disabilities are unable to participate fully in the justice system as they do not fully understand court procedures and the duties of the various role players (Bornman et al., 2015; Msipa, 2015).

Others believe that the difficulties faced by persons with disabilities could be related to the physical environment of the courthouse; for instance, barriers posed by infrastructure, such as staircases instead of ramps (Fitzsimons, 2016; Zimbabwe Lawyers for Human Rights [ZLHR] (2020). Yet others think that barriers relate to rigid rules and procedures that have to be followed when presenting evidence that may pose challenges for persons with communication disabilities who wish to express themselves freely (Msipa, 2015). Owing to these and other reasons, the general public believes that persons with disabilities are at an increased risk of being denied fair and equal treatment within the country's justice system.

While on the surface, the challenges faced by persons with communication disabilities (e.g., the deaf, hearing impaired, hard-of-hearing and the deaf-blind) may seem to be solely a Zimbabwean problem, research in other parts of the world has reported similar challenges (Kalaluka, 2013). Findings from studies conducted in South Africa, for example, reveal how persons with communication disabilities, such as the deaf and the hard-of-hearing, face different normative, physical, and informational barriers when they find themselves in South Africa's courts of law (Bornman et al., 2015; Viljoen, 2018; White et al., 2020).

Still concerning South Africa, researchers concur that, despite existing foreign and national legislation, persons with communication disabilities and their families still find it difficult and even overwhelming to access and participate effectively in the criminal justice system, irrespective of whether as a witness or an alleged perpetrator (Archer & Hurley, 2013; Bornman et al., 2015). This could be because of the limited and constrained resources, accommodations and support offered to persons with communication disabilities who need to access the court system (Fitzsimons, 2016). Docrat, Kaschula and Ralarala (2017:275) underscore the complexity of the problem, and they argue that:

> ...even though there is an overtly empowering legal and constitutional framework for Deaf and hearing-impaired persons, covert policies remain in place on the ground. There is therefore a disjuncture between these overt language policies and the disempowering covert implementation (or lack thereof) of policy at all levels when it comes to sign language, from police investigations to the way [d]eaf people are treated in the South African criminal courts...

Flynn (2016) highlights three distinct inaccessible features in the UK's court system that unfairly affect persons with disabilities: (1) the physical infrastructure (instead of ramps, architectural features such as staircases, which act as environmental barriers); (2) procedural barriers (instances when persons with disabilities do not, or are unable to, understand court procedures and communicate effectively with key role players in the court system), and (3) evidentiary barriers (those rules of evidence and procedures that are not adapted to facilitate effective communication with persons living with communication disabilities who may be witnesses in court, for example).

In Zambia and Kenya too, studies reveal how persons with disabilities face challenges accessing court premises and infrastructure. Kalaluka (2013) reports that, in Kenya, a High Court judge was taken round the court building by a wheelchair-bound litigant to demonstrate how difficult it was for persons with disabilities to access the court building without ramps. The Kenyan High Court was therefore challenged for having inaccessible court premises that may have denied the petitioner access to justice. Thus, the current barriers posed by the physical structure of the law courts in Kenya remain a serious hindrance for persons with disabilities to the extent that accessing courts remain a Herculean task. Lawyers with physical disabilities face the same difficulties, yet some of these physical obstacles could be minimised simply through the construction of ramps to ensure that persons in wheelchairs can easily access all buildings.

Similar challenges for persons with disabilities are also reported as a common occurrence among European Union (EU) member states. The FRA Annual Report 2011 (EU FRA, 2011), highlights serious concerns, practices, and concrete obstacles to accessing justice for persons with communication disabilities in EU member states. Some of the key concerns include unnecessarily strict time limits on bringing claims. The strict time limits do not give persons with disabilities enough time to prepare their claims. This is, for instance, the case in 22 of the 27 EU member states. Other notable difficulties include excessive legal costs and the complexity of legal procedures, which in most cases are not understood by persons with disabilities.

## The research problem

On a regular basis, there are accusations against the courts for not safeguarding the rights of persons with disabilities within Zimbabwe's justice system. While most of these crying voices disappear unheard, a few are still 'heard' through daily and weekly newspapers. In Zimbabwe, one such story, 'Justice eludes people with disabilities', was reported by the Zimbabwe Human Rights NGO Forum (commonly referred to as 'the Forum') (2016) in the *Financial Gazette*. Although the researchers will not go into details of the story due to space constraints, the story mirrors that perpetrators evade justice while persons with disabilities face many unfortunate circumstances because of the country's skewed justice delivery that seemingly fails to serve them.

Critics (e.g., Msipa, 2015) argue that, for far too long, the justice system in Zimbabwe has been inaccessible to people with a range of disabilities because investigative and judicial procedures fail to adapt to meet their needs. For instance, The Law Society of Zimbabwe (LSZ) (among other organisations) agrees that, at present, persons with disabilities are not receiving any preferential treatment from lawyers; yet lawyers, due to their privileged understanding of the law, should be at the forefront in the fight for the rights of disadvantaged groups in society.

The Law Society of Zimbabwe further acknowledges that, although it often deals with cases involving deaf litigants, court cases have been postponed several times because of the absence of a sign language interpreter (Legal Resources Foundation, 2020). For these and other reasons, the society agrees that the justice system needs to be improved so that it makes provisions for persons with disabilities. The failure of courts to provide interpreters for the deaf is echoed by the Zimbabwe Forum, a federation of human rights' non-governmental organisations, which provides free legal counsel and representation to persons whose rights would have been violated. The Forum observes that not all courts have employed court interpreters who are competent in sign language.

Another story that demonstrates the plight of people with communication disabilities was published in the *Newsday* newspaper on 24 April 2020. The story authored by the ZLHR (2020) carried the headline, 'Zimbabwe court orders ZBC and government to ensure people living with disabilities access vital information on coronavirus in a friendly format'. Although the story is situated in a slightly different context, it also demonstrates glaring inequalities and injustices that persons with communication and other disabilities face on a day-to-day basis.

From the few examples cited, the stark reality is that persons with communication disabilities still face many barriers when accessing courts in Zimbabwe. As a result, they sometimes choose not to report their victimisation as, all too often, the process seems to be more of an obstacle than a benefit. Likewise, perpetrators with communication disabilities may experience profound disadvantages in preparing and presenting their defence if not provided with appropriate accommodations during both the pre-trial and trial processes.

## Research objectives

This study aimed to:

(a)   Examine constitutional, statutory and other provisions made for persons with disabilities in Zimbabwe's justice delivery system;

(b)   Examine whether Zimbabwe's constitutional, statutory and other provisions enhance or impede access to justice by persons with disabilities; and

(c)   Suggest how Zimbabwe's justice delivery system could be transformed to reduce any identifiable barriers to justice for persons with disabilities.

## Significance of the study

Various international and national laws forbid discrimination against persons with communication disabilities and make it clear that they should be given fair and equal access to the court system (see, for instance, the Convention on the Rights of Persons with Disabilities (CRPD) (United Nations (UN), 2006); the Protocol to the African Charter on Human and Peoples' Rights on the Rights of Persons with Disabilities in Africa (hereinafter, 'African Charter') (African Union, 2018); and the Constitution of Zimbabwe Amendment Act No. 20 of 2013 (hereinafter, 'the Zimbabwe Constitution' or 'the Constitution')) (GoZ, 2013). Scholars generally agree that, for transformative equality to be achieved, certain rules and laws need to be changed to include specific accommodations for witnesses and accused persons with communication disabilities to enable them to participate effectively in the justice system (Fredman, 2005, 2007; Goldschmidt, 2017).

Furthermore, it is the responsibility of individual courts to ensure effective access to justice. When all people participate effectively in court processes, benefits accrue for both the victim and the perpetrator because all parties are allowed an opportunity to present their version of events and feel believed. More importantly, when access to justice is guaranteed, it assists both victims and perpetrators to experience the effective fulfilment of their human rights.

To contribute to addressing the issues raised above, this study therefore explores the statutory provisions that Zimbabwe's laws make for persons with communication disabilities. These provisions are examined in terms of these factors: legal or policy provisions; procedural (and evidential) provisions; physical provisions; information and communication provisions; and economic provisions. These provisions are examined to ascertain whether they aid or make it difficult for persons with communication disabilities to access Zimbabwe's justice system.

Apart from addressing any identifiable impediments to access to justice by persons with communication disabilities, the study also suggests possible court accommodations that may assist persons with communication disabilities to participate more effectively in the court system. By so doing, the study, hopes to contribute to the advancement of transformative equality policies and, hence, the promotion of justice for all citizens, regardless of their ability or disability.

## Scope of the study

While the focus of this study is on access to Zimbabwe's justice system by persons with communication disabilities, in a way, the study overlaps into disability studies. In this study, we borrow the definition from the Disabled Persons Act [Chapter 17:01] in the Constitution of Zimbabwe, which defines a disabled person as, a person with a physical, mental or sensory disability, including a visual, hearing or speech functional disability, which gives rise to physical, cultural or social barriers inhibiting him from participating at an equal level with other members of society in activities, undertakings or fields of employment that are open to other members of society (GoZ, 2013).

While various sections of Zimbabwe's Constitution (and the Disabled Persons Act) make provisions for persons with disabilities in general, this study mainly focused on sections that mention disabilities which affect a person's chances of fully participating in the trial process as a witness or as an accused person, e.g., from the time of arrest, police questioning statement and during the court trial because they are deaf, hard-of-hearing, and blind. The catchy words or phrases we found in the Constitution, which relate to persons with communication disabilities (PWCDs) were:

> (1) persons with disabilities,

(2) persons with physical and mental disabilities,

(3) mentally disordered or defective persons *(note the word 'defective' is used in a derogatory way)*,

(4) persons who are deaf or mute or both.

However, in this study we sometimes refer to persons with communication disabilities (PWCDs) as simply persons with disabilities (PWDs).

## The methodology

The researchers adopted document analysis as the primary method of data collection. Document analysis primarily involved researchers' identification, collection and use of case law/recent judgments that have relevant information about the matter under investigation. For Zimbabwe, the researchers analysed documents that included, but were not limited to, the Constitution of Zimbabwe (GoZ, 2013), The Criminal Procedure and Evidence Act (GoZ, 2016), and The Magistrates' Act. The selected documents were analysed to identify the stated guarantees and provisions for persons with disabilities and with a view to understanding how the guarantees and provisions in these documents compare with regional and international protocols for persons with disabilities. Regionally or on the African continent, the study examined provisions made by the African Charter on Human and People's Rights (African Union, 2018) and at the international level, the study analysed provisions made by the the UN's Convention on the Rights of Persons with Disabilities (UN, 2006). Document analysis was meant to provide the researchers with an appreciation of the procedural and physical provisions, which various legal and constitutional documents made for persons with disabilities and the extent to which courts in Zimbabwe safeguarded those provisions during the trial processes. Put differently, the researchers were therefore, able to compare the guarantees various laws made on paper for persons with disabilities and the realities in Zimbabwe's justice system.

Alongside document analysis, data for the study were collected through observation of open court proceedings involving persons with disabilities in Zimbabwe's courtrooms. Zimbabwe's courts have an open system: members of the public can freely visit courtrooms and observe proceedings, as long as they observe rules of the courts. The study capitalised on this and benefited from observation of cases, which involved persons with various communication and other disabilities. The aims of observation of court proceedings were twofold: first, to identify any obstacles that could impede the full participation of persons with communication disabilities in the trial process; and second, to focus on identifying any accommodations that courts made in the open court proceedings to assist persons with communication disabilities to participate actively in those proceedings.

## Theoretical framework

The data collected for the study were analysed in terms of transformative equality (Goldschmidt, 2017), an approach rooted in law that is critical for understanding the equality and non-discrimination obligations in conditions of systemic power inequality (e.g., the court system) (UN, 2006). Transformative equality recognises the need to change rules and laws to include different perspectives and not only dominant views and experiences (Goldschmidt, 2017). As such, transformative equality targets certain structures and systems (including the court system) to bring about change through introducing a variety of positive measures for persons with disabilities (Degener, 2016). An international rights treaty that emphasises transformative equality for persons with disabilities is the United Nations Convention on the Rights of Persons with Disabilities (UNCRPD) (UN, 2006), which emphasises three types of obligations: formal equality (equal treatment as a matter of law); substantive equality (measures to equalise the enjoyment of human rights); and transformative equality (measures to remove the causes of inequality) (Minkowitz, 2017). Formal equality is needed to have equal status as members of society; substantive equality is needed to redistribute power and resources proactively; and transformative equality is needed to transform opportunities, institutions and systems so that they are no longer grounded in historically determined paradigms of power (Minkowitz, 2017).

For this chapter, the focus was mainly on examining language use, communication, and barriers to effective communication between court officials and persons with communication disabilities, who participated in the trial process with the aim of contributing to transformative equality in the legal domain. According to Hepple (2013), while one of the main aims of equality initiatives is to increase the participation of disadvantaged groups in institutions, the introduction and implementation of the schemes to accommodate the needs of persons with disabilities only rarely involves the active participation of those groups. Instead, most such initiatives are designed by the holders of power (government, employers, etc.) and rely on top-down, command-and-control mechanisms for their enforcement. The result is that many schemes end up producing enormous paper documents that are ineffective (Hepple, 2013).

The researchers therefore viewed transformative equality as a very useful tool for analysing any inequalities in Zimbabwe's justice delivery systems, which prevent persons with communication disabilities from fully accessing and enjoying their fundamental human rights and possibly suggest measures to remove the various barriers to equality within Zimbabwe's justice system.

## Discussion and findings

In the sections below, the researchers analysed the Constitution of Zimbabwe and its related Acts, the African Charter on Human and People's Rights (ACHPR) and UN's Convention on the Rights of Persons with Disabilities (CRPD) in terms of the physical, procedural, legal and any other guarantees and provisions they make regarding access to justice by persons with disabilities. The provisions these statutes make were then analysed according to the tenets of transformative equality.

The rationale in studying the guarantees and provisions that the various statutes make was three-fold. First, the analysis was meant to allow the researchers to arrive at an informed point of view, regarding the extent to which these statutes make safeguards to access to justice by persons with communication disabilities. Secondly, the analysis also enabled the researchers to explore the extent to which institutions such as the police and the courts protect access rights by persons with communication disabilities. Finally, by examining these statutes, the researchers were able to identify gaps – be they physical, procedural, legal, attitudinal, economic and communication – affecting access to justice for persons with communication disabilities so as to advocate the necessary policy reforms to ensure that persons with disabilities have equal access to justice as people without disabilities. Below, we present our key findings from the analysis of the selected legal documents and our observation of court proceedings in Zimbabwe's courtrooms.

### *Legal provisions on access to justice by PWDs in national, regional and international statutes*

The Constitution of Zimbabwe, the African Charter on Human and People's Rights (referred to as the African Charter in short) and the UN's Convention on the Rights of Persons with Disabilities make very clear provisions for access to justice by persons with disabilities. The African Charter was adopted in 2018, with Zimbabwe being among the signatories. In this protocol, Article 13 addresses the 'Right to Access Justice' and also highlights that states have an obligation to ensure that persons with disabilities have access to justice on an equal basis, including the provision of appropriate age, gender and procedural accommodations (African Union, 2018).

In principle, Zimbabwe has passed the relevant legislation that specifically accommodates persons with (communication) disabilities who need to access the court system and that allows equal participation in all legal proceedings. For example, Zimbabwe's Constitution (GoZ, 2013:11) foregrounds equality and states that "[e]veryone is equal before the law and has the right to equal protection and benefit of the law, including persons with disabilities". The express inclusion of the phrase "persons with disabilities" in this clause implicitly includes persons with communication disabilities, such as the deaf, the hard-of-heading, the blind and the deaf-blind.

Furthermore, Zimbabwe's Constitution clearly emphasises that no one should be discriminated against on the grounds of disability; and it underscores that "failing to eliminate obstacles that unfairly limit or restrict persons with disabilities from enjoying equal opportunities or failing to take steps to reasonably accommodate the needs of such persons" is unconstitutional (GoZ, 2013: 13). However, during the observation of court proceedings, we encountered a case in which a deaf accused person who was in a wheelchair complained about how he was treated during the time of his arrest and at the police station. He complained about how police officers carried him while sitting in his wheelchair and shoved the wheelchair into the back of their police van. He further complained about how he fell off the wheelchair while being carried into the charge office for questioning because the police station building did not have a ramp for wheelchairs, just staircases. While this may appear an isolated case, a descriptive study on wheelchair accessibility in Harare's public buildings, conducted by Useh, Moyo and Munyonga (2001) confirms that this challenge is widespread in Zimbabwe. According to the study, parking areas have the lowest average wheelchair compliance percentage of 18%, followed by ramps (at 39%). Thus, physical obstacles like staircases, while disabled persons need to access buildings using ramps, impede dignified access to justice for persons with disabilities.

The Constitution through the Disabled Persons Act (Chapter 17:01) further proclaims that persons with communication disabilities (the deaf, hard-of-hearing, deaf-blind and the blind) may not be discriminated against in a court of law because of their inability to communicate; and key role players in the court system should provide court accommodations to assist such individuals to be able to communicate and testify in court (GoZ, 2013).

The implications of the above clause are very clear regarding persons with communication disabilities. The first is that courts and justice officials should recognise that the rights of persons with communication disabilities (e.g., the deaf, the hard-of-hearing and the deaf-blind) are constitutionally given and should therefore be respected at all times. The second implication is that courts and other justice officials should do everything in their power to assist such persons. Regarding this important provision for persons with communication disabilities, during the observation of court proceedings, we witnessed two cases involving deaf witnesses. In both instances, the cases could not proceed because the courts had not provided sign language interpreters in time. While these observed cases may, once again, appear isolated, at a 2021 workshop conducted in Zimbabwe by the United Nations Development Programme (UNDP) and the United Nations Partnership on the Rights of Persons with Disabilities Project (UNPRPD), which drew participants from the magistracy, police services, prison services and other government departments, such postponements were confirmed to be common occurrences in most courts due the unavailability of sign language interpreters (UNDP, 2021). Such delays in providing the required intermediaries amounts to a denial of justice in the context of the 'justice delayed is justice denied principle', (Mwela, 2013).

Following after relevant sections of both the CPRD (UN, 2006) and the African Charter (African Union, 2018), Zimbabwean law further provides for the appointment of an intermediary for a person with a communication disability, as highlighted in the Criminal Law (Sexual Offences Act (Chapter 9: 12), it is stated:

> [W]henever criminal proceedings are pending before any court and it appears to such court that it would expose any witness under the biological or mental age of eighteen years to undue mental stress or suffering if he or she testifies at such proceedings, the court may appoint a competent person as an intermediary in order to enable such witness to give his or her evidence through that intermediary.

While the provision cited in this paragraph may not be directly related to persons with other disabilities, it serves to show that Zimbabwean law makes provisions for various disadvantaged groups like children and those with disabilities.

Contrary to the provisions of the UN's CPRD (UN, 2006) and the African Charter (African Union, 2018), Zimbabwe is yet to make clear provisions regarding overcoming physical barriers in accessing institutions, such as courts of law and police stations. While the CRPD (UN, 2006) and the African Charter emphasise the need to have physical accommodations for persons with disabilities, for example, those with communication disabilities and in wheelchairs, facilities such as ramps, and rooms equipped with closed-circuit television systems, are still a pipe dream in most institutions in Zimbabwe.

### Language and communication provisions on access to justice by persons with disabilities in Zimbabwe's Constitution

To comprehend the various language and communication provisions that the Constitution of Zimbabwe (GoZ, 2013) makes regarding access to justice by persons with disabilities, Sections 6, 22 and 70 of the Constitution of Zimbabwe (GoZ, 2013) were analysed. Section 6, for instance, makes very clear language provisions for all citizens of the country, regardless of race, ethnicity, class, and status. Section 6(1) stipulates Chewa, Chibarwe, English, Kalanga, Khoisan, Nambya, Ndau, Ndebele, Shangani, Shona, sign language, Sotho, Tonga, Tswana, Venda and Xhosa as the officially recognised languages of Zimbabwe. The same section further stipulates that an Act of Parliament may prescribe other languages as officially recognised languages and may prescribe languages of record. Of interest is Subsection 3, which clearly states:

> The State and all institutions and agencies of government at every level must:
>
> (a) ensure that all officially recognised languages are treated equitably; and
>
> (b) take into account the language preferences of people affected by governmental measures or communications (Section 6, Constitution of Zimbabwe, 2013).

This subsection places sign language on the same footing as other official languages. By this provision, deaf persons have the constitutional right to be heard in the justice delivery system and it is therefore the responsibility of courts to ensure that they can participate in the trial process, just like speakers of the other languages listed in the same clause. This provision is meant to ensure equal access to justice by all citizens, regardless of their ability or disability.

Further to the above important provision, Subsection 4 of Zimbabwe's Constitution emphasises the need for the state to promote and advance the use of all languages recognised in Zimbabwe as official languages, including sign language, along with the creation of conditions that facilitate the development of those languages.

While Section 6 of the Constitution of Zimbabwe (GoZ, 2013) makes important language provisions for all citizens, including those with disabilities, Section 22 focuses on provisions specific to persons with disabilities. For instance, Section 22(1) states: "The State and all institutions and agencies of government at every level must recognise the rights of persons with physical or mental disabilities, in particular their right to be treated with respect and dignity." Although this section does not state any specific areas in which persons with physical or mental disabilities should be treated with respect and dignity, this means that such persons deserve to be treated with respect and dignity in all spheres of life, including when they wish to access the justice system.

Further to the above, Section 6, read in conjunction with Subsections 2, 3 and 4 of the Constitution of Zimbabwe GoZ, 2013), also emphasise that persons with physical and mental disabilities should be assisted by the state, state institutions and agencies of government at all levels. Of particular interest are Subsections 3(b) and 3(c), which state:

> The State and all institutions and agencies of government at every level must:
>
> (3b) consider the specific requirements of persons with all forms of disability as one of the priorities in development plans;
>
> (3c) encourage the use and development of forms of communication suitable for persons with physical or mental disabilities.

When one considers the provisions made for persons with disabilities in the subsections above, it is fully clear that the constitution is very sensitive to the needs of persons with disabilities. However, there is a mismatch that is observed when one considers the practical realities that apply in institutions of justice when persons with disabilities attempt to access police stations and courts of law. For instance, cases involving persons with disabilities have been found to drag on for years because specific requirements for such persons' communication are not available (UNDP, 2021).

Related to the above requirements for persons with disabilities, Subsection (4) adds: "The State must take appropriate measures to ensure that buildings and amenities to which the public has access are accessible to persons with disabilities." However, while the laws of the land are very clear about the kind of rights that PWDs should be accorded, it is disheartening to note that most court buildings and amenities remain barely accessible by PWDs, while other members of the public access them with ease.

Also relevant for the current study is Section 70 of the Constitution of Zimbabwe (GoZ, 2013), which explains the rights of accused persons. In our examination, we considered Subsection 2, which makes the following important submissions regarding the rights of accused persons:

> (2) Where this section requires information to be given to a person –
>
> (a) the information must be given in a language the person understands, and
>
> (b) if the person cannot read or write, any document embodying the information must be explained in such a way that the person understands it.

The above section clearly explains the rights of accused persons and does not exclude any accused persons based on their physical or mental status. This means that all accused persons in Zimbabwe should enjoy the same rights, like having the information about their crime given in a language they understand, or having the same information explained in a way the person understands.

However, the reality about the courts in Zimbabwe is such that, where cases involve the deaf, for instance, the availability of persons who can present the information in the language of the deaf, or at least explain in the language they understand, is not guaranteed, unlike for accused persons who are able to hear. According to our observations and interviews with court interpreters, cases involving deaf persons are sometimes postponed and courts often take a long time to find suitable persons to assist accused persons who are deaf. However, if training for sign language interpreters was available in Zimbabwe's universities and colleges, trained sign language interpreters would be in full-time employment in Zimbabwe's law courts to avoid the 'justice delayed is justice denied' situations referred to earlier.

## Procedural provisions regarding access to justice by PWDs in The Criminal Procedure and Evidence Act and The Magistrates' Act

Both the Criminal Procedure and Evidence Act (Chapter 9: 07) and The Magistrates' Act (Chapter 7:10) provide for the rights of PWDs and the procedures to be followed in connection with trials and detentions involving mentally disordered or defective *persons* (*note the use of the word defective in the constitution, which in itself is inappropriate*) and persons who are deaf or mute, or both (GoZ, 2016). The overarching provision is made in Section 190 of the Criminal Procedure and Evidence Act, which explains the right to legal representation of accused persons. It states:

> Every person charged with an offence may make his defence at his trial and have the witnesses examined or cross-examined –
>
> (a) by a legal practitioner representing him; or
>
> (b) in the case of an accused person under the age of sixteen years who is being tried in a magistrate's court, by his natural or legal guardian; or
>
> (c) where the court considers he requires the assistance of another person and has permitted him to be so assisted, by that other person.

The above section of the Act makes it very clear that all accused persons, regardless of social class, have the same right to legal representation. However, of the three provisions, it is the third one that caught the researchers' attention. It makes it abundantly clear that it is the prerogative of the court to decide if an accused person requires the assistance of another person. This is often necessary when the accused person has some kind of communication (or other) disability. Unfortunately, in the case of Zimbabwe, it is not the accused person who decides, but the court that decides as it sees fit.

Apart from the above, Section 192 of the Criminal Procedure and Evidence Act (GoZ, 2016) also makes provisions for the trial of mentally disordered or defective persons (*see our previous comment regarding the inappropriateness of the word defective*), while Section 193 of the same Act also makes provisions for the detention of persons who are deaf or mute, or both. While Section 192 calls upon the magistrates to proceed with the trial by following the dictates of the Mental Health Act, Section 193 states:

> …in any criminal proceedings, if it appears to the court that the accused is unable to conduct his defence properly by reason of deafness or muteness or both, the court may, if it is satisfied, after hearing such evidence as the State may lead and such other evidence as the court may think necessary or desirable, decide that it is necessary in the interests of the safety of the public or for the protection of the accused that the accused should not be released from custody or should be kept in custody, as the case may be, or order the accused to be kept in custody in some prison pending the decision of the President in terms of subsection (3).

While the above provision may require the accused to be detained in a prison before the case is finalised, the provision makes some safeguards regarding the safety of the accused. Thus, whether the accused person who is deaf or mute, or both, gets released or continues to be detained in a prison, it is for his or her good and that of the public.

Apart from the above provisions, another procedural accommodation that clarifies what courts ought to do when they are confronted by language and communication barriers in their processes is mentioned in the Criminal Procedure and Evidence Amendment Act (Chapter 9:07). This provision relates to language accommodations. It recommends that, in the case of deaf, mute and hard-of-hearing witnesses and accused persons, persons who are appointed intermediaries for persons with these communication disabilities should be conversant in the language of the witnesses or the accused persons. The use of sign language (and a competent sign language interpreter), as well as other means of communication methods, should be provided for. Section 161(2) of the Criminal Procedure and Evidence Act states that the expression, *'viva voce'*, shall, in the case of a 'deaf and dumb witness' (terminology used in the Act), include Sign language, and, in the case of a witness younger than 18 years (including a mentally challenged patient aged below 18 years), include demonstrations, using anatomical dolls, gestures or any other form of non-verbal expression.

Similarly, the Children's Act (Chapter 5:06 of GoZ, 2001) makes reasonable procedural provisions for all children, including victims with communication disabilities who are younger than 18 years old and who are appearing in a children's court or participating in a trial process through the Victim Friendly Procedure or Court. The Victim Friendly Court was enacted by Zimbabwean law to allow vulnerable witnesses to give evidence through closed circuit television (away from the actual courtroom) and through other special survivor sensitive ways. The Children's Act also mentions appropriate questioning techniques that may be used in the court. Nevertheless, while these procedural provisions are commendable, to date, no specific guidelines have been developed as to how these differential questioning techniques should be employed.

## Gaps in access to justice by PWDs: Towards transformative equality in Zimbabwe's justice delivery system

While the CRPD (UN, 2006), the African Charter (AU, 2018) and Zimbabwe's constitutional and statutory provisions explained above, make worthwhile provisions regarding access to justice by persons with disabilities, the findings presented have shown some gaps that still exist in the implementation of these provisions. The researchers have shown that, while various national, regional and international statutes emphasise social inclusion and participation of all human beings in the justice system of their country, including those of persons with disabilities, Zimbabwe still needs to upscale the implementation of various constitutional and statutory provisions to ensure that persons with disabilities have equal access to justice. If this does not happen, the country will lag far behind others in meeting the principles of the UN's (2006) CRPD, which are equality, accessibility, autonomy, participation and inclusion (Fredman, 2007; Goldschmidt, 2017).

To ensure that there is equality, for instance, the government of Zimbabwe has to transform the legal system into a more balanced structure by taking asymmetrical power structures into account. This can be achieved by, for example, making reasonable physical and procedural accommodations, modifications, and adjustments to the justice system to ensure that all citizens enjoy, or exercise their rights and freedoms on an equal basis. The importance of reasonable accommodations is specifically listed as an obligation in Article 5 of the UNCRPD; and refusal to provide reasonable accommodation constitutes discrimination (UN, 2006). Similarly, special temporary measures that are necessary to accelerate or achieve equality of persons with disabilities shall not be considered discrimination. These measures are actually regarded as part of the duty to promote equal treatment.

Another important principle of the CRPD on which Zimbabwe still lags is that of accessibility (UN, 2006). According to Fredman (2007), accessibility is not only a human rights principle, but also a precondition to exercise other rights. If one cannot access a court of law, for instance, because there are physical barriers, this prevents one from exercising one's right to be heard in a court of law. This means that accessibility is linked to equality. According to the tenets of transformative equality, states have an obligation to provide accessibility as an essential part of the new duty to respect, protect and fulfil equality rights (Fredman, 2005). Barriers to access to essential objects, facilities, goods, and services meant for the public should be removed gradually in a systematic manner and continuously monitored with the aim to achieve full accessibility. This close link between accessibility and equality means that a denial of access may amount to discrimination.

With regard to the principle of autonomy (Goldschmidt, 2017), various international and local statutes examined earlier recognise the importance of according persons with disabilities their own autonomy and independence, including the freedom to make their own choices. In fact, the first principle mentioned in the CRPD (UN, 2006) is respect for inherent dignity, individual autonomy (including the freedom to make one's own choices), and independence of persons (UN, 2006). Although this principle has a more individual focus, it is related to the principles of accessibility and participation.

In terms of transformative equality, persons with disabilities should decide what is best for them, instead of having others (e.g., a magistrate, a prosecutor, an interpreter and other officers of the courts, as in Zimbabwe's justice system) decide what is good for deaf, hard-of-hearing and deaf-blind persons for example. The right to be an independent person with legal capacity, who is entitled to have as much say as possible on all matters related to his or her own private and public life, is crucial to realise human rights. At the basis of personal autonomy for all human beings lie freedom of choice and the attribution of agency. In the capability approach (what people are actually able to do or to be), and in the CRPD, the perspective has changed towards recognising, "what people CAN do, what they are capable of, instead of what they can NOT do" (Goldschmidt, 2017:9). The capability approach is rooted in disability studies and acknowledges that society is made up of individuals with unequal abilities and needs (Nussbaum, 2011).

Apart from the above principles, another principle is that of participation (Goldschmidt, 2017). This principle is best summarised by the common slogan, 'Nothing about us without us', which is very common in disability conventions. This principle calls for the active involvement of persons with disabilities in all the processes of the court. The question one may pose in connection with this is: To what extent are disabled persons actively involved in the processes of the courts in Zimbabwe? While the above question is likely to draw various responses from different sections of the society – some of which may be highly charged – it is clear that participation is also related to equality. If one can fully participate in the activities of one's country, then one is an equal member of society. Without full and effective participation, one is excluded from society. If disabled persons in Zimbabwe fail to participate fully in their trials in criminal law courts, for example, then several of their other human rights are violated.

In view of the above, steps clearly have to be taken to enable all citizens to participate in Zimbabwe's court system. Institutions of justice should put in place mechanisms aimed at assisting persons with disabilities to participate actively in the country's justice system; and active measures have to be taken to consult or involve them and their representative organisations. Thus, from the brief explanation above, it is clear that participation is intricately linked to inclusion and personal autonomy, an issue which we did not delve into in detail.

The principles mentioned and explained above reflect what Fredman (2007) describes as 'the four dimensions' of substantive equality: redressing disadvantage (the redistributive dimension); addressing stigma, stereotyping and prejudice (the recognition dimension); facilitating voice and participation (the participative dimension); and accommodating difference, including through structural change (the transformative dimension). It is only when all these dimensions of equality are addressed that we begin to see all citizens participating as equals in the various activities of the country, including when they are accused persons and witnesses in the courts of law.

## Policy recommendations

From the discussion above, it is clear that, if courts and other institutions for justice in Zimbabwe are serious about increasing access to justice for persons with disabilities, there is an urgent need for them to adopt a number of legal, physical, language and procedural changes within their areas of jurisdiction. For instance, physical and language accommodations identified and explained in this chapter ought to be made to increase access to justice by persons with disabilities in Zimbabwe. Furthermore, institutions for justice should provide practical and feasible guidelines to ensure that courts, for example, are deaf-aware and sign language inclusive to reduce gaps associated with failed and delayed communication with persons who are deaf or who have hearing impairments.

In terms of physical accommodations, private testifying rooms and rooms that are accessible by wheelchair are some of the areas that require urgent attention. As regards communication accommodations, alternative ways of communication with persons with communication disabilities are an important recommendation. One such way is through using anatomical dolls (particularly in cases involving minor persons), which should always be available when needed. The second strategy could be using simple questioning techniques to assist persons with communication disabilities to participate effectively in the trial process. Apart from this, expert evidence has to be given in court for persons with disabilities.

Further to the above, specific training for professionals to address aspects regarding knowledge, awareness and patience needs to be conducted so that victims can access the court system in a fairer manner. According to the UN (2016), in some cases, lawyers lack training to work with or best serve clients with disabilities and this can affect the quality of service obtained by the client. For example, according to one law firm in South Africa, very little attention is given to training young lawyers on how to provide legal services to people with mental health problems. The same toolkit further explains that lawyers may not be trained on the rights of persons with disabilities. The UN cites an example of the 2012 report prepared by the Open Society Institute for Southern Africa, which found out that, of the nine countries reviewed, "currently … a specialized disability rights law course is being offered in three universities in the region, Midlands State University in Zimbabwe, Eduardo Mondlane University in Mozambique and Chancellor College in Malawi" (UN, 2016:10). According to the UN (2016), training is also a critical remedy in dealing with attitudinal barriers to justice by some officers in the justice system. Attitudinal barriers refer to negative attitudes and false beliefs or assumptions on the part of relevant actors (including police, lawyers and judges), which may result in persons with disabilities being considered and treated as less credible at all stages of legal processes – including when reporting a crime – and in terms of whether one can serve as a witness, or in making legal decisions, seeking remedies for alleged violations of one's rights, or otherwise participating in legal proceedings (UN, 2006:6).

Training could also go along with refresher courses in which the responsibilities of specific professionals in the court system are re-explained. For example, responsibilities of such critical professionals like prosecutors, social workers, interpreters, and the police, should be re-examined, particularly in the contexts where they work with persons with disabilities.

Finally, work-related challenges faced by professionals in the court system should be addressed. Most professionals report being overworked, having caseloads that are too large, etc. This results in witnesses, particularly those with a disability, not being able to fully access the court system.

## Conclusions

The discussion in this chapter has established that, while most of Zimbabwe's legal documents make very important provisions in terms of rights and access to justice by persons with disabilities, many barriers to access justice still exist in Zimbabwean society. This mismatch between constitutional provisions and the practical realities in the justice delivery system confirm some of the perceptions that some sections of society have about the country's justice delivery that they view as being unfair to persons living with various forms of communication (and other) disabilities.

The findings in this chapter reveal that, contrary to the principles of transformative equality, Zimbabwe's constitutional and statutory provisions regarding access to justice by persons with communication disabilities still remain paper documents lacking practical action. The chapter therefore concludes that, because most of Zimbabwe's constitutional and statutory provisions lack practical implementation in the justice delivery system, they continue to perpetuate deep structural inequalities that impede access to justice by a significant number of persons living with communication disabilities.

In this study, the researchers focused on access to justice by persons with communication disabilities who constitute a very small fraction of persons with disabilities who encounter the justice system. However, the researchers assume that the violations of the rights of persons with disabilities that occur in Zimbabwe's justice system are endemic and symptomatic of a disregard by justice officials of the rights and needs, not only of the deaf, the hard-of-hearing, and the deaf-blind, but of all people who live with disabilities.

Finally, although the findings of this study are based on data from Zimbabwe's justice delivery system, it is hoped that many of the issues raised in this chapter are of interest to other justice delivery systems where persons with communication and other disabilities are a common occurence.

## Acknowledgements

This work is based on the research supported by the National Institute for the Humanities and Social Sciences (NIHSS) and the Andrew W. Mellon Foundation. However, the opinions, findings and conclusions or recommendations expressed in this publication are those of the authors, and the NIHSS and the Andrew W. Mellon Foundation accept no liability in this regard.

## References

African Union. 2018. *Protocol to the African Charter on Human and Peoples' Rights on the Rights of Persons with Disabilities in Africa.* https://au.int/en/treaties/ protocol-african-charter-human-and-peoples-rights-rights-persons-disabilities-africa [Accessed 10 November 2022].

Archer, N. & Hurley, E.A. 2013. A justice system failing the autistic community. *Journal of Intellectual Disabilities and Offending Behaviour*, 4(1-2):53-59. https://doi.org/ 10.1108/JIDOB-02-2013-0003

Bornman, J., White, R., Johnson, E. & Bryen, D.N. 2015. Identifying barriers in the South African criminal justice system: Implications for individuals with severe communication disability. *Acta Criminologica: Southern African Journal of Criminology*, 29(1):1-17.

Degener, T. 2016. Disability in a human rights context. *Laws*, 5(3):35. https://doi.org/ 10.3390/laws5030035

Docrat, Z., Kaschula, R.H. & Ralarala, M.K. 2017. The exclusion of South African sign language speakers in the criminal justice system: A case-based approach. In: M.K. Ralarala, K. Barris, E. Ivala & S. Siyepu (eds.). *Interdisciplinary themes and perspectives in African language research in the 21st century.* Cape Town: Centre for Advanced Studies of African Societies. 261-277.

EU FRA (European Union Agency for Fundamental Rights). 2011. Access to justice in Europe: An overview of challenges and opportunities. Luxembourg: Publications Office of the European Union.

Fitzsimons, N.M. 2016. Justice for crimes victims with disabilities in the criminal justice system: An examination of barriers and impetus for change. *University of St. Thomas Law Journal*, 13(1):33-87.

Flynn, E. 2016. *Disabled justice? Access to justice and the UN Convention on the Rights of Persons with Disabilities.* New York: Routledge. https://doi.org/10.1007/978-3-319-43790-3_17

Fredman, S. 2005. Providing equality: Substantive equality and the positive duty to provide. *South African Journal of Human Rights*, 21(2):163-190. https://doi.org/10.1080/19962126.2005.11865132

Fredman, S. 2007. Human rights transformed. Nordic *Journal of Human Rights*, 19(12). https://doi.org/10.1093/acprof:oso/9780199272761.001.0001

Goldschmidt, J.E. 2017. New perspectives on equality: Towards justice through the disability convention? *Nordic Journal of Human Rights*, 35(1):1-14. https://doi.org/10.1080/18918131.2017.1286131

GoZ (Government of Zimbabwe). 2001. *Children's Act* (Chapter 5: 06). Harare: Government Printers.

GoZ (Government of Zimbabwe). 2013. *Constitution of Zimbabwe Amendment Act*, No. 20, 2013. Harare: Fidelity Printers.

GoZ (Government of Zimbabwe). 2016. *The Criminal Procedure and Evidence Amendment Act, 2016* (No. 2 of 2016) [Chapter 9:07]. Harare: Fidelity Printers.

Hepple, B. 2013. Transformative equality: The role of democratic participation. Paper presented at Labour Law Research Network (LLRN) Inaugural Conference: *Facing Development: The North-South Challenge to Transnational Labour Law*. 13-15 June, Barcelona. https://www.upf.edu/documents/3298481/3410076/2013-LLRNConf_SirBobHepple.pdf/d2fc160a-5b89-456a-9505-bffa977796de [Accessed 10 November 2022].

Kalaluka, L. 2013. Towards an effective litigation strategy of disability rights: The Zambian experience. *International and Comparative Disability Law and Policy*, (1):165-189.

Legal Resources Foundation. 2020. *The recognition of paralegals and access to justice in Zimbabwe.* Harare: Legal Resources Foundation.

Minkowitz, T. 2017. CRPD and transformative equality. *International Journal of Law in Context*, 13(1):77-86. https://doi.org/10.1017/S1744552316000483

Msipa, D. 2015. How assessments of testimonial competence perpetuate inequality and discrimination for persons with intellectual disabilities: An analysis of the approach taken in South Africa and Zimbabwe. *African Disability Rights Yearbook*, 3:63-90. https://www.adry.up.ac.za/articles-2015/msipa-d [Accessed 10 November 2022].

Mwela, F. 2013. *Justice delayed is justice denied principle: Tanzania Primary Courts: The case study of Iringa Municipal.* Saarbruecken, Germany: Lambert Academic Publishing (LAP).

Nussbaum, MC. 2011. *Creating capabilities: The human development approach.* 1st Edition. Cambridge: Cambridge University Press. https://doi.org/10.4159/harvard.9780674061200

UN (United Nations). 2006. The United Nations Convention on the Rights of Persons with Disabilities (UNCRPD). https://www.un.org/disabilities/documents/convention/convention_accessible_pdf.pdf [Accessed 10 November 2022].

UN (United Nations). 2016. Free toolkit on disability for Africa: Access to justice for persons with disabilities. Department of Economic and Social Affairs (UNDESA), Division for Social Policy and Development (DSPD). https://freeresources.fundsforngos.org/how-to-guides/a-free-toolkit-on-disability-for-africa/ [Accessed 20 July 2022].

UNDP (United Nations Development Programme). 2021. Promoting an inclusive justice delivery system in Zimbabwe. 17 March. https://www.undp.org/zimbabwe/news/promoting-inclusive-justice-delivery-system-zimbabwe [Accessed 10 November 2022].

Useh, U., Moyo, A.M. & Munyonga, E. 2001. Wheelchair accessibility of public buildings in the central business district of Harare, Zimbabwe. *Disability and Rehabilitation*, 23(11):490-496. https://doi.org/10.1080/09638280010008924

White, R.M., Bornman, J., Johnson, E., Tewson, K. & Van Niekerk, J. 2020. Transformative equality: Court accommodations for South African citizens with severe communication disabilities. *African Journal of Disability*, 9(0):651. https://doi.org/10.4102/ajod.v9i0.651

Zimbabwe Human Rights NGO Forum. 2016. Justice eludes people with disabilities. Press release. *Financial Gazette*, 22 January. https://www.hrforumzim.org/justice-eludes-people-with-disabilities/ [Accessed 10 November 2022].

ZLHR (Zimbabwe Lawyers for Human Rights). 2020. Zim court orders ZBC and government to ensure people living with disabilities access vital information on coronavirus in a friendly format. *Newsday*, 24 April.

# PART II

## Language and gender-based violence

# THE IMMORAL COMPLAINANTS

## A critical discourse analysis of appeal decisions on cases of marital rape


*Débora de Carvalho Figueiredo*
*Ana Luiza Soares Barcelos*
*Luiza Ferreira da Costa*


## Introduction

The debates associated with violence against women go hand in hand with the public perception of women's autonomy over their bodies and of women's rights in general. While feminist movements defend women's right to their bodies and choices, many societies continue to exhibit sexist attitudes and beliefs, which are difficult to deconstruct, despite the history of feminism and feminist struggles. In Brazil, although the constitution grants equal rights to men and women, the country continues to experience an epidemic of violence against women, with numbers on the increase. According to the latest Brazilian Yearly Report on Public Security (Brazil, 2022), in 2021 Santa Catarina was the state with the highest rate of rapes of adult women per 100 thousand inhabitants in the country. Furthermore, Brazilian society continues to hold sexist views regarding the nature and meaning of sexual consent. A 2014 survey by the Institute for Applied Economic Research (Instituto de Pesquisa Econômica Aplicada – Ipea) showed that at least 27.2% of the Brazilian population believes, totally or partially, that "a married woman must satisfy her husband in bed, even when she doesn't want to" (Brasil, 2014:11). This misunderstanding of the concepts of access to a woman's body and of consent to sex represents a public security issue, which is reflected in the alarming numbers of sexual assaults in the country. The issue of sexual violence is frequently addressed in popular media, but this media attention fails to spark a broader and deeper national debate on the social and cultural causes of sexual violence in the Brazilian society.

Driven by the persistence of sexual violence against women, especially in the domestic sphere, this chapter seeks to explore, the reasonings used in appeal decisions produced by Santa Catarina's Court of Justice (Tribunal de Justiça de Santa Catarina – TJSC) in cases of marital rape. Our objective is to analyse critically TJSC's judicial discourse on marital rape, including references to previous speeches by lawyers, complainants, defendants, witnesses, and lower court judges, considering that all these voices are filtered by TJSC to represent the state's view on women's rights and the state's official understanding of sexual consent within intimate relations. A critical analysis of the judicial discourse on this matter is necessary to investigate the position of the judiciary in relation to victims of marital rape, in seeking to understand how judges interpret and apply sexual violence legislation to cases of domestic sexual abuse and, by extension, how effective the judicial system is for women seeking justice. This investigation was done by analysing appellate decisions through the lens of Critical Discourse Analysis (CDA), as this theoretical and methodological approach addresses the ideologies hidden in discourse. According to Fairclough (2013:08), CDA focuses on "discursive aspects of power relations and inequalities: on the dialectical relations between discourse and power and their effects on other relations in the social process and its elements." For this reason, in this chapter, we also analyse the reported speech of lay people (appellants, defendants, and witnesses) involved in the cases investigated, as a way of contrasting their understanding of the facts and how they portray the events with the representations produced by those in positions of power, such as police officers and members of the judiciary.

## Critical discourse analysis (CDA)

According to Fairclough (1992:125), CDA is a form of critical social science that focuses on issues confronted by those who are in some way socially vulnerable, for instance "the poor, the socially excluded, those subject to oppressive gender or race relations, and so forth". CDA is a way to approach social issues evidenced in the semiotic aspect of social practices, and it proposes a critical view that is not always obvious for those who cannot relate directly to the social problem under discussion. Discursive investigations that take a critical approach aim to identify social wrongs and offer, if not solutions, at least a new perspective to engage in further and (hopefully) productive debates about how to deal with these challenges.

This method of analysis finds its importance in the societal demand to reach, systemically and scientifically, a level of debate in which we can combine social activism and social consciousness, without mistaken assumptions or being irresponsible towards the subject in question. Whether our opinions and life experiences might take us to common-sense views of certain topics, this method of analysis grounds the critical views in theoretical discussions and concepts, and allows the analysts to be rigorous and scientific, while meeting the need to initiate debates about difficult subjects within the scientific community – mostly those which are urgent and require changes in our social context.

In addition to that, when applied to the discourse of the judiciary, CDA allows us to understand better how this system frequently benefits privileged people to the detriment of those who are already marginalised, as reflected in the research outputs in this chapter. While, through its complex use of language, the judiciary can function as a means to keep ordinary people unaware of their own rights, CDA, combined with theoretical support from other social science disciplines, allows scholars to explore and explain the meanings and implications concealed within legal texts.

## The transitivity system and the analysis of appeal decisions

From the perspective of systemic functional linguistics (Halliday & Matthiessen, 2004), language is a semiotic system, a resource for meaning making; hence, texts represent processes of meaning making in context. As such, a text can be explored and analysed in many ways, focusing on its meanings or on its context, or on both, as they are complementary and inseparable. For this analysis, we investigate transitivity in appeal decisions.

According to Halliday and Mathiessen (2004), the transitivity system addresses how clauses encode our experiences through process, participants and circumstances that attend to the process and qualify it. This semiotic approach to language allows us to identify how the reality of sexual abuse, in the case of this research, is constructed in legal texts by judges, lawyers, and prosecutors.

Official texts, such as appellate decisions, contain technical and specific terms that differ from the language we use in everyday life, especially for those who are disenfranchised and treated as minority groups (racialised people, the poor, etc.). Referring to the common view that sees legal language as impenetrable, Coulthard and Johnson (2007) observe that the understanding of legal language is one of the skills necessary for the attribution of meaning to legal texts; and that legal discourses aim at producing precise, clear texts that do not open up possibilities for ambiguity. However, this precision only applies to (or is targeted at) legal practitioners, since texts from the judiciary employ terminologies and unusual syntactic structures in such a way that a considerable part of the population does not understand them. Appellate decisions, the official documents chosen to be analysed in this chapter, are collegiate decisions produced by a second instance court; and, although their format might vary, certain elements are required by the Brazilian law: the report, the argument, and the vote. The report contains the name of the parties, a summary of the appellant's request, a response and a record of the main occurrences in the process; the argument contains the magistrates' analysis of issues of fact and issues of law; finally, in the vote the magistrates resolve the issues submitted by the parties (art. 458 of the Code of Civil Procedure [CPC], BRASIL, 1973) (Coacci, 2013).

By investigating the transitivity system in legal decisions, and guided by a critical discursive approach, this chapter seeks to analyse how violence against women is represented in legal texts, more specifically in appellate decisions from the Court of Justice of Santa Catarina (TJSC), considering that these judicial texts represent the view of the state of Santa Catarina on matters of sexual violence against women.

## Methodological choices: data collection and analytical procedures

As stated above, the texts analysed in this chapter are appellate decisions. More specifically, the data consist of three appellate decisions in cases of marital rape produced by the Court of Justice of Santa Catarina (TJSC) between 1 January and 30 June 2018 and made available on the court's official website (TJSC, n.d.). The time frame corresponds to the first semester of the year when the research study that grounds this article was originally conducted.[1]

To undertake a microanalysis of the representations of rape in these court decisions, we made use of the transitivity system, as proposed by Systemic Functional Linguistics (Halliday & Matthiessen, 2014). After selecting the main clauses that build the court's narrative in each case, we analysed them in terms of representational meanings. The transitivity system was applied to observe how agency and action were construed by the magistrates. After the microanalysis, the findings were subject to the more interpretive/explanatory steps associated with Critical Discourse Analysis (Fairclough, 1992:2013).

Considering the high number of rape cases in the state of Santa Catarina, the appellate decisions analysed were those selected following a set of requirements to restrict the corpus to the scope of this chapter. The first requirement was that the appeals should be cases involving article 213 of the Brazilian Penal Code, which typifies the crime of rape.[2] The second requirement was that the appeals should have been heard between 1 January and 30 June 2018. The first search on TJSC's website produced 61 appeals on rape cases in that period. However, the objective of this work is specifically to discuss cases of rape of women over 18 years of age; so, after applying this filter, the initial

---

1  The data used in this chapter were collected in 2018 as part of the End of Letras/Inglês Course Work by Barcelos (Barcelos, 2020), carried out between 2018 and 2020.

2  The legal definition of rape in the Brazilian Penal Code is: "Art. 213: To constrain someone, through violence or serious threat, to have carnal knowledge or to practice or allow other libidinous acts to be performed upon them." (Wording given by Law No. 12.015, of 2009). http://www.planalto.gov.br/ccivil_03/Decreto-Lei/Del2848.htm#art213

number was significantly reduced. In addition, during the selection stage, attention was drawn to the appeals in which there was a pre-existing marital relationship between victim and assailant. Thus, of the 61 appeal decisions initially found, only three fit the desired profile – rape cases of adult married women assaulted by their partners, heard between 1 January and 30 June 2018 by the TJSC.

## Data analysis and discussion

The structure of this section is based on the three appellate decisions analysed, followed by a final segment on the topic, which we named "The 'immoral' complainants". Despite the different dates, judges, and even cities that identify each appeal, a common feature in the three cases is the defendants' attempt to compromise the complainants' image as a tactical means to justify their acts of violence.

### Appeal 1: Apelação Criminal n. 0001114-57.2016.8.24.0005

This appeal decision concerns a case in which the defendant (identified in this work by his initials 'CG') was acquitted of the rape charge by a lower court. In the original trial, CG (the husband) was accused of raping his wife (DAF) after an argument. According to the victim's allegation, he acted violently towards her, and she only 'consented' to his sexual advances because she feared that, otherwise, her children would overhear CG assaulting her. Although the defendant was acquitted of the crime of rape by the first instance court, he was found guilty of other crimes that were included in the same trial. He appealed the lower court decision to change the legal basis on which he was acquitted. The legal basis for the acquittal was Article 386, Item VII of the Brazilian Code of Criminal Procedures ("there is not enough evidence for the conviction"); and the objective of the defence was to change it to Article 386, I/tem I ("the inexistence of the fact is proven"). To analyse the appeal and decide whether the appellant's request should be granted, the Court of Justice included in its decision reports from the first trial.

In Example 1, we can follow the transitivity analysis of the first part of this appeal decision, in the 'report' section. The judges began the section by reviewing the facts:

**Example 1: Apelação Criminal n. 0001114-57.2016.8.24.0005 (p. 7)**

> "According to the complainant, on the day [date], around [time], at the residence located in the street [address], in the Municipality of Balneário Camboriú, the appellant CG, **in theory**, using force, holding his companion DAF by the arm and removing her clothing, **would have constrained her to have carnal intercourse with him.**"

Following the transitivity analysis, there are several issues to be observed in this example. First, most of the violent elements of the event – such as "using force" and "holding his companion DAF by the arm and removing her clothing" – are represented through

Circumstances of Mode (Halliday & Mathiessen, 2004), meaning that it was through them that the defendant supposedly carried out his action, described as "would have constrained her". Circumstances do not carry the same weight within the structure of the clause as the 'Process', that is, the verb(s) that describe the action(s). As it follows, the structure of the clauses that describe CG's actions towards the victim places her in the position of an almost active participant in a sexual act ("would have constrained her to have carnal intercourse with him"), since CG's action is to 'constrain' the victim, and the alleged rape is referred to as the victim 'having carnal intercourse with the defendant'.

In constructing the clause this way, after textualising the violent elements of the events as circumstances, an unusual lexical choice is made to condense the defendant's entire action. *Constranger* (freely translated as 'to constrain'), in its colloquial sense in Brazilian Portuguese, is used much more frequently, meaning 'to embarrass' someone, rather than with the meaning expressed in this appeal decision, which is 'to coerce', 'to force' or 'to restrain' someone. This illustrates how legal discourse makes unfamiliar/outdated lexical choices selected from the prestige linguistic variety. Such choices are often uncommon in colloquial language, even when referring to actions that occur in everyday life. Linguistic choices like the one above, are unfamiliar to the lay public who, in this case, would have to depend on the circumstantial elements of the clause to understand the verb *constranger* as 'to force', 'to coerce' or 'to restrain' the victim.

Finally, the use of the expression "in theory" and the verbal phrase "would have constrained" represent the situation as hypothetical, which contributes to the idea that the complainant's words cannot be entirely trusted or taken as absolute truth, since her claims could be fraudulent. It is common to use hypothetical terms in legal decisions to guarantee that defendants will not textually be found guilty before the end of the trial. This also occurs in this appeal decision, because the defendant had already been acquitted of the crime of rape. For this reason, events are portrayed in terms and tenses that indicate that the accusations had not been confirmed. In short, these discursive strategies are used to ensure that the criminal justice system follows the *in dubio pro reo* principle ('When in doubt, for the accused'), fundamental to guaranteeing the rights of the accused, regardless of the accusation.

To continue the analysis, we look at the following comments about the victim:

**Example 2: Apelação Criminal n. 0001114-57.2016.8.24.0005 (p. 7)**

> "The victim, **despite trying to get away from him and prevent the conduct, allegedly ended up giving in** to the **appellant's lascivious will** out of **fear for her minor children.**"

As in Example 1, the narrative in Example 2 continues to portray the victim as active ("ended up by giving in"), indirectly recognising her as the agent in the final words of this segment. This discursive strategy deserves attention – especially in legal texts – because, although it is clear, from the point of view of consent, that the actions described are unacceptable, focusing on the actions of the victim rather than on the actions of the accused changes the perspective on the facts, and it may give the impression that the victim allowed the attack to take place. That is, the excerpt above, as the previous one, associates the victim's violation to her act of 'consent by conduct', casting her fear for her children as a mere circumstance in her submission. Moreover, what she 'consented to' was not directly linked to the actions of the assailant; rather, it was attributed to an almost supernatural and unconscious force ("lascivious will"), which removes CG's guilt and attributes it to his 'uncontrollable lust'. In other words, this passage shifts the responsibility for the events from the accused and places it on a non-existent agent, i.e., the accused's 'uncontrollable' impulses, aided by the 'compliance' of his victim. On the topic of marital rape, Couto and Schraiber (2011:177) comment:

> ...in this process of naturalization of the social, categories such as 'instinct', 'impulsiveness', 'fatality' and 'fate' are adopted to give meaning to aggressions against wives (Couto et al., 2007), which, consequently, helps to cover up the identification of these actions as violence (Rosa et al., 2008).

According to Figueiredo (2000:190), descriptions of sexual assaults as motivated by uncontrollable sexual desire are "disconnected from social issues such as gender violence, domestic violence, gender asymmetry and [the] high level of social tolerance to the problem of violence against women." Figueiredo also highlights that, considering that most sexual assaults are carried out by men against women, children, and persons with some type of disability or vulnerability, the cause of this type of abuse is not just lust, but rather the vulnerability of the victim and the access and power of the assailant over the victim (Figueiredo, 2014:146). On the same issue, Ehrlich (2001) points out that, when the justice system depicts, in its official statements, violent male actions as resulting from 'uncontrollable' sexual impulses, it licenses "a view of sexual masculinity that portrays violent men as not being 'agents' of their own actions" (Ehrlich, 2001:58). In the case of the excerpt analysed above, the fact that the victim 'consented' to this 'agentless' desire due to fear for her children was not acknowledged as sufficient grounds for a conviction in the first trial. The victim was discursively placed in a position where she made conscious choices by 'consenting', as a person who had full control of the situation, while the aggressor, following his instinctual nature, is not represented as the alleged author of the acts, since the agent supposedly responsible for them is an incorporeal and uncontrollable entity (his 'lascivious will').

## *Appeal 2: Apelação Criminal n. 0001418-34.2015.8.24.0056*

Unlike the first appeal discussed earlier, the second appeal refers to a case in which the accused was found guilty of rape in the first instance trial due to the presence of physical evidence. However, despite the evidence supporting the conviction, on appeal, the defence requested that LV de L, the defendant, be acquitted of the crime due to "lack of evidence" and "decay of the victim's right to representation", arguing that EMC, the victim, had not expressed willingness to represent legally against the accused. The appeal court dismissed this argument, as the victim had officially reported the rape to the police and had assisted the justice system during the trial. There was no doubt, in the eyes of the judiciary, that the victim intended to pursue the case to the end. In addition to the victim's willingness to report the assault, the court presented jurisprudence that states that formal representation is not necessary if the victim notifies the police authorities of their desire to report the crime.

In the report section, Appeal Decision 2 states that the Public Prosecution Office accused the defendant of the crimes of rape and torture. It also includes extracts from the accused's statements to the police, in which he admits to behaving violently against the victim during the events under trial and also on other unrelated occasions. For the purposes of this analysis, we must remember that the violent acts admitted by the accused are typified as crimes by the Brazilian penal code.

**Example 3: Apelação Criminal n. 0001418-34.2015.8.24.0056 (p. 14)**

| |
|---|
| A. "[...] has been in a stable relationship with EMC for four years; [...] who has been living in Santa Catarina for two months [...]; that about a month ago he began to suspect that his partner had an extramarital relationship; that since then the interrogated **began to threaten E. with death** and sometimes **tried to hang and strangle her** so that she would tell who she was having a relationship with;" |
| B. "[...] that due to this suspicion, when the respondent went out to work, he **closed the door and put a padlock on the outside, preventing the victim from leaving the house during the night.**" |
| C. "[...] that before that, the respondent **started to threaten E. and beat her on the head with a stick** so that she would point out where W's house was." |
| D. "that the respondent states that he also **choked E. and slapped her** breasts;" |
| E. "that the respondent claims that he **tied the victim's arm to his own** with a power cable to be able to sleep, so that she would not leave the house;" |

This testimony was given by the defendant in the pre-trial stage, in his statement to the police, before the Public Prosecution Office started the criminal proceedings against him. In his own words, there are descriptions of a series of crimes established by the Brazilian Penal Code that were not included in the trial process: threats, forced confinement and physical injuries (arts. 147, 148 and 129 of the Brazilian Penal Code).

**Example 4: Apelação Criminal n. 0001418-34.2015.8.24.0056 (p. 4)**

A. On November 14, 2015, between 9 am and 6 pm, at the residence located on [street], in the municipality of Santa Cecília/SC, LV de V, the accused, trying to obtain a confession from EMC, his partner, that she was having a romantic relationship with another man, constrained her, with the use of violence and major threats, stating that he would kill her, **causing her great mental and physical suffering**.

B. To do so, with the victim **still tied** to the bed, after raping her, the accused LV de V inserted a wood stick into EMC's vagina and, with a knife, hurt the victim's left breast and vagina.

C. As if that was not enough, at each new cut the accused LV de V made on the victim's vagina, he **also** threw acetone on the cuts, increasing her suffering, **in addition** to threatening to cause her graver bodily harm by setting her genitals on fire.

D. Finally, the accused LV de V, **not satisfied with everything he had already done**, introduced the acetone bottle on the victim's rectum, keeping her like that, **under intense physical and mental suffering, for approximately 9 hours**, causing on the victim the bodily injuries described on pages 19/31 of the technical reports.

In Appeal 2, the judicial text has a tone of empathy in relation to the victim's anguish and suffering during the rape and torture session, as presented in Example 4. The main characteristic of these excerpts is the use of attributes to the physical and mental consequences suffered by the victim. The court points out, in various formulations, that the victim was under intense suffering, not only regarding the torture, but also from the beginning, when describing how the defendant raped her. The court acknowledges this suffering as they apply value judgment both to the torture and the forced physical penetration, pointing out the intensity of the physical pain and the mental torture. The use of the same attribute to both parts ("under intense physical and mental suffering") evidences this acknowledgement. Additionally, the appeal decision is emphatic when pointing out the extension of the torture and the actions of the defendant as never-ending and cruel, with the use of "still tied", "As if that was not enough", and "not satisfied with everything he had already done". This differentiates this report section from the report section in Appeal 1, since here the magistrates do not use the technical and formal language usually employed to narrate facts in the reporting section of appeals: here we observe a sense of empathy towards the victim and outrage at the cruelty she suffered. This same view of the events appears in the vote section; but, due to size limitations, we chose not to present these examples here. Suffice to say, that the defendant was sentenced to eleven years and four months for the crimes of rape and torture.

In addition, it is also important to discuss the ease with which the defendant described his actions. Through transitivity analysis, we can observe that the acts of rape and torture were attributed to LV de L as the main actor in material processes that make up his deposition to the police ("the interrogated began to threaten E. with death and sometimes tried to hang and strangle her"; "the respondent started to threaten E. and beat her on the head"; "he also choked E. and slapped her"; "that he tied the victim's arm"). In his deposition, the assailant did not try to separate himself from his actions using passive forms of description. Instead, he seemed to acknowledge his behaviour in such a way that it became almost 'natural'; he was seemingly unaware of the gravity of what he had done, apparently unconcerned about the consequences.

### Appeal 3: Apelação Criminal n. 0003697-62.2015.8.24.0033

In the third case analysed, the defendant was accused of forcing his wife to perform oral sex after trying to penetrate her, causing injuries and bleeding. As in the cases analysed above, this appeal was requested by the defendant, alleging lack of evidence of rape and the "deterioration of the victim's right to representation". He received a sentence of seven years and seven months in the first trial for the crimes of rape and threats (art. 147 Penal Code) to the life of the complainant NDSDS but was granted release pending appeal. His release was justified based on the following argument: "the requirements that authorize his preventive detention are absent, according to arts. 312 and 313 of the Code of Criminal Procedure" (Criminal appeal n. 0003697-62.2015.8.24.0033, from Itajaí, p. 4). This means that, in the first trial, the judge convicted ADRS of the crimes he was accused of (rape and threats to the life of the complainant) but evaluated the evidence as insufficient to keep him in prison while awaiting the appeal decision, as determined by art. 312 of the Code of Criminal Procedures. However, the first instance judge failed to consider art. 313, paragraph 3 of the same Code, which recommends preventive detention in cases of domestic violence.

The facts of the case were exposed in the report section as such:

**Example 5: Apelação Criminal n. 0003697-62.2015.8.24.0033 (p. 8)**

> "The victim stated that the defendant, when they were ready to sleep, **threw himself on her, choked her and tried to have sexual intercourse, giving up after she started bleeding, when he then forced her to perform oral sex**."

We can observe in this excerpt that the actions attributed to the defendant are not textualised in passive forms and/or with inactive agents in the representation, which means that this narrative establishes a specific agent for the material processes related to the events. However, when talking about the assailant's violence against the victim, the crime of attempted rape is described as 'sexual intercourse', despite the victim's bleeding as a result. Another point to consider is the distinction made in the appeal decision between 'sexual intercourse' and 'oral sex'. In other words, although the court recognised the crime of rape, in Example 4, there is a normalisation of this crime in referring to it as "have sexual intercourse" and "perform oral sex".

In her doctoral research, Figueiredo (2000:70) discussed the presence of a romantic lexis in some appellate decisions related to sexual crimes, arguing that "the use of affective and erotic terms [in court decisions in rape cases] exposes aggression in a framework of consensual sexual acts, undermining the violence and unilaterally of the act." In such cases, the judicial writers apply to the description of sexual crimes the same vocabulary used to describe consensual sexual acts, blurring the distinction between sexual practices between consenting adults and forced sex. From our perspective, when referring to rape, the terms chosen should point directly to the intimate violation of the victim, focusing on issues such as the use of force, psychological violence, coercion, humiliation, and other actions committed by rapists and sexual predators as a result of their sense of entitlement over their victims and their bodies, especially in the context of marriage.

## The 'immoral' complainants

During the development of this chapter, we identified a common element in the cases analysed: all contained claims from the accused about the complainants' supposed infidelity. In the three cases, allegations of infidelity were used by the accused to justify their violent actions and to undermine the complainants' reliability in court. This section carries out a brief discussion on how the appeal decisions analysed addressed the issue of the alleged infidelity of the victims. We begin with examples from Appeal 1:

**Example 6: Apelação Criminal n. 0001114-57.2016.8.24.0005 (p. 8)**

"That CG is an alcoholic and suspects that the deponent is cheating on him with another man";

"we went to sleep, and he started to try it, I told him I didn't want to have sex, because the way he was acting, it wouldn't happen; he said I was seeing someone else, that was I didn't want anything to do with him anymore"

In Appeal No. 1, the accusation made by the defendant about the alleged infidelity of the victim was exposed in the victim's statements. According to her, these accusations were being used as a psychological weapon to force her to 'prove' her fidelity by having sex with him. In the same excerpt from her deposition, we find reference to other instances of psychological violence by the defendant in the form of threats against the victim's life, while accusing her of infidelity, as in the following example:

**Example 7: Apelação Criminal n. 0001114-57.2016.8.24.0005 (p. 11)**

That, on [date], around [time], C. took the deponent to work and **as the deponent refused to kiss him, he began to accuse her saying that there was a man watching them**; That, then, C. returned home, but soon called the deponent saying, **'I'm going to kill you and whoever is with you'**.

This type of accusation, followed by forced 'consent' to sexual advances, is not at all uncommon in cases of marital sexual violence. Dantas-Berger and Giffin's (2005) research on women who reported sexual abuse in the state of Rio de Janeiro showed the presence of the same strategy. The authors reported that the women they interviewed 'consented' to sex for fear of other forms of violence from their partners: "overall, despite trying to 'resist' – say no – they ended up 'giving in' to sexual intercourse, sometimes for fear of physical aggression, loss of financial support, or accusations of infidelity" (Dantas-Berger & Giffin, 2005:426).

The allegations of infidelity in the analysed cases were not limited to the moment the crime took place. In Appeals Nos. 2 and 3, the defendants presented these suspicions as a way of discrediting the image of the complainants as victims and of raising doubts about the victims' character. An example is the defendant's speech in Appeal 2. In his deposition, in spite of recognising the authorship of physical forms of violence, the defendant always justified himself by referring to his suspicions ("[...] he began to threaten E. with death and sometimes tried to strangle and suffocate her so that she would tell who she was having an affair with"), and by taking the position of a victim of adultery who has been accused of crimes committed by another man, as we can see in the example below:

### Example 8: Apelação Criminal n. 0001418-34.2015.8.24.0056 (p.15)

> "that when they got home E. started crying and said that during the night the person she was having an affair with arrived at the house and she opened the door; **that she had sexual relations with that person on the couch and in bed**; that E. said that this person was W, who lives near [location]; she later said that she did not have sexual intercourse with W, **but that [W] had hurt her a lot, inserting a stick into her vagina**; that he had spread cream on the piece of wood and introduced it several times into her vagina, **as well as thrown acetone and threatened to set her vagina on fire**; that before that, **the interrogated started to threaten E. and hit her on the head with a stick so that she would point out where W's house was** [...] that after he got home, he ingested alcohol; that the respondent alleges that around 11:00 am today, after the fight he had with E., **he had, at her request, sexual intercourse with her**".

During the trial, the defendant declared:

### Example 9: Apelação Criminal n. 0001418-34.2015.8.24.0056 (p. 15)

> "she told me 'yeah, I was with him, I told your brother and cousin that he broke the door, but I opened it'; [...] what I did to her was to slap her, and I pulled her hair, **I wanted to drag her out and bring her to the hospital or the police station, but she didn't want to**; I didn't torture her at any time; that the daughter, the eldest, saw me beating her; **that he did not have sexual intercourse against her will; she was already injured, she just wasn't inflamed, she had a purple ear; she said it was the lover**".

In his statements to the police and during the trial, the defendant insisted that the victim had admitted she was having an affair and that the man with whom she was having this affair (identified as 'W') was the person behind the crime of torture. In his version, LV de L also included details, such as his wife crying as she told him about this other man, the neighbourhood where 'W' resided, and that he tried to take the victim to the hospital after she was tortured by 'W', but that she refused to go. To justify the presence of his sperm in the evidence collected, the defendant stated that, after the discussion (which included the violent acts that he reported to the police), he only had sex with the victim after she asked for it, despite her injuries. During his defence, LV de L justified his violence through his aim of extracting from the victim a confession of infidelity, at the same time trying to undermine the complainant's reputation by turning the image of a victim of rape and torture into the image of a manipulative person who was trying to 'frame' him.

A similar allegation was made by the defendant in Appeal No. 3, in which he claimed that the victim made the charge of rape to harm him, reversing the positions of victim and assailant. In Appeal No. 3, we can see once again the representation of the victim as someone who broke the accused's heart and exposed him to danger, betraying him with a person who was trying to harm her husband physically.

The fact that the betrayal argument is used in court by different men accused of marital rape leads us to consider that violent men, capable of violent crimes, may try to take advantage of the damage that an image of promiscuity and infidelity can do to a woman's character, even in the presence of physical evidence of rape. In such cases, they not only try to damage the victim's reputations, they rely on it as their main line of defence.

## Conclusions

The main objective of this study was to investigate how the TJSC, the main court of justice in Santa Catarina, a state with one of the highest rates of rape in Brazil, understands and represents marital rape. Departing from this objective, the analysis resulted in the identification of valuable points for discussion and an investigation into the subject of intimate sexual violence. First, we noted the low number of appeal decisions in the TJSC, recorded under art. 213 of the Penal Code (rape) that involved conjugal partners, considering that only three cases fit the interests of this analysis, among the other 61 rape appeals judged between January and June 2018. Unfortunately, this does not mean that this type of crime is rare in Santa Catarina specifically, or in Brazil as a whole. According to a survey by the organisation Énois Inteligência Jovem (2015), 47% of women and adolescents interviewed reported that, at some point, they had been forced by their partners to have sex. The actual number of women who are forced (by physical or psychological pressure) to have sexual relations with intimate partners cannot be pinpointed precisely, because of the characteristics of this type of rape, the lack of information on marital rape, the difficulty many women have in identifying what has happened or is happening to them as abuse, and the victims' fear of disbelief and humiliation if they report the assault. Whilst the literature generally confirms that this type of abuse is one of the most common, the real numbers cannot be accurately estimated.

As for the discourses and voices analysed in this study, both from legal professionals and lay participants (complainants and accused), the analyses point to a specific theme for each case. In Appeal No. 1, we could observe that the criminal justice system had great difficulty in attributing legitimacy to a crime of rape in the absence of physical evidence of injury to the victim's body, grounded in the myth of the 'real' rape, a crime of physical and sexual violence performed by an unknown person. The decisions analysed were based mainly on physical evidence, demanding the victims to show evidence of physical injuries to identify rape and, therefore, disregarding other forms of coercion that are often used by men towards women, such as manipulation and psychological torture. Other examples of rape myths appeared in the analysed cases, such as Appeal No. 3's disconnection from the reality of the crime of rape through the use of romanticised lexical choices, representing acts that constitute rape as consensual sexual activities, such as in "have sexual intercourse" and "perform oral sex".

The point here is that, even though violent behaviour is inherently social, we should also keep in mind that it is unilateral rather than mutual, since it involves the actions of one person that are contrary to the wishes and wellbeing of another person. However, in spite of that, it is not uncommon for magistrates to represent sexual assault as erotic, romantic or affective acts. This has two consequences. The first, and more immediate, is the partial blaming of the victim. According to Coates and Wade (2004:501), "language that mutualizes violent behavior implies that the victim is at least partly to blame and inevitably conceals the fact that violent behavior is unilateral and solely the responsibility of the offender." The second is less immediate, but potentially more harmful to society: the linguistic blurring of the line between consensual sexual acts and forced/coerced sex makes it more difficult for women to identify abuse, to see themselves as victims of abuse, and to report it.

Whilst Appeals 1 and 3 were based, each in its own way, on stereotypes and myths about rape, the analysis of Appeal 2 gravitated towards the accused's speech and the lack of interest from the public prosecution in accusing him of other crimes (threatening to cause unjust and serious harm; depriving someone of their freedom; offending the psychological or physical integrity of others), which he himself confessed to during his police interview. The fact that such crimes were mentioned without major consequences for the defendant conveys the message that his violent actions were acceptable in the eyes of the law, even those that extended to the point of extreme violence. In addition, the analysis also discussed the ease and naturalness with which the defendant described his violent acts.

From the appeal decisions analysed in this chapter, we can say that, in these three cases, the criminal justice system in Santa Catarina did not explore or delve into the concepts of consent and psychological violence when dealing with marital rape; rather, it worked based on stereotypes and myths grounded on mistaken ideas about sexuality and physical violence within marriage. Referring to the sexual mythology articulated in legal reasoning, Figueiredo (2000:34) makes this argument:

> This set of myths, stereotypes and ideological assumptions about male and female sexuality and gender relations was incorporated into statutory and common law, as well as into the discourse of legal professionals (lawyers, judges, etc.). There is an interaction between legal discursive practices and broader social practices: cultural/ideological views of gender and sex relations shape legal practices and court texts, which in turn build and reinforce common views of sexual and social behavior (Edwards, 1996).

However, as our data was limited, further research is necessary to assess if our results represent a general trend in the way the judiciary in Santa Catarina understands and represents sexual violence within intimate relationships.

## References


Barcelos, A.L.S. 2020. *A critical discourse analysis of Santa Catarina State Court's perspective on marital rape*. End of course work. Universidade Federal de Santa Catarina, Florianópolis. https://repositorio.ufsc.br/handle/123456789/204354 [Accessed 14 November 2022].

Brasil. 2014. Tolerância social à violência contra as mulheres. *Sistema de Indicadores de Percepção Social (SIPS)*, IPEA. Brasília.

Brasil. 2022. *Anuário Brasileiro de Segurança Pública 2022*. Brasília.

Coacci, T. 2013. A Pesquisa com Acórdãos nas Ciências Sociais: Algumas reflexões metodológicas. *Revista Mediações*, 86-109. https://doi.org/10.5433/2176-66 65.2013v18n2p86

Coates, L. & Wade, A. 2004. Telling it like it isn't: Obscuring perpetrator responsibility for violent crime. *Discourse & Society*, 15(5):499-526. https://doi.org/10.1177/ 0957926504045031

Coulthard, R.M. & Johnson, A. 2007. *An introduction to forensic linguistics*. London: Routledge. https://doi.org/10.4324/9780203969717

Couto, M. & Schraiber, L.B. 2011. Representações da Violência de Gênero Para Homens e Perspectivas Para a Prevenção e Promoção da Saúde. In: R. Gomes (ed.). *Saúde do Homem em Debate*. Rio De Janeiro: Editora Fiocruz. 175-199.

Dantas-Berger, S.M. & Giffin, K. 2005. A Violência nas Relações de Conjugalidade: Invisibilidade e Banalização da Violência Sexual? *Cad. Saúde Pública*, 21(2):417-425. https://doi.org/10.1590/S0102-311X2005000200008

Ehrlich, S. 2001. *Representing rape: Language and sexual consent.* London: Routledge.

Énois Inteligência Jovem, Instituto Vladimir Herzog, Instituto Patrícia Galvão. 2015. *"Menina pode tudo: Como o machismo e a violência contra a mulher afetam a vida das jovens das classes C, D e E"* Survey. https://dossies.agenciapatriciagalvao.org.br/fontes-epesquisas/wpcontent/uploads/sites/3/2018/08/ENOIS_meninapodetudo2015.pdf [Accessed 14 November 2022].

Fairclough, N. 1992. *Discourse and social change.* Cambridge: Polity Press.

Fairclough, N. 2013. *Critical discourse analysis: The critical study of language.* 2nd Edition. London: Routledge. https://doi.org/10.4324/9781315834368

Figueiredo, D.C. 2000. Victims and villains: Gender representations, surveillance and punishment in the judicial discourse on rape. Doctoral thesis. Florianópolis: Universidade Federal Santa Catarina. http://repositorio.ufsc.br/xmlui/handle/123456789/79275 [Accessed 14 November 2022].

Figueiredo, D.C. 2014. Discurso, gênero e violência: Uma análise de representações públicas do crime de estupro. *Linguagem e Direito/Language and Law*, 1:141-158.

Halliday, M.A.K. & Matthiessen, C. 2004. *An introduction to functional grammar.* London: Routledge.

# LANGUAGE EVIDENCE OF CHALLENGES IN THE ADMINISTRATION OF JUSTICE FOR VICTIMS OF DOMESTIC VIOLENCE DURING THE COVID-19 PANDEMIC

*Ndikaru Wa Teresia*

## Introduction

The effects of the outbreak of the Covid-19 pandemic permeated all spheres of life, wrecking economies and upending social structures. In its wake, the pandemic brought what some referred to as "a shadow pandemic" (International Development Law Organization, 2020) in the exacerbation of domestic violence.

To understand the intersection between the Covid-19 pandemic and domestic violence, an exploration of domestic violence as a construct is imperative. Consensus is still lacking on a comprehensive, universally accepted definition of domestic violence. Some scholars have embraced broad-based definitions of domestic violence that feature structural violence, including unequal access to education, healthcare services, and poverty (Montesanti & Thurston, 2015; Renzetti, Follingstad & Coker, 2017; Sinha et al., 2017). This is plausible, considering that poverty contributes to domestic disputes, involves a lack of access to healthcare services by victims, and children are denied educational opportunities. Scholars, however, have omitted to focus on access to justice, which is an equally important structural feature associated with domestic violence.

In this chapter, Amnesty International's definition stands out due to its attempt to conceptualise domestic violence comprehensively. Amnesty International considers domestic violence as a violent attack on individuals or groups of people in the family context, involving psychological, physical, and/or sexual violence (Appiah & Mohammed, 2013). Domestic violence is, therefore, characterised by sexual abuse, battery, marital rape, dowry-related violence, female genital mutilation, or any other traditional practice that can be physically or psychologically injurious to a member of a household (Appiah

& Mohammed, 2013). In Kenya, the Coalition on Violence Against Women (COVAW) concurs that domestic violence is characterised by forms of violence such as battery, verbal insults, and sexual violation (COVAW, 2020). While these definitions infer the legal dimensions associated with domestic violence, they do so only in a rather indirect manner. This may be attributed to the social angle within which domestic violence is often debated and handled.

Domestic violence is not unique to a particular region or country of the world but is a worldwide phenomenon (Javier & Herron, 2019). About one in every three women across the globe has experienced sexual or physical violence. The prevalence of domestic violence in sub-Saharan Africa is about 36% (Muluneh et al., 2020). The 2014 Kenya Demographic and Health Survey indicated that 39% of women who have ever been married and about 9% of men between 15 and 49 years old have experienced sexual or physical forms of domestic violence (Wado, 2021).

Despite the lack of consensus on how to define domestic violence, all agree on the consequences of domestic violence: in Kenya, domestic violence is a major cause of non-accidental and preventable deaths of mainly women and children (National Council on the Administration of Justice (NCAJ), 2020). The cases of domestic violence increased significantly with the outbreak of Covid-19 in March 2020 (COWAV, 2020). The NCAJ indicated that the sexually violent nature of offences increased by 36% in the first quarter of 2020, follwoing the pandemic's outbreak. The perpetrators of these offenses were parents, close relatives, guardians, or people living with the victims (NCAJ, 2020). A national hotline set up for gender-based violence (GBV) reported an increase between March and April 2020, of about 301% of GBV events experienced by women and girls before lockdown. Reports by the National Crime Research Centre (NCRC) indicated an increase of about 88% of GBV cases between April and June 2020, most of which occurred at home and were perpetrated by close family members (Jerving, 2021).

Police statistics also revealed that the incidence of domestic violence increased by 92% between January and June 2020; and that 71% of the 2416 cases reported were perpetrated by men aged between 18 and 33 years (Ahmed, Changole & Wangamati, 2021). This demonstrated that women were adversely affected and had to depend on their husbands or partners, a factor that increased the level of physical and sexual domestic violence, even as the restriction on mobility limited their access to treatment and protection services, as well as their access to justice (Human Rights Watch, 2021).

The outbreak of the pandemic, therefore, provided an atmosphere in which domestic abuse thrived in the home. This increase could be attributed to the various measures adopted by the Kenyan government in March 2020 to prevent the spread of the Covid-19 pandemic in the country. These measures included outlawing public meetings; the closure of educational institutions and businesses, particularly in the hospitality industry; restrictions on movement, and curfews (Human Rights Watch, 2021). While these interventions were effective in slowing the spread of the pandemic in the country, they brought with them various associated economic and social issues that negatively affected families (Ahmed et al., 2021). The pandemic disrupted livelihoods and increased economic hardships, particularly for those who lost their jobs (Ahmed et al., 2021). In particular, jobs in the informal sectors, such as selling food, cleaning homes, and sex work, which normally employ a significant number of women, were lost (Jerving, 2021). The pandemic, therefore, not only confined victims at home with their abusers, it also made them dependent on their abusers at a time of economic difficulty. The victims also could not access critical health services due to the restrictions.

The rampant occurrence of domestic violence in Kenya during the pandemic was also occasioned by the lack of existing structures to address the problem. Before the pandemic, Kenya had recorded an increased incidence of domestic violence, which mostly affected women and girls, yet the authorities had failed to devise measures to prevent an exacerbation of the same, even as they instituted nightly curfews and lockdowns at the outset of the Covid-19 pandemic (Human Rights Watch, 2020). This chapter focuses on the legal dimension of domestic violence, and more particularly, on the access to justice by victims during the pandemic.

## Literature review and theoretical underpinnings

### *The place of language in the criminal justice system*

Language is a critical component of the criminal justice system. Solan and Tiersma (2006) concur that the criminal justice system is replete with language events: the initial spoken and written encounters between crime victims or suspects and the police; the presentation of testimonies to the court, which capture speeches recorded in earlier language events; the interpretation of statutes, and the presentation of a court verdict. The rules of evidence, the principle of statutory interpretation, and constitutional doctrine all present a tacit assumption that language events are recalled accurately, and language is interpreted precisely. This implies that, without language, it becomes difficult to conceive of the criminal justice system, its tenets, and operationalisation.

There are various ways in which language interacts with criminal law or, rather, the criminal justice system. For example, the language used by police officers and crime suspects is essential in determining whether someone should be detained for a suspected crime (Solan & Tiersma, 2006). Language is a critical tool that the police use during interrogation to ascertain the involvement of a suspect in a crime. More specifically, linguistic evidence is a major area of interaction with the criminal justice system. Generally, any writing or speech can be regarded as linguistic evidence.

However, the criminal justice system focuses on linguistic issues that impact the evidence that could be admissible in a trial (Solan & Tiersma, 2006). Essentially, Solan and Tiersma (2006) reveal that language is a critical building block of the practice, theory, and philosophy of the criminal justice system. This is evident, considering that the legal structures upon which the legal system is based are founded on texts referred to as 'statutes', are interpreted based on those statutes, and are implemented, based on the same. This study, however, focuses on the language used by the victims of crime and, in this case, domestic violence that, in most cases, disproportionately affects women and children and is perpetrated by people to whom they are closely related.

Consideration of context is critical when examining speech in the legal system. Context is considered almost all the time while making judicial judgments, not just as a way of gleaning the several possible senses the particular words were intended to mean but also as a way of determining why the speaker used those words in the first place (Solan & Tiersma, 2006). Analysis of the relationship between language and law is currently undertaken by social scientists and linguists. As language is a social phenomenon, its use is highly instrumental. Various social institutions are established through the use of language, including the legal justice system (Freeman & Smith, 2013). The linguistic contribution of legal parlance is limited to the meaning of single words in some cases. This is often applicable where a word is fairly common in its usage (Coulthard & Johnson, 2017).

In particular, linguistic knowledge is essential in facilitating an understanding of the substance of the law. The knowledge of linguistics and language has significantly influenced legal interpretation and, more particularly, interpretation of statutes. For instance, judges or other judicial officers are required to determine the meaning of particular texts, and they accomplish this by developing maxims of interpretation, such as *exclusio alterius, expressio unius*, and *eiusdem generis* (Freeman & Smith, 2013).

Sociolinguistics involves studying the use of language in its social contexts. Linguistics primarily focuses on the structure of a language, while sociolinguistics analyses the use and function of language. Therefore, the major concern of sociolinguistics is understanding the complex relationship between language and the society in which it is used. There are three major ways in which this particular relationship is conceptualised. These will now be discussed. The axiomatic assumption posits that language reflects the society in which it is used (Eades, 2010:5-6). In this chapter, the use of language by domestic abuse victims to verbalise their frustration in bringing their abusers to justice provides a subtle hint about the society in which they live and its particular apathy towards addressing, as they would any other, the crime of domestic violence that, in its extreme perpetration, claims lives.

Secondly, there is a view that language determines aspects of culture or society, which is diametrically opposed to the axiomatic assumption (Eades, 2010:5-6). This would mean that the accounts by victims of domestic violence about their abuse – and particularly their quest for justice – determine whether the society becomes just. This view is highly contestable, considering that domestic violence victims are mostly discriminated against by the very legal systems that have been put in place to protect them.

The third view is that there is a reciprocal and dynamic relationship between language and society, to the extent that language use simultaneously shapes and reflects society. As opposed to the first two dimensions, this third perspective is broadly adopted in social sciences and has led to the understanding that the two components are inextricably related. The agency of individuals within social groups creates, maintains, reinforces, changes, and shapes the social structure that, in turn, enhances or limits the agency of individuals (Eades, 2010:5-6). This view suggests that domestic violence victims have the power to use language to rally society to appreciate the gravity of the crime committed against them and actually activate the legal mechanisms meant to protect them. This would be a more proactive use of language by the victims, rather than verbalising their abuse without calling people to action.

The Kenyan social linguistic context is richly complex, considering that there are 42 languages spoken in the country. There is a distinct divide between the endoglossic and the exoglossic Kenyan languages. On one hand, the exoglossic language is largely English, which is used in official communication in government and private organisations. On the other hand, the endoglossic language is Kiswahili; however, even though it is used in official communication, this is not to the same extent as English is used. The hegemonic rise of the importance of English as a language of instruction and visual communication in Kenya is occasioned by the unequal treatment of the indigenous languages in the country (Docrat, Kaschula & Ralarala, 2021). This language dominance may be a barrier to those seeking to access justice, particularly if seekers emanate from disadvantaged socioeconomic backgrounds, lack legal representation, and cannot express themselves effectively in English (which is, arguably, the lingua franca within the corridors of justice).

In criminal justice parlance, language is considered a tool of crime as criminals may use language to commit a crime (and, with respect to domestic violence, emotional abuse falls into this category). Language is also a tool used to report a crime, with domestic violence victims verbalising their abuse and recording statements with the police (Docrat, Kaschula & Ralarala, 2021). This study went further than these known roles of language in the criminal justice system to examine how the language that victims of domestic violence use to talk about their abuse and abusers inadvertently reveals the challenges involved in their gaining access to justice.

## Legal responses to domestic violence in Kenya

Kenya ratified the Convention on the Elimination of All Forms of Discrimination Against Women (CEDAW) in 1984 and this has seen to the establishment of measures to ensure that the rights of women are upheld accordingly. Various laws in Kenya are aimed at curbing domestic violence. For one, the 2010 Kenyan Constitution (Republic of Kenya, 2010) guarantees the right to freedom and security of every Kenyan. This right includes protection against any forms of violence from private or public sources; and protection against psychological or physical torture, or degrading or inhuman treatment (Ahmed et al., 2021).

In particular, various statutes have been enacted by the Kenyan Parliament to curb domestic violence. The Protection Against Domestic Violence Act of 2015 provides a framework for protecting vulnerable individuals and providing victims of domestic violence with the life that they require (Republic of Kenya, 2014). While this is a positive move to curb the prevalence of domestic violence in the country, the implementation of the provisions of this legal structure is quite poor or even non-existent (CREAW, 2021). For instance, law enforcement officers largely consider domestic violence to be a domestic issue and only step in after grievous harm, such as homicide, has occurred.

Furthermore, some of the approaches adopted by law enforcement officers to handle domestic violence victims impede them from receiving the assistance that they seek. This is evident in the casual manner with which police handle victims of domestic violence – to an extent, they implicate them in their own victimisation or want to be bribed begore they will pursue the offenders. Other challenges associated with the implementation of laws to protect victims of domestic violence include financial hurdles, characterised by the very high court fees and other legal fees, and the evidentiary threshold demanded by the Protection Against Domestic Violence Act, which has resulted in the denial of protection orders for deserving and urgent cases (COWAV, 2020).

There is also the 2006 Sexual Offences Act, which provides for the protection of everyone from harm associated with sexual acts, and also provides the framework for ensuring that victims access psychological support and justice (Kenya Law, 2006). Notably, the Act is conspicuously silent in regard to marital rape (Republic of Kenya, 2014). This implies that, based on the existing legal frameworks, sexual violence within the domestic context cannot be successfully tried and convicted.

Besides these challenges, comprehensive domestic violence prevention and response services that exist in Kenya are limited and mostly found in peri-urban and urban areas; in rural areas, they are almost non-existent (Ahmed et al., 2021). Available services are too few to cater for the increased number of domestic violence victims; the services are also usually crowded and found in urban areas only (Ahmed et al., 2021). There have been reported cases in which some police officers have been bribed to protect the perpetrators of domestic violence, resulting in further victimisation of the victims. Furthermore, the judicial system in Kenya is fraught with a backlog of cases, resulting in lengthy court proceedings that force victims to cover transportation costs that are occasioned by regular court adjournments (Ahmed et al., 2021).

## Legal responses to domestic violence during the Covid-19 outbreak in Kenya

The Kenyan government took various legal measures to curb the spread of the pandemic. These measures overlooked the associated shadow pandemic of domestic violence that was ravaging families at household level (Bhalla, 2020). For instance, Executive Order Number 2 of 2020, which was established on 28 February 2020 by the National Emergency Committee on Coronavirus, did not have any representation from the Ministry of Public Service, Youth and Gender Affairs (Office of the President, 2020) and therefore did not feature in any domestic violence issues in the response plan (Aluga, 2020).

Additionally, the Community Engagement Health Strategy that was established in April 2020 by the Ministry of Health to respond to the pandemic did not cover domestic violence. In response to pressure from civil society, in May 2020, the Ministry released guidelines for healthcare providers responding to domestic violence victims (Bhalla, 2020). The guidelines provided a framework for community-based interventions to resume prevention work and awareness activities at community level. However, these guidelines did not feature comprehensive programmes and services required by domestic violence victims (Ahmed et al., 2021).

At the outset of the Covid-19 outbreak in Kenya, essential police and judicial services, social services, community-based prevention programmes and medical and psychological services were invariably disrupted. There were reported cases of police turning away domestic violence victims and asking them to report their cases later (Ahmed et al., 2021), which compromised the collection of evidence in cases of sexual violence.

As the reported cases of domestic violence increased, in June 2020, the National Police Service set up a toll-free hotline so that domestic violence victims could report incidents of abuse. However, this hotline was limited its operational hours due to curfew restrictions, thereby hindering domestic violence victims from reporting incidents of abuse (Ahmed et al, 2021), thus denying victims the opportunity to seek help during the prime hours when domestic violence is most often perpetrated.

There were also limited transportation services due to lockdowns and curfews; and domestic violence victims also feared mistreatment by the police and contracting the coronavirus if they ventured into public spaces. Due to this, in August 2020 the National Police Service launched PoliCare, a one-stop model police station that provided domestic violence victims with critical multisectoral services. However, these services were only available to residents of Nairobi County (Ahmed et al., 2021). Besides these issues, at the height of the pandemic, the administration of justice was also significantly challenged by the court processing and proceedings scaling down, which brought about limited access to courts during the pandemic. Amongst the most affected by these changes aimed at curbing the spread of the pandemic were the victims of domestic violence (Shikongigi, 2020).

Upon reopening in July 2020, the courts held a few sessions and provided lenient bail to domestic violence perpetrators as a way of curbing overcrowding in remand prisons (Bhalla, 2020). In most cases, the courts only handled rape and child abuse cases, which they termed 'essential services' and delegated all other domestic violence cases to be handled at police station level. The slower operation of courts contributed to repeat offences and witness tampering. In July 2020, courts established electronic filing of cases and virtual court hearings in compliance with their social distancing health guidelines. These services were, however, only available to middle-class domestic violence victims who could afford the internet services (Ahmed et al., 2021).

In May 2020, the Ministry of Health declared that emergency clinical and post-rape care services would be classified as essential services; but the services were not accessible, since most healthcare facilities had been converted into quarantine centres and most healthcare providers had also been deployed to isolation centres. Domestic violence victims also feared accessing healthcare facilities due to the possibility of contracting the virus or being forced to be tested for Covid-19 and afterwards being subjected to mandatory quarantine at their own cost if they tested positive (Ahmed et al., 2021).

The few shelters that remained after the outbreak of the pandemic were reluctant to admit additional victims due to limited resources; they also demanded that, to confirm their negative status, victims had to obtain a Covid-19 medical certificate (Ahmed et al., 2021). Kenya has yet to establish functional public shelters for domestic violence victims; and, with the continuation of the pandemic, women have been increasingly exposed to psychological and physical violence due to their economic vulnerability, isolation, and family confinement (International Development Law Organization, 2020).

## Methodology

The methodology adopted for the review of accounts by victims of domestic violence was informed by the interpretivism research philosophy. The interpretivism approach presumes that reality is socially constructed and varied, and the goal of the researcher is to understand meanings (Willis, Jost & Nilakanta, 2007). In particular, this study adopted the critical discourse analysis (CDA) method (Willis, Jost & Nilakanta, 2007). Notably, CDA transcends traditional discourse analysis, going beyond descriptions of language to analyse, interpret and explain important relationships of representation embedded in the discourse being analysed (Salter & Mutlu, 2013). In this research, victims' accounts and those of officials from organisations that support domestic abuse victims, were examined, focusing on elements, such as the overall structure of the interactions, word use, and sentence structure in relation to the perpetuation of domestic violence and the administration of justice during the Covid-19 pandemic.

The adoption of CDA in this study was also informed by the fact that it also supplies effective insights into the relationships between language and social linguistic context (Willis, Jost & Nilakanta, 2007). Critical discourse analysis identifies semantic categories or linguistic mechanisms through which ideology is developed, thereby revealing the hidden ways that authors use within their discourse to package, consciously or unconsciously, their representation of the world (Salter & Mutlu, 2013).

Therefore, in this study, the researcher considered the language used by the victims of domestic violence, and by professionals working in various agencies and non-governmental organisations that provide social and legal support to victims of domestic violence. This language was considered a tool for exploring and highlighting the challenges that the victims encountered in their quest to access justice during the Covid-19 pandemic.

## Data collection

Empirical material on victims' access to justice during the pandemic was based on a mapping of news media articles, news media broadcasts, and reports by organisations supporting victims of domestic violence. The discourse, in this case, included both direct and reported speech by the victims about their quest for justice during the pandemic.

## Inclusion and exclusion criteria

- ### Inclusion criteria

  - The articles, reports and broadcasts published between March 2020 and October 2021 (the latter date was when the Kenyan government lifted the night curfew – a watershed event because it was at night that most abuses were perpetrated).
  - Reports published by reputable organisations or agencies that support domestic violence victims.

- ### Exclusion criteria

  - Articles, reports or broadcasts published before March 2020 and after October 2021.
  - Accounts published in personal blogs.

## Data analysis

The analysis of study data was based on Fairclough's system of discourse analysis, which comprises three dimensions. The first dimension includes analysis of the text of written and spoken accounts, which may involve visual images (Amoussou & Allagbe, 2018). The visual images scrutinised in this study included video clips of victim accounts and interview discussions featuring professionals from government agencies and non-governmental organisations. The second dimension involves analysis of discourse practices evident in the production, consumption, and distribution of text (Amoussou & Allagbe, 2018). This study included an examination of the vocabulary chosen by research participants to express the challenges involved in accessing justice for victims of domestic violence. The third dimension is the social-cultural practices of the research participants. This aspect is further mapped onto a three-dimensional framework for analysing text and discourse. It therefore includes participants' linguistic descriptions of the properties that make up the text; the interpretation of the relationship between the text and the discursive processes or interactions involving the victims, and explanations of the relationship between the discourse and the victims' cultural or social reality (Amoussou & Allagbe, 2018). Finally, the third dimension involves analysis of how research participants link their accounts of domestic violence to their social-cultural context.

## Ethical considerations

The anonymity of research participants is a key ethical requirement in social research (Creswell & Creswell, 2018). This analysis included text that had previously been published in news media articles, organisational reports, and news broadcasts and was therefore accessible to the public. Some of the participants whose accounts were used for analysis in this study were identified by their actual names, while others had already been anonymised in the respective publications in which they featured. Therefore, the need for, or possibility of, making their accounts anonymous, though duly considered, was not applicable in such cases.

## Discussion and findings

The findings of this study were based on analysis of published accounts by the victims of domestic violence at the height of the Covid-19 pandemic in Kenya. The findings were also based on the perspectives of government officials and the professionals who helped or engaged with the victims of domestic violence during the pandemic.

### Increase in domestic violence during the Covid-19 pandemic

At the height of the Covid-19 pandemic, news accounts of domestic violence used language that indicates the prevalence of the crime. According to Fanis Lasiagali, the head of the 1195 Helpline by Healthcare Assistance Kenya, from February to June 2020, the number of cases handled by the Helpline rose from 86 to about 1 100. Lasiagali added that approximately a third of the callers were men who reported psychological abuse from their families and spouses, claiming that they were being harassed and abused due to their inability to provide for their families (Bhalla, 2020). A *Business Daily* report published in April 2020 quoted the Health Chief Administration Secretary (CAS), Dr Mercy Mwangangi, acknowledging a sharp increase in domestic violence cases recorded by the National Council on Administration of Justice (NCAJ) and the Gender Violence Recovery Centre (GVCR). Dr Mwangangi claimed that the crime was characterised by sexual and gender-based violence and its perpetration was largely attributed to close relatives and guardians (Kivuva, 2020). In the same vein, Prof. Margaret Kobia, the Cabinet Secretary, Ministry of Public Service, Youth and Gender Affairs in Kenya, admitted in an interview on *NTV Kenya* that the "Office of the Director of Public Prosecution (ODPP)" had raised the "issue of increased cases of domestic violence" in the country (*NTV Kenya*, 2020).

The use of language by stakeholders who handle victims of domestic violence, such as Lasiagali, as captured by Bhalla (2020) was instructive in understanding the prevalence of domestic violence occasioned by Covid-19 that, incidentally, affected male victims at unprecedented levels. The increased domestic violence was acknowledged by government agencies, such as the National Council on Administration of Justice (NCAJ) and Gender Violence Recovery Centre (GVCR), the Ministry of Health, and the Ministry of Ministry of Public Service, Youth and Gender Affairs. Therefore, a consequence of the pandemic was that it affected the social fabric of Kenya, manifesting in some cases as domestic violence.

Accounts by stakeholders, victims and government officials also illustrated various social and economic factors that exacerbated domestic violence during the pandemics. Key amongst these were tough economic times. Rose, a small-scale business trader at Kibuye market in Kisumu City, was featured in the *2021 Human Rights Watch Report*. Rose claimed that her abusive marriage had become unbearable during lockdown. Her husband became more abusive, physically, and emotionally, even as she relied on him more to provide for the family from his carpentry business (Human Rights Watch, 2021). Magdalene, a twenty-two-year-old domestic violence victim, was evicted from home by her husband, along with her three-year-old daughter who had psychological and physical disabilities (Odhiambo, 2020). The closing down of the economy adversely affected the informal sector, as observed by Ms Agnes Odhiambo, a senior women's rights researcher and head of the Nairobi office at Human Rights Watch. She noted that informal sector opportunities that disproportionately employ women for jobs, such as cleaning homes, selling food, and sex work, were impacted heavily by the lockdowns (Jerving, 2021). Besides, as reported by the Human Rights Watch, the measures adopted by the government to counter the pandemic spread had the unintended consequence of elevating gender-based violence risk: 45% of girls and women aged between 14 and 49 years experienced some form of physical violence; and about 14% experienced sexual violence (Human Rights Watch, 2020). Therefore, in confining women such as Rose and Magdalene to their homes, Covid-19 made these women wholly reliant on their abusive partners, with very few options for recourse. Limited financial resources implied that the victims could not afford the required medical attention in cases of physical and sexual abuse.

### *The Covid-19 pandemic compromised legal structures for seeking redress for domestic violence*

In April 2020, the Health CAS, Dr Mwangangi, reminded the public that the "law has not been suspended" and would "catch up with those who mete violence on others" during the pandemic (Kivuva, 2020). She urged Kenyans to handle domestic disputes using the available civil structures, without resorting to violence (Kivuva, 2020). However, the challenge of accessing justice was compounded by movement restrictions that made it difficult for victims to report abuse and seek help so that relevant service providers could respond to their needs effectively and efficiently (Odhiambo, 2020). Dr Christine Nasilia, a health specialist, acknowledged in an interview on *Citizen TV* that, when domestic violence occurs, the perpetrator may not allow the victim to use their phone "because of the suspicion of 'Who are you calling?'". In the same interview, Dr Oscar Githu, a forensic psychologist, acknowledged that this limited the help victims could get, because the phone is "the only tool which you can use to get some help" (*Citizen TV Kenya*, 2020a). Even outside the home during curfew hours, victims' options were limited as they could "get beaten and locked up by the police" (Jerving, 2021). According to the 2021 Human Rights Watch Report, the victims' interviews indicated that they needed a safe place before they could report abuse to authorities or pursue prosecution of their abusers since they feared reprisal. The lack of safe shelters condemned them to continue living with their abusers. Charlotte, an interviewee, feared reporting her husband to the police while she still lived with him since he would possibly retaliate with more violence. Fatima, another interviewee, said that, without safe houses, "women cannot pursue justice" since their abuser can track them and even kill them (Human Rights Watch, 2021).

The other critical impediment to domestic violence victims accessing justice related to the scaling down of operations in the judicial system in Kenya. In acknowledging this challenge, Prof. Margaret Kobia indicated that the Ministry of Public Service, Youth and Gender Affairs was "liaising with the judiciary to make the domestic violence cases urgent and prosecute them with the technology that they are currently using, such as Skype hearings" (*NTV Kenya*, 2020).

The context of the pandemic also led to the closure of critical services in the judiciary, which affected access to justice by the victims. The prevalence of the pandemic compromised the existing legal structures for addressing domestic violence. The use of words such as "suspended" and "catch up" refers to the lack of availability of law and order during the pandemic and makes it clear why domestic violence victims would have experienced difficulties in accessing justice. Dr Mwangangi's statement reflects what Eades (2010:5-6) considers the usage of language in particular contexts (sociolinguistics). From Dr Mwangangi's choice of language to describe the situation of legal structures being unavailable, we can infer that victims of domestic violence had little or no access to legal structures during the pandemic; further, we can infer the possible disregard of the law by domestic violence perpetrators, as it was easier for them to get away with their crimes. Other contextual issues are apparent in Charlotte and Fatima's accounts, revealing the inadequate provision of safe houses, and the fear of further victimisation in the victims' quest for justice.

## Justice and legal access worsened during the pandemic

Evidently, the high rates of domestic violence during the pandemic drew the attention of the highest government authorities. In July 2020, President Uhuru Kenyatta acknowledged that, due to the pandemic, women had become more vulnerable to "physical, sexual and psychological violence", even as their access to "protective and recovery services" was restricted. He ordered the National Crime Research Centre (NCRC) to investigate the worrying trends, develop an advisory for security agencies on remedial action to be undertaken within 30 days, and also begin prosecuting the perpetrators (Bhalla, 2020). While Judy Gitau, Regional Coordinator for the movement Africa for Equality Now, welcomed this development, she called for more action to ensure that the victims were provided with justice and safe spaces (Bhalla, 2020).

However, Ms Odhiambo observed, "there is a real lack of political will to address gender-based violence", because political commitment "has to come with resources and proper planning" (Jerving, 2021). She cited a case from March 2021 when, in announcing new movement restrictions, the government had not included domestic violence (GBV) service providers, such as safe houses. The government had increased helpline services, but the programmes were poorly coordinated and confusing, with poorly trained personnel. Ms Odhiambo said that the "poor implementation did not really help as many people as it was supposed to help". The government failed to provide "critical early warning, detection, data collection, and protection measures in national and county-level contingency plans and budgets for containing the Covid-19 pandemic" and it "contributed to an increase in cases of gender-based violence" (Jerving, 2021). The same sentiments are held by Glady's Koskei, a community activist, who claims that the government has "never given me any support" in her work of rescuing children who are victimised in domestic violence (Human Rights Watch, 2021).

The police culture preceding the pandemic contributed to victims' limited access to justice. Charlotte (interviewee) said that she feared reporting her husband to the police because they would "obviously ask" for money before they would help; that police assistance is faster when one provides a bribe; and that the speed of their action is determined by the amount of the bribe. She reported her incident to one police station and, after two weeks in which no action was taken, reported it to another police station (Human Rights Watch, 2021).

A report by the Human Rights Watch cited interference by the police in the handling of domestic violence of cases. Grace, a rape victim from Machakos County, presented her clothes to the police; but, since she had been abused by a former police officer, the police refused to accept, record, and store her evidence until 11 days after the crime had been committed. This delay was calculated to destroy or compromise her evidence to make it inadmissible in court. The police also refused to provide her with P3 medical examination forms, insisting she negotiate a monetary settlement with her offender. They argued she would lose the case in court. She eventually gave in, due to a lack of finances to travel to court multiple times (Human Rights Watch, 2021). Grace's case reflects the necessity of examining language use in the legal system as Solan and Tiersma (2006) suggest, as it is important to examine how particular words or phrases are used by a speaker in a particular context. By urging Grace to resolve the matter out of court, the police were expressly preventing the perpetrator from facing criminal charges. The resolving of this matter is reflective of the societal perception that the violence meted against victims at home does not have to be taken to court for resolution – a perception that police authorities uphold in cases such as this.

Therefore, failure by relevant authorities to support access to justice by domestic violence victims preceded the pandemic. The accounts by government officials, such as President Uhuru Kenyatta and Cabinet Secretary, Prof. Margaret Kobia, demonstrate the government's awareness about the gravity of domestic violence during the pandemic and the need to recommit to deal with the crime, as well as help the victims. The view by Ms Gitau (Regional Coordinator of Africa for Equality Now), that it was time the government swung into action to hold perpetrators accountable, reflects that domestic violence worsened during the pandemic and the government has not paid much attention to it. However, despite the pledges by senior government officials, the problem persisted at a time when domestic violence cases had risen to unprecedented levels and the victims needed to be supported socially and economically and given access to legal services.

## Cultural stigma dissuades victims to consider legal channels to resolve domestic violence cases

The cultural stigma attached to domestic violence has made it increasingly difficult for support structures to be created for perpetrators to be brought to book. In an interview on *Citizen TV*, Dr Christine Nasilia, a health specialist, said, "We are already documenting quite a lot of people who are locked within their homes, and they have no valve for letting out pressure. They are roasting within, but they have no support system that can reach them" (*Citizen TV Kenya*, 2020a). Prof. Margaret Kobia also acknowledged that "most of these domestic violence cases are never reported because of the stigma attached to them" (*NTV Kenya*, 2020). Fanis Lasiagali, the head of the 1195 Helpline by Healthcare Assistance Kenya acknowledged a significant proportion of men reported being abused, although they only reported psychological abuse. This reluctance to report abuse by their female spouse is indicative of the cultural stigma that abused men face, which inhibits them from seeking justice for their abuse.

## The lack of recognition of domestic violence as a crime like any other

The majority of victims whom Ms Odhiambo interviewed did not report the crimes against them due to scepticism that they would receive support, or a belief they would have to bribe the authorities to get justice. Kenyan police and other state security agents have been implicated in many rape cases – "particularly during times of crisis" – and have not faced justice. Victims are often bound with "a lot of other psychological chains, which prevent them from reporting their abuse". Rose, a GBV victim, said that she was unaware that she could report the domestic violence to the police. She did not know where to seek help until a friend told her about a community-based organisation. That eventually sensitised her to report the abuse (Human Rights Watch, 2021). In an interview on *Citizen TV*, Milka Okiya, another GBV victim, expressed her cluelessness on what she could do about her abusive husband. She said, "If these things continue where will he take us? And we are with him there. He can beat us or commit suicide" (*Citizen TV Kenya*, 2020b). Grace also claimed that her husband used to take advantage of the lockdown and curfew to beat her badly, but she did not consider pressing charges against him (Human Rights Watch, 2021). Therefore, in these cases, because victims did not regard domestic violence as a crime, they felt helpless.

## Minimal or absent health services critical in administering justice to victims

Ms Odhiambo commented that the failures of the government included not providing timely access to quality healthcare, including emergency sexual, reproductive and psychosocial care. The abused women whom she had interviewed and who had received health and legal support acknowledged that this support was "inadequate"; and they were also limited by inadequate finances (Jerving, 2021). In the same vein, Dr Githu observed that the "health-seeking behaviour" of the victims "during the Covid pandemic" was affected because "people are afraid to seek critical health services" (*Citizen TV Kenya*, 2020a). Most women did not report domestic abuse cases to the relevant authorities; when they did, only a few women received medical care or the justice they deserved (Odhiambo, 2020). Leticia, a victim, said that she was charged for the medical services that she sought at the Kisumu General District Hospital after her husband had attacked her with a machete. Amelia, another victim, said that the Jaramogi Oginga Odinga Teaching and Referral Hospital in Kisumu referred her to a private health facility for follow-up gynaecological services since the government facility could not provide those services. She could not, however, afford the private gynaecologist (Human Rights Watch, 2021). Dr Githu further observed that, "since most resources have already been diverted to handling the pandemic", providing state support to domestic violence victims "may not be a priority at the moment" (*Citizen TV Kenya*, 2020a).

Since the pandemic disrupted the provision of health services, many domestic violence victims have not had access to them and therefore have been unable to document crucial evidence that they could use to charge their abusers. In addition, the depressed economy during the pandemic has contributed to victims' lack of funds required for accessing healthcare services. This has been complicated by an increase in the cost of medical services during the pandemic.

## Conclusions

Accounts by the victims, professionals supporting the victims, and government agencies indicated that the Covid-19 pandemic provided a perfect atmosphere for domestic violence to thrive. Domestic violence thrived during the pandemic as restrictive governmental measures enacted to contain the spread of the virus resulted in negative social and economic effects. Secondly, at the height of the Covid-19 outbreak in Kenya, access to and administration of justice was problematic for victims of domestic violence, and this environment emboldened perpetrators of domestic crime as they were assured that they would get away with their crimes.

The challenges associated with access to justice for victims before the outbreak, such as apathy by government agencies and authorities, and limited shelters for victims, persisted and even worsened as the pandemic restrictions intensified. Besides, the legal channels were not considered by victims appropriate for the resolution of domestic violence cases, a perspective that preceded the pandemic and was informed by the social and cultural perspectives and stigma associated with the crime.

The lack of recognition of domestic violence by the government as being as serious as any other crime heightened the helplessness of the victims during the pandemic since they could not seek legal redress, yet they were trapped with their abusers due to lockdowns and curfews. Additionally, the restricted or lack of access to critical healthcare services during the lockdown and curfews made it difficult for victims of domestic violence to acquire critical evidence that they could use to pursue legal justice against their abusers.

## References

Ahmed, S.A., Changole, J. & Wangamati, C.K. 2021. Impact of the Covid-19 pandemic on intimate partner violence in Sudan, Malawi and Kenya. *Reproductive Health*, 18(222). https://doi.org/10.1186/s12978-021-01272-y

Aluga, M.A. 2020. Immunology and infection Coronavirus Disease 2019 (Covid-19) in Kenya: Preparedness, response and transmissibility. *Journal of Microbiology*, 53:671-673. https://doi.org/10.1016/j.jmii.2020.04.011

Amoussou, F. & Allagbe, A.A. 2018. Principles, theories, and approaches to critical discourse analysis. *International Journal on Studies in English Language and Literature*, 6(1):11-18. https://doi.org/10.20431/2347-3134.0601002

Appiah, S.C. & Mohammed, A. 2013. *Domestic violence and its effect on women*. Elsevier: SSRN. https://doi.org/10.2139/ssrn.2364190

Bhalla, N. 2020. Kenya orders probe into rise in violence against women and girls during pandemic. 6 July. *Reuters*. https://www.reuters.com/article/us-health-coronavirus-kenya-women-trfn-idUSKBN2472ER [Accessed 8 December 2022].

*Citizen TV Kenya*. 2020a. Citizen weekend interview: Cases of domestic violence on the rise during Covid-19 pandemic. https://www.youtube.com/watch?v=7pw_0MDkcqg [Accessed 8 December 2022].

*Citizen TV Kenya.* 2020b. Gender based violence increases with Covid-19 restrictions. https://www.youtube.com/watch?v=9I4XpYeyayw&t=26s

Coulthard, M. & Johnson, A. 2017. *An introduction to forensic linguistics: Language in evidence.* New York: Routledge. https://doi.org/10.4324/9781315630311

COVAW (Coalition on Violence Against Women). 2020. *Advisory opinion/statement. The shadow pandemic: Demanding concrete actions to protect women and girls from gender-based violence during the Covid-19 pandemic.* https://covaw.or.ke/advisory-opinion-statement-the-shadow-pandemic-demanding-concrete-actions-to-protect-women-and-girls-from-gender-based-violence-during-the-covid-19-pandemic/ [Accessed 8 December 2022].

CREAW (Centre for Rights Education and Awareness). 2021. *CREAW Kenya statement condemning the sexual assault and subsequent murder of Velvine Nungari.* Centre for Rights Education and Awareness. https://home.creaw.org/2021/03/19/creaw-kenya-statement-condeming-the-sexual-assault-and-subsequent-murder-of-velvine-nungari/

Creswell, J.W. & Creswell, J.D. 2018. *Research designs: Qualitative, quantitative, and mixed methods approaches.* Newbury Park, CA: Sage.

Docrat, Z., Kaschula, R. & Ralarala, M.K. 2021. *A handbook on legal languages and the quest for linguistic equality in South Africa and beyond.* Stellenbosch: African Sun Media. https://doi.org/10.52779/9781991201270

Eades, D. 2010. *Sociolinguistics and the legal process.* Bristol, UK: Multilingual Matters. https://doi.org/10.21832/9781847692559

Freeman, M. & Smith, F. 2013. *Law and language.* Oxford: Oxford University Press.

Human Rights Watch (HRW). 2021. *"I had nowhere to go": Violence against women and girls during the Covid-19 pandemic in Kenya.* https://www.hrw.org/report/2021/09/21/i-had-nowhere-go/violence-against-women-and-girls-during-covid-19-pandemic-kenya [Accessed 8 December 2022].

Javier, R.A. & Herron, W.G. 2019. *Understanding domestic violence: Theories, challenges, and remedies.* Lanham, MD: Rowman & Littlefield.

Jerving, S. 2021. Report: Kenya failed to protect GBV survivors during pandemic. Devex. Retrieved from https://www.devex.com/news/report-kenya-failed-to-protect-gbv-survivors-during-pandemic-101634

Kenya Law. 2006. Sexual Offences Act No. 3 of 2006. Retrieved from http://kenyalaw.org:8181/exist/kenyalex/actview.xql?actid=No.%203%20of%202006

Kivuva, E. 2020. Domestic abuse on the rise amid coronavirus fight. 14 April. *Business Daily.* https://www.businessdailyafrica.com/bd/news/domestic-abuse-on-the-rise-amid-coronavirus-fight-2286982 [Accessed 8 December 2022].

Montesanti, S.R. & Thurston, W.E. 2015. Mapping the role of structural and interpersonal violence in the lives of women: Implications for public health interventions and policy. *BMC Women's Health*, 15(100). https://doi.org/10.1186/s12905-015-0256-4

Muluneh, M.D., Stulz, V., Francis, L. & Agho, K. 2020. Gender based violence against women in sub-Saharan Africa: A systematic review and meta-analysis of cross-sectional studies. *International Journal of Environmental Research and Public Health,* 17(3):903. https://doi.org/10.3390/ijerph17030903

NCAJ (National Council on the Administration of Justice, Kenya). 2020. *Statement on justice sector operations in the wake of the Covid-19 pandemic.* https://www.judiciary.go.ke/download/statement-on-justice-sector-operations-in-the-wake-of-the-covid-19-pandemic/ [Accessed 8 December 2022].

*NTV Kenya.* 2020. Cases of domestic violence in Kenya have increased during coronavirus period – CS Kobia. https://www.youtube.com/watch?v=MxJcIU4_v9A

Odhiambo, A. 2020. Tackling Kenya's domestic violence amid Covid-19 crisis: Lockdown measures increase risks for women and girls. Human Rights Watch. https://www.hrw.org/news/2020/04/08/tackling-kenyas-domestic-violence-amid-covid-19-crisis

Renzetti, C.M., Follingstad, D. & Coker, A.L. 2017. *Preventing intimate partner violence: Interdisciplinary perspectives.* Bristol, UK: Polity Press. https://doi.org/10.1332/policypress/9781447333050.001.0001

Republic of Kenya. 2010. Constitution of Kenya, 2010. http://www.parliament.go.ke/sites/default/files/2017-05/The_Constitution_of_Kenya_2010.pdf

Republic of Kenya. 2014. *National Policy for Prevention and Response to Gender Based Violence.* http://psyg.go.ke/docs/National%20Policy%20on%20prevention%20and%20Response%20to%20Gender%20Based%20Violence.pdf [Accessed 8 December 2022].

Salter, M.B. & Mutlu, C.E. 2013. *Research methods in critical security studies: An introduction.* London: Routledge. https://doi.org/10.4324/9780203107119

Shikongigi, A. 2020. Covid-19: Courts and domestic violence cases in Kenya. https://www.africanwomeninlaw.com/post/covid-19-courts-and-domestic-violence-cases-in-kenya

Sinha, P., Gupta, U., Singh, J. & Srivastava, A. 2017. Structural violence on women: An impediment to women empowerment. *Indian Journal of Community Medicine*, 42(3): 134-137. https://doi.org/10.4103/ijcm.IJCM_276_15

Solan, L. & Tiersma, P.M. 2006. *Speaking of crime: The language of criminal justice.* Chicago, IL: University of Chicago Press.

Wado, Y.D. 2021. Violence against women in Kenya: Data provides a glimpse into a grim situation. 19 October. *The Conversation.* https://theconversation.com/violence-against-women-in-kenya-data-provides-a-glimpse-into-a-grim-situation-170109 [Accessed 8 December 2022].

Willis, J., Jost, M. & Nilakanta, R. 2007. *Foundations of qualitative research: Interpretive and critical approaches.* London: Sage.

# THE SOCIOLINGUISTIC ANALYSIS OF LOADED LANGUAGE DURING CROSS-EXAMINATION IN SOUTH AFRICAN CRIMINAL TRIALS

## A case-based approach


*Russell H. Kaschula*
*Zakeera Docrat*


## Introduction

With the number of rapes on the increase, a gender-based violence (GBV) crisis and femicide in South Africa, complainants are often reluctant to report cases due to cultural taboos, linguistic barriers and stigmatisation that often relate to the power dynamics in the legal system. This is also true of other criminal cases that may be related to politically, culturally or otherwise sensitive issues. In a criminal case, a complainant is required to lay a charge with the police, with the statement recorded in English (Docrat et al., 2020), regardless of the fact that only 9.6% of the population speaks English as their mother tongue (Census, 2011; RSA SSA, 2011). The majority of complainants cannot read nor verify what is recorded in the English statement because they only speak one or more of the nine official African languages, or they do not have sufficient proficiency in English.

The discrepancies between the written statement (evidence) and the oral evidence provided in court are often brought to the fore in court cases. These discrepancies may impact negatively on the credibility of the witness, as well as the state's case, when proving or disproving charges. In South Africa, cases in which linguistic discrepancies are highlighted are minimal (Docrat et al., 2021). This, however, is not because there are minimal cases where linguistic discrepancies result in procedural irregularities or affect the outcome of the case, but rather that this is an area with which legal practitioners do not appear to be well acquainted. The concomitant cultural underpinnings of language also play an important role here, as it may not be possible to translate or interpret certain words or concepts from one language into another without losing the essence of what is being said or alluded to. From a sociolinguistic point of view, this is known as 'cultural asynchrony'; in other words, a situation where there is no equivalence in cultural concepts, for example, in relation to death or marriage (Carbaugh, 1990; Kaschula, 2021).

In this chapter we seek to engage with case law, particularly the case *State* v *Omotoso* (2018), where cultural taboos are brought to the fore during cross-examination and complainants are reluctant to use terms and phrases such as 'rape', 'sexual penetration', 'penis size' and 'consent'. There is also a reluctance even to refer to the genital organs directly (Ehrlich, 2001; MacKinnon, 1988). This has an effect on the success of the trial and discharging the onus, where the relevant legislation, the Sexual Offences and Related Matters Amendment Act 32 of 2007 (RSA, 2007), lists penetration and consent as two of the four elements of the crime. Although the focus of this chapter hinges on the *Omotoso* case (2018), from a perspective of the linguistic limitations to cross-examination and how linguistic discrepancies between the written statement and oral evidence were contradictory, we also highlight three additional cases. These include *State* v *Pistorius* (2014), *State* v *Van Breda* (2019), as well as *Kewana* v *Santam Insurance*. These cases highlight the stark disparities between written statements and oral evidence, where the statements were either provided in a language other than English or translated by a police officer before recording them in English. Reference will also be made to the ongoing case of *Afriforum* v *Julius Malema* (2022), which involves the use of political language that could be interpreted as loaded language.

The objective in this chapter is to apply a sociolinguistic analysis of the criminal cases, where we will, *inter alia*, apply Grice's Maxims (Grice, 1975). The Gricean approach will be applied in the context of the cross-examination in the *Omotoso* case (2018). The work of Ehrlich (2001) will also be applied in analysing the content of the questions posed during cross-examination and the answers provided in relation to the written statement. Through the sociolinguistic analysis, we discuss the parameters and linguistic limitations of cross-examination in relation to the relevant legislative and policy frameworks. There are also two case studies (a court case and a movie) that are analysed from a sociolinguistic perspective. The chapter concludes with relevant recommendations.

What follows is the constitutional and legislative frameworks relevant for the discussion and analysis of the case law involving linguistic and cultural taboos arising during cross-examination and within courtroom discourse more generally.

## Constitutional framework supporting use of language

Loaded terms, underpinned by taboo and euphemism, make it difficult to implement the right to a fair trial. In almost all instances, research relating to crime and criminal related offences concerns an accused's right to a fair trial, including the right to be tried in a language the accused fully understands (Docrat et al., 2021). Section 35(3) of the Constitution (RSA, 1996) guarantees an accused's right to a fair trial, which includes the right:

> (i) to adduce and challenge evidence.

This constitutional right conferred on an accused person may be limited when questions posed during cross-examination affect the complaint's Section 10 constitutional right to dignity and their ability to have the state discharge the onus by proving the crime. The court in the case of *State* v *Baleka* (1988) ruled that courts have the power to curtail cross-examination in "… situations where cross-examination is abused and degenerates to a treadmill of repetition and a quagmire of irrelevancies …".

Section 10 of the Constitution states that "everyone has inherent dignity and the right to have their dignity respected and protected". This right must be borne in mind and protected when a complainant is being cross-examined, especially in rape and other sexual offences cases. The competing rights of Section 35(3)(i) and Section 10 must therefore be balanced carefully during cross-examination. This right to dignity again becomes questionable when one is dealing with issues of taboo and euphemism and where the language of record, English, expects one to be succinct and to the point, even when speaking an African language.

## Legislative framework supporting use of language

Section 35(3)(i) of the Constitution must be read together with Section 166 of the Criminal Procedure Act 51 of 1977 (CPA) (RSA, 1977), which regulates the process of cross-examination:

> (1) An accused may cross-examine any witness called on behalf of the prosecution at any criminal proceedings or any co-accused who testifies at criminal proceedings or any witness called on behalf of such co-accused at criminal proceedings, and the prosecutor may cross-examine any witness, including an accused, called on behalf of the defence at criminal proceedings, and a witness called at such proceedings on behalf of the prosecution may be re-examined by the prosecutor on any matter raised during the cross-examination of that witness, and a witness called on behalf of the defence at such proceedings may likewise be re-examined by the accused.

For the purposes of this chapter, we are concerned with the italicised part of the extract in Section 166(1) of the CPA (RSA, 1977), given that one of the cases, namely *State* v *Omotoso* (2018), focuses on the sociolinguistic and legal analysis of the cross-examination of a complainant.

Although the process of cross-examination is both constitutionally and legislatively safeguarded, Section 166(3) of the CPA (RSA, 1977) allows for the curtailment of the cross-examination of a witness:

> (3) (a) If it appears to a court that any cross-examination contemplated in this section is being protracted unreasonably and thereby causing the proceedings to be delayed unreasonably, the court may request the cross-examiner to disclose the relevancy of any particular line of examination and may impose reasonable limits on the examination regarding the length thereof or regarding any particular line of examination.

The court has a responsibility to ensure that the purpose of cross-examination is to elicit facts that are favourable to the cross-examiner's case and to challenge the truth and accuracy of the witness's version of the disputed events. Cross-examination must be curtailed where it becomes vexatious, abusive, oppressive, or discourteous and where such questions may be disallowed (Joubert, 2014:300). Much will depend, however, upon the demeanour of the witness who is being cross-examined. The case of *Omotoso* (2018), discussed below in this chapter, will provide practical insight into when and how cross-examination should be limited where an advocate's (cross-examiner's) line of questioning impacts the witness's Section 10 constitutional right to dignity and descends into a barrage of unwarranted and irrelevant questions. Again, this can be particularly complex when seen against the sociolinguistic principles outlined above. The Legal Professional Ethics Code of Conduct: Uniform Rules of Professional Ethics of the General Bar Council of South Africa provides the following on the conduct of advocates during cross-examination:

> (a) In all cases it is the duty of the advocate to guard against being made the channel of questions which are only intended to incense or annoy the witness...

Following on from the limits of cross-examination, evidence is adduced and challenged for the purposes of proving or disproving a charge. The elements of a crime are often clearly outlined in the various statutes and should guide the line of questioning. In the case of *State* v *Omotoso* (2018), the elements of the crime of rape were to be proved or disproved. As will be evidenced below, the cross-examination went beyond disproving the elements of the crime, where unnecessary graphic details were sought by the accused's council. Section 3 of the Sexual Offences and Related Matters Amendment Act 32 of 2007 (Sexual Offences Act, RSA, 2007) defines the crime of rape as follows:

> Any person who unlawfully and intentionally commits an act of sexual penetration with another person without the latter's consent, is guilty of the offence of rape.

The elements of the crime are therefore:

(a)   Sexual penetration of another person;

(b)   without the consent of the latter person;

(c)   unlawfulness; and

(d)   intention.

Of further relevance to the analysis of the cross-examination in the *Omotoso* case (2018) is the definition of sexual penetration, defined in Section 1(1) of the Sexual Offences Act (2007):

> Sexual penetration includes any act which causes penetration to any extent whatsoever…

This theoretical legislative framework, read together with the various constitutional rights, must be borne in mind as the chapter progresses.

The following section in the chapter outlines the sociolinguistic perspective on taboo and euphemism relevant to the case law and case studies.

## A sociolinguistic perspective regarding taboo and euphemism

Certain words, when used under certain circumstances, may have meanings that are regarded as indecent and disrespectful; and these are usually forbidden by a particular society. This language usage is found in all societies, and it is a linguistic universal. These are social constructions that have nothing to do with the words or the linguistic terms used. Emotional and social reasons, such as politeness, respect, decency and so on, that force the speaker to avoid phrases or words considered to be disrespectful, rude, or indecent. Such behaviour can have implications within courtroom discourse where participants come from different cultural and linguistic backgrounds (Kaschula, 2021).

Fromkin and Rodman (1983:266) refer to the forbidden terms or phrases as 'taboos', meaning that these are "words that are not to be used or at least not to be used in 'polite society'". This use of language forbids linguistic forms, especially those relating to sexual organs; and this has consequences in courts of law, in rape or sexual assault cases. Trudgill (2000:18) supports this point by proclaiming that a taboo is something that is prohibited from being articulated and is usually believed to be forbidden or regarded as immoral or improper. Trudgill (2000) even views taboo as behaviour that is prohibited or inhibited in a seemingly irrational manner. Avoided (taboo) words are substituted by using words of avoidance. The avoided words are usually substituted by, for example, loans words, euphemisms, circumlocutions, or metaphors. These words may lack equivalence in a court of law.

The use of taboo and euphemism or avoided words also differs from culture to culture and this is again reflected in language. Taboo then refers to words that may not be uttered and to topics that may not be publicly discussed. Swear words are often taboo in many languages and the way in which such terminology is used can differ from one language to another. What may be considered an innocent term in one culture may be a swear word in another. The term 'camel herder' used in North Africa, or the Middle East may be an innocent term to many, but in these countries, it has taken on pejorative connotations. People take offence to being called 'camel herders' as the term depicts a lack of social class and standing. It is seen as an insult to someone's family. Likewise, to swear by your mother in isiXhosa is perhaps the worst taboo swear word that you can use, *umsunu kaNyoko,* as it invokes your mother's genitalia. Mbaya (2002:225) provides further examples of euphemisms where sexual acts are not referred to directly: "… in Chiluba, sex is referred to as *mwsu* (eyes). In Wolof, the expression 'to chat up a girl' is translated as 'to ask for a face' (*gnam kanam*). Likewise, death is associated with euphemisms, such as 'to sleep' in Wolof, 'to leave' in Lingala, or 'to disappear' in Chiluba (Mbaya, 2002:225).

If we do not have names for certain entities or refer to these entities by different names, then it shows the power that such entities have in our respective societies. This may even be true of diseases, such as HIV/AIDS. In southern Africa, it is referred to as *ugawulayo,* 'the one who chops down'. This personification of the disease and the fact that a different word is used reveals the mystery and power afforded to the disease. In Uganda, it is referred to as 'slim' disease due to the weight loss that people often suffer. Evil entities such as the devil are referred to using avoidance terms for fear of invoking evil. Metaphysical or mythical entities, such as the one used in southern Africa, *uthikoloshe* (referring to a short-bearded being with a massive penis who secretly visits women at night), do not have real names. People even place their sleeping beds on bricks to heighten them so that the *uthikoloshe* cannot get onto the bed to have sex with them. This term is further discussed below in the case study analysis of a movie, *A Reasonable Man.* Other southern African mythical or real beings, associated with evil and the devil perhaps, have been named as *uhili, isithunzela,* and *umthakathi,* as part of *ubuthakathi* (witchcraft or evil spells).

There are also certain secret languages that have been developed for certain contexts. AmaXhosa male initiates, for example, make use of such a secret language where certain words are avoided or replaced with others. This is true of female initiates undergoing *intonjane* as well. Tsotsi-taal, a language spoken by gangsters, criminals, and prisoners in South Africa, could also be regarded as such a secret language, as it serves to exclude others (Kaschula, 2021).

There seems to be no question that languages are as much culturally based as they are innate, and that language is a part of cultures and identities. It expresses cultural values but also, to some extent, determines culture, one's identity and the way one perceives and interprets the world. The close link between language and culture explains why we assume that any communicative competence in a language involves both linguistic and cultural competence.

In a multicultural society, it is not easy to become linguistically and culturally competent in all the languages with which one may come into contact. Intercultural communication, where various cultures are involved, is often required in Africa and the world today. This calls for awareness of differences, for appreciation of the variety of views and values, and for tolerance when we are confronted with language and cultural practices, which at first may seem strange. In the discussions that follow in this chapter, we see how such lack of awareness can also contribute to what we now call 'linguistic prejudice' and other forms of discrimination and prejudice, which are based on the way that a person speaks and the way that others interpret others' identities through speech acts.

The interchange of taboo words and euphemistic expressions becomes prescriptive by its nature since the latter words are regarded as 'correct' at the level of a particular language community. Having strict rules that prescribe euphemistic terms or expressions for particular situations and environments may be perceived as a form of social censorship, specifically by more liberal and uninhibited speakers of a language. These prohibited words or phrases might be associated with superstitions, principles and beliefs that reflect a particular societies' customs, traditions, and views.

The use of taboos is highly influenced by the culture of a particular society, and this is just as prescriptive in nature. Wardhaugh (2010:211) points out that a society's culture is the 'know-how' of whatever it is one has to know or believe in order to operate in a manner acceptable to its members, "and to get through the tasks of daily living". This is an indication of the influence of society on language use. The fact that the words used rely on the culture and the user's knowledge of their world is an indication that language and culture are intertwined.

The cultural norms and values of a society can have an influence on its language. Take, for example, the case of *Kewana* v *Santam Insurance* (discussed more fully below), which concluded that, because the interpretation of the isiXhosa word *ukukhulisa*, 'to grow', equated 'fostering' in law, then the case could not be one of adoption. The legal duties are different for adoption and fostering and there is no specific word for adoption in isiXhosa, though the concept most certainly exists (Kaschula, 2021). This case therefore excluded the child from being adopted and the conclusion based on this cultural and linguistic misunderstanding resulted in the child not receiving damages as they were regarded as being fostered and not adopted by the deceased mother or caregiver.

Taboo can also reflect what is seen as improper usage of language and cultural values of a language. This is reflected in all people's languages and cultures. The words 'penis' or 'vagina' might be more liberally used in English as opposed to their equivalent in an African language. The euphemistic expressions define and reflect the sociocultural structure of a community. One universal type of taboo includes the terms associated with body parts, especially genitalia; and this taboo is based on social constraints that are reflected in the languages. Most languages use euphemism for these concepts; and using their proper terms might be regarded as improper and offensive to the listener, depending on the environment. This is part of sociocultural prescriptivism. For example, it is accepted that the proper terms for genitalia are needed when dealing with health-related matters. It is also interesting to note that, in most languages, the terms for death and dying are taboo. For example, in South Africa, in the Afrikaans language, there is a difference between the term for the death of an animal (*vrek*) and the word for a person (*dood*). Similarly, in Nguni languages (isiXhosa, isiZulu, isiNdebele and siSwati), *ukufa* is used for animals while *ukubhubha*, *ukusweleka* and *ukutshona* are used with reference to humans. Respect for death is a linguistic universal. This constant change and evolution in the use of taboo and euphemism can have an impact within courtrooms and on the outcome of specific culture-bound cases.

Arguably, in the African and South African legal context, it is still the monolithic Western paradigm or category that rules. There is, therefore, little awareness or open-ness to any other perspective or category, other than that of the monolingual legal practitioner. Majeke (2002:153) characterises this as follows:

> We all know that no legal system will ever succeed in establishing itself as a social system efficiently if it is not founded on the fundamental cultural rhythms of the majority of the population in its borders. Yet we continue to teach young indigenous Africans how to be good Roman, Dutch, and English law specialists. They are becoming foreigners in their own land.

This is pertinent to African legal practitioners and the point made at the beginning of this chapter; and the extrapolation to African witnesses and non-legally trained participants is obvious. Langer (1989) continues to point out that human beings naturally create categories to make sense of the world around them: "Any attempt to eliminate bias by attempting to eliminate perception of differences is doomed to failure" (Langer, 1989:154).

From a comparative point of view, Eades (2005:304-314) supports this stance when analysing the Australian court system in relation to Aborigines and the use of their dialect of English within the system. The cultural differences embedded in Aboriginal English, "the perception of differences", often contribute to miscommunication in the courts. Eades continues to point out that, among Aborigines, direct questions are not important in information seeking; and that silence as an interaction is not an indication that communication has broken down (Eades, 2005:305). These points are true too of many African languages and cultures where direct forms of questioning are seen as rude, such as in isiXhosa. These cultural underpinnings run contrary to standard Australian or South African English culture and can be problematic in courts of law. Eades also points out that a lawyer's handbook has been published to create awareness and "mindfulness" (Eades, 2005:306). This 'mindful' communication can be particularly complex when intercultural communication takes place, especially when the communicative event suffers from 'cultural noise'. Gibson (2002:9) states that "[i]ntercultural communication takes place when the sender and the receiver are from different cultures. Communication can be very difficult if there is a big difference between the two cultures; if there is too much 'cultural noise', it can break down completely".

On occasion, 'cultural noise' occurs among mother-tongue speakers of isiXhosa themselves, where members of the bench, as well as the witnesses or accused, are isiXhosa mother-tongue speaking, but the court medium of communication is English only, to the detriment of those isiXhosa speakers who do not understand English (Kaschula & Ralarala, 2004:257). The participants are then differentiated by what Ting-Toomey (1999:6) refers to as "secondary dimensions of diversity". In other words, 'primary dimensions of diversity' would be those differences that are visible and unchangeable, such as race, whereas 'secondary dimensions' are aspects of socialisation, such as educational levels.

African courtrooms contain both primary and secondary dimensions of diversity, depending on the participants involved. Furthermore, Ting-Toomey (1999:22-24) presents certain assumptions, which will increase an individual's understanding of the intercultural communication process. These assumptions include the fact that intercultural communication always takes place in a context and within an embedded system. It does not happen in a vacuum. Courts or hospitals in Africa mostly represent a system where a Western paradigm is *de facto* entrenched, adding wider responsibilities for translation structures, namely the need for language to be translated in context (Kaschula & Maseko, 2012).

Donald Carbaugh (1990:151) recognises that multilingual scenarios – as in those that pertain to most African countries with selected language bias towards English or

French – present a particular situation of intercultural contact that is fundamentally problematic. These problems are exacerbated in many African law courts, hospitals and surgeries where cultural preferences for speaking do exist in these contexts, but where some patterns are valued, and others are rendered somehow problematic. Arguably, it is these very 'practical' problems, as outlined by Carbaugh, that are encapsulated in the term 'practicable' in Section 6 of the South African Constitution, which has undermined indigenous language usage in the workplace. This has threatened not only the equality to speak but also to be heard in one's own language and context.

In a legal context, court proceedings should take place with the use of an effective and properly trained interpreting team. In 2017, the Chief Justice instructed that English would be the only language of record in South Africa. This is problematic, as sworn statements are often given in an African language and then translated by a policeman into English. This process can be flawed as the policeman may not have good English skills and is not a trained translator, thereby allowing for the statement to be disregarded in a court of law where everything happens in English (Docrat & Kaschula, 2019).

Inherent in concepts such as 'mindfulness', 'primary and secondary diversity', 'multi-lingualism' and 'intercultural communication' is the need to acknowledge the relationship between language and thought. Sociolinguistic theory recognises a continuum between language and thought, 'mould theories' and 'cloak theories'. Mould theories characterise language as "… a mould in terms of which thought categories are cast" (Bruner et al., 1956:11), while cloak theories offer the role of language as "… a cloak conforming to the customary categories of thought of its speakers" (ibid.). This distinction is further developed when addressing the 'Sapir-Whorf hypothesis', which is associated with the two principles of linguistic determinism and linguistic relativity, where, in the case of the former, our thought patterns are determined by our language, while, in the case of the latter, speakers of different languages perceive and interface with the world differently (Chandler, 1995:89). It is, however, essential that the role of translation in the conveyance of message acts be explored. Multilingual courtrooms where a single language may dominate could present a situation where the standard Whorfian problems associated with translation from one language to another exist and are further complicated by problems of context and perspectives. The latter could be as extreme as differences in the concept of justice as underpinned by what is deemed to be right or wrong. This could apply, for example, to perspectives on property ownership, community versus individual rights, rights of elders over others, and so on (Kaschula & Maseko, 2012). If a less Whorfian perspective is adopted, such as that presented by universalism, then it is acknowledged that totally different languages are not untranslatable, as "most universalists do acknowledge that translation may on occasions involve a certain amount of circumlocution" (Chandler, 1995:92). However, this circumlocution may be central to the conveyance of context and the avoidance of 'lost in translation' problems.

This can be seen in examples of cross-examination of a witness where members of the bench are confronted with an answer of 'no', whereas the interpreter and witness engaged in a lengthy dialogue. Much of the discussion was then contextual and attempting to establish a suitable framework for posing a dichotomous question. This is explored further in the chapter.

The section that follows focuses on the case of *State* v *Omotoso* (2018), while further examples are drawn that highlight discrepancies between written witness statements by the South African Police Services (SAPS) and the oral evidence provided in court.

## *State* v *Omotoso (2018): cultural taboos and the linguistic limitation of cross-examination*

Briefly, the facts of the case concern a Nigerian-born evangelist, Timothy Oluseun Omotoso, Senior Pastor at Jesus Dominion International Church. The Pastor held various youth empowerment projects for members of his church, including a project, Grace Galaxy Music Group. It is alleged that the pastor sexually assaulted and raped young women who were part of this group. Omotoso was arrested on 20 April 2017 at Port Elizabeth Airport, in the Eastern Cape, in South Africa. His 63 charges include racketeering, rape, sexual assault, and human trafficking. Omotoso is alleged to have committed the crimes with the aid of his two female co-accused who are alleged to have groomed the young women before the rapes and sexual assaults. It must be noted that, for the purposes of this chapter, we have focused on the evidence (specifically the cross-examination) of the first witness, Cheryl Zondi. This testimony was heard in the Port Elizabeth High Court before Judge Makaula who, following the testimony by Zondi, recused himself from the trial given a potential conflict of interest. The case is thus ongoing before another judge.

In this chapter, we are concerned with the cross-examination employed by Advocate Dauberman of witness Zondi, and Makaula's curtailment of the cross-examination against the theoretical, constitutional and legislative framework we have advanced above.

Three questions that Dauberman posed, in our view, infringed on the witness's right to dignity and went beyond the scope of discrediting her version of the events concerning the crime of rape:

1. By going on the next crusade, you were prepared to be raped?
2. You foresaw the possibility of being raped again?
3. How many centimetres of his penis penetrated your vagina?

Reading these three questions with the legislative framework in mind, it is clear that the questions are of no relevance to the elements of the crime of rape, where the depth of penetration is irrelevant. The questions were intrusive, imposed on the witness's dignity, attempted to invalidate the crime, and lessen the severity of the crime and the implications thereof. From a cultural perspective, the cross-examination and the intrusive and non-dignified questions raised concerns about cultural taboos concerning genital organs. Given the heinous nature of the crime, it is a given fact that the genital organs need to be referred to; however, in certain cultures and for some religious purposes, communities forbid direct reference to terms such as 'vagina' and 'penis' and provide euphemisms or other 'culturally' sensitive and acceptable terms. An example of the genital organs in isiXhosa (for the amaXhosa people) is *umphambili*.

Regardless of the cultural taboos, Zondi proceeded to answer all questions directly, referring to the genital organs. It is our argument that, if an interpreter had been employed and Zondi was not competent in English (the language of proceedings and record) and had provided testimony in isiXhosa, she would have used the term *umphambili*. This, in our opinion, would have sparked further intrusive, irrelevant questions from Dauberman that no penetration of the vagina had taken place. These observations are drawn based on the line of questioning adopted during cross-examination.

The court, through Makaula J, intervened when all three of the aforementioned questions were posed to Zondi. In fact, the second question was a rephrased version following Makaula J's instruction to Dauberman that the first question be disallowed. Judges are afforded more latitude in criminal cases to intervene to see that justice is done and the truth is ascertained (Schwikkard & Van der Merwe, 2010:374-375). The ability to intervene and curtail the cross-examination is guided by three principles:

> (a) The judge must conduct the trial so that his impartiality and fairness manifest to all concerned;
>
> (b) a judge should refrain from questioning in such a way or to such an extent as to lose judicial impartiality and objectivity; and
>
> (c) a judge should desist from questioning in a way that may intimidate or disconcert a witness so as to affect his demeanour or impair his credibility.

## The linguistic discrepancies between written statements and oral evidence

The case of *Omotoso* (2018) also casts the spotlight on police statement taking, specifically the discrepancies arising from the written statement and the oral evidence provided by Zondi. On several occasions during cross-examination, Dauberman referred to Zondi's written statement, pointing out that her oral evidence differed factually. According to Zondi, the statement she provided to the police was rewritten by a police officer in English and she did not read the rewritten version in detail. Zondi disputed facts emerging from the statement, which placed the accused at the venues of the alleged crimes at the times recorded. Zondi maintained her position on the facts of the case and stated that Dauberman had asked the police officer why the statement was recorded as such, given that she did not say that. Zondi stated further that she merely provided her statement, which the police officer recorded (written form) and she signed it.

This example once again shines light on police statement taking in South Africa and the inaccuracies arising in statements written by police officers who have limited language skills and linguistic training. Language and literacy courses are not offered during police training. Police qualifications require six months of basic training, coupled with a valid driver's licence and matriculation certificate attesting to the completion of schooling (Docrat et al., 2017)

The situation is often complicated by the fact that the police officer is required to record a statement in English and may not be proficient in the language. A complainant may also be relaying the facts in a language other than English, requiring the police officer to interpret and translate. The police officer therefore acts as a transpreter. Our observations are based on the fact (Census, 2011) that a mere 9.6% of South Africans speak English as their mother tongue (RSA SSA, 2011).

According to Docrat et al. (2020), the fact that police officers are not sworn translators or interpreters has serious implications for justice when, in the South African context, a statement takes precedence over any oral narrative when evidence is led in court. It is argued that statement construction is a complex process:

> It combines translation, where more than one language is spoken, with retelling and reconstruction. The police officer must synthesise everything he/she's being told to ensure the facts are accurately recorded; a process called subjective synthesis. (Docrat et al., 2020)

The situation is exacerbated further where a complainant is either not in a position to read the statement, if they cannot read English, or is having difficulty doing so, where there are handwriting barriers.

These discrepancies have the potential of affecting the witness's credibility in terms of the facts of the case and discrediting Zondi's account of the events. The demeanour of witnesses in criminal trials and, in a rape trial in this instance, is important during cross-examination where the power dynamics unfairly favour the accused. Zondi, however, stood firm, maintained her position, and answered the questions.

We explore the power dynamics in rape trials in further detail in the following section of this chapter.

## The sociolinguistics of cross-examination in rape trials

The criminal justice system defines the characteristics of a legitimate victim, and a legitimate perpetrator as follows:

> Legitimate perpetrators … are strangers to their victims, carry a weapon, and inflict physical injury upon their victim, beyond the sexual violence; legitimate victims are women raped by precisely these kinds of perpetrators. The discourses of rape … construct stranger rape 'as 'real rape' and render the vast majority of rapes invisible. (Ehrlich, 2001:20)

Language has a considerable impact on the way listeners interpret and visualise events – a fact that becomes extremely important in a sexual assault trial. Ehrlich (2001:152) explains that stereotypes and power relations shape and constrain complainants' ability to tell the story of their sexual assault or rape. Defence attorneys ask questions that frame and structure the complainant's 'talk' about the sexual assault experience. This was evident in the *Omotoso* case (2018) and relates to the Quality and Quantity Maxims – informative and true. During cross-examination, Zondi was constantly asked whether she clearly stated she did not consent to sexual relations with the accused; and it was put to her that she failed to communicate her lack of consent. Complainants are therefore held accountable for rape for not clearly communicating their lack of consent and this relates to the Manner Maxim – avoiding obscurity. The cross-examination of Zondi also exposed the fact that complainants are subjected to a revictimisation, forcing them to retell (and relive) the story of their attack. This links to the Relation Maxim – relevance.

Given the power dynamics that exist in courtroom discourse, MacKinnon (1988) argues that women only report rapes that they consider to be believable. The criminal justice system is seen as one that protects male sexual interests through culturally powerful legal discourse, which controls the female victims themselves, as was evident in the case of *Omotoso* (2018).

In the case of *Afriforum* v *Julius Malema*, the loaded political slogan, *dubul'ibhunu*, or 'kill the boer', is presently under scrutiny. Malema claims it is not aimed at white farmers but rather at a system. An expert witness, a linguist, has also argued that this slogan can be traced back in relation to songs that were used in the struggle and that it is not aimed at any particular person, but rather at the system of apartheid. This case also shows the importance of context in analysing loaded language in courts of law. In the proceeding section of the chapter, we provide two further case studies that highlight the linguistic and cultural challenges within criminal cases in a monolingual courtroom discourse setting.

## *Case study:* A Reasonable Man

A classic case of cultural misunderstanding, which is portrayed in a South African film (*A Reasonable Man*, by Gavin Hood) develops the point that is made above. At a consultation room in prison, in which the lawyer offers to represent the accused (a boy) in a murder case, the lawyer and the interpreter converse as follows:

> **Lawyer**: …tell him, he is charged with the murder of a baby.
>
> **Interpreter**: *Utholwa unetyala lokubulala umntwana, uyezwa? Indaba ukuthi wabulala umntwana. Wambulala! Wambulala!* (You have been found guilty of murdering a child, do you understand? The point is, you killed a child. You killed him! You killed him!)

At another point in the courtroom, the judge queried the interpreter's translation of the accused's answers:

> **Judge**: Ask the accused whether he accepts his counsellor's admission that he killed the baby.
>
> **Interpreter**: *Uyakuvuma ukuthi ubulele ingane?* (Do you admit that you killed a baby?)
>
> **Accused**: *Ngibulele uTikoloshe!* (I killed a Tikoloshe!)
>
> **Interpreter**: He says yes, My Lord.
>
> **Judge**: He has said a good deal more than that, what exactly did he say?
>
> **Interpreter**: My Lord, he says he killed a Tikoloshe.
>
> **Lawyer**: An evil spirit, My Lord.

It should be noted here that it is the multilingual lawyer who intervenes on behalf of the accused to clarify what the accused is actually saying. Beyond circumlocution, the notion of bias is characteristic of many courtroom cross-examinations; and this is, in part, displayed by the interpreter's intent in purposefully and consciously (or unconsciously and unknowingly) twisting and turning the evidence being given by the accused, and thereby contributing to a perception of guilt (with the consequential impact on the application of justice).

The notion of bias is crucial in the judicial context; it needs to be revisited as a frame for devising some form of intervention towards achieving a system that is sensitive and responsive to the complex South African language and cultural situation in courts. For this reason, multilingual competence by any judicial officer in South Africa would place them in a better position to achieve social justice and to contribute to a more just and understanding society.

Mertz shows that there has been extensive debate regarding language as an "…instrument or reflection of social dynamics and language as an active participant in social construction" (Mertz, 1994:436). Within the legal context it is imperative to formalise the distinction between language used to convey information through semantic meaning, and language which "…expresses and reflects social divisions and inequalities…" (Mertz, 1994:436). In other words, this refers to the contextual meanings associated with any experience or conveyance of a perception of reality (Kaschula & Maseko, 2012). However, individual context and thought may inform language and communication, and thus have relevance to the final outcomes through evaluation of the evidence. This dichotomy is best reflected by Eagleton in discussing the concept of reality in literature, as perceived by the structuralists and semioticians. He recognises that reality is not necessarily reflected by language "but produced by it"; and that the way humans perceive the world is dependent on the sign-system (language) that they have at their command (Eagleton, 1983:55).

A further example is provided in the legal case study that follows in relation to the notion of adoption and how it is perceived in southern African Nguni society. In fact, there is no equivalence for the term 'adoption' in the Nguni languages, such as isiZulu or isiXhosa. This case study was first presented in Kaschula and Anthonissen (1995) and has been referred to elsewhere, for example, in Kaschula and Ralarala (2004). However, it remains pertinent and relevant for this chapter as it speaks directly to the link between language, identity, and intercultural communication (Kaschula, 2021).

## *Case study: Kewana v Santam Insurance*

The above notion of reality being produced by language is supported by examining the facts of the Kewana case. Prior to undertaking an intercultural analysis of this case, a brief summary of the facts and relevant data is included. This case was presided over by the Honourable Mr Chief Justice Beck of the Transkei Supreme Court, with Kaschula, in his legal capacity as a registered advocate of the Supreme Court of South Africa, sitting as assessor in an advisory capacity.

Advocate T.L. Skweyiya (Senior Counsel) appeared for the plaintiff, while Advocate P.A.C. Rowan appeared for the defendant. The interpreter in this case was Mr Z. Dywili, who interpreted from isiXhosa into English and vice versa. Only Advocate Skweyiya and the assessor were able to follow both the original isiXhosa and the English interpretation. Professors Bennett (from the University of Cape Town) and Mqeke (from the then-

University of Transkei) were called as expert witnesses. Most of the witnesses, as well as the plaintiff, were uneducated and not competent in English.

In this case, the plaintiff (Nodanile Kewana) is the mother of L.N. Xaji (born Kewana) who was a fare-paying passenger on a bus insured by the defendant. The bus overturned near Lady Frere in the Transkei/Eastern Cape. The driver was driving recklessly, and he failed to avoid an accident when, by the exercise of reasonable care, he could have done so. Ms L.N. Xaji suffered severe injuries and died on the same day. The deceased was not married and had been employed as a housekeeper in Cape Town. A sister of the plaintiff, Ms N.N. Mangali, a widow and the mother of Andile Mangali, had previously become insane and had to be taken care of by another sister, Ms M.N. Mdazuka. When Ms Mdazuka experienced difficulties in maintaining both her sister and her sister's son, she suggested that Andile Mangali should be adopted by the deceased.

The deceased was, at the time of her death, supporting and maintaining her mother (Nodanile Kewana), N. Xaji (her daughter), as well as Andile Mangali (her nephew). In the first instance, the court found that the defendants were liable to pay damages to Nodanile Kewana and the deceased's daughter. With regard to Andile Mangali, the matter was set down for hearing. The plaintiff claimed she would not have been able to support Andile without the deceased's financial assistance, and that the deceased took care of Andile because he had no one else to maintain him. Andile was to be regarded as the deceased's son. The 'eye' (someone appointed as a keeper or caretaker) of the homestead at the time had been called and informed that Andile was being taken into the Kewana homestead as a child of the deceased. When the deceased had returned home to Cala in the Transkei from Cape Town (on holiday), a ceremony was held where family and neighbours, as well as the local chief, were invited. A goat and a sheep were slaughtered, and a public declaration was made that the purpose of the ceremony was to accept Andile as the deceased's second child.

This invited the question: Can an unmarried twenty-year-old woman adopt a child in amaXhosa custom? Is there such a concept as adoption, bearing in mind that (according to Professor Mqeke) there is no English equivalent for the terms *ukondla/ukukhulisa*, which would best be interpreted as 'maintaining' or 'causing to grow'? Professor Mqeke, however, felt that adoption is a known concept in customary law and that women were increasingly adopting children in this way. He saw this as a welcome development, which was not contrary to public policy or morals. Counsel for the plaintiff submitted that the requirements for adoption in these circumstances (publicity, presence of their chief, and public declaration) had all been fulfilled and that a formal adoption had taken place. Furthermore, it was submitted that this carried with it a legal duty of support on the part of the deceased.

Wolfsen (1992) points out that, in cross-cultural communication, there is a tendency to judge the speech behaviour of others by one's own standards. He states further:

> With no other frame of reference at their disposal, such speakers have little choice but to interpret what they hear according to the rules of speaking of their own native speech communities. And since the rules are very likely to be quite different, misunderstandings are almost inevitable. (Wolfsen, 1992:202)

Kewana's case revolves around the terms *ukondla* and *ukukhulisa*. These terms form part of the plaintiff's culture and worldview. It would seem that the concept of adoption is not in dispute, but rather the way in which it is perceived to operate in amaXhosa society and customary law as opposed to in South African common law. The interpreter then has to face the problem of interpreting cultural concepts into English. The focus of this discussion will be on the problems associated with such a process. The following comments are made regarding cross-cultural interpreting: Whether, if, and how one can come to co-ordinate conduct in particular situations of intercultural contact is, of course, a fundamentally practical problem. "As is especially pronounced in some courtrooms and classrooms ... cultural preferences for speaking do exist in contexts, where some patterns are valued, others are rendered somehow problematic, with translations from one into another being difficult at best" (Carbaugh, 1990:151).

It would seem, therefore, that an individual's view of the world may be influenced by his or her language. In turn, this would complicate cross-cultural translating and inter- preting. The Whorfian hypothesis is concerned with the possibility that an individual's views of their environment may be conditioned by their language and vice versa. Here, 'environment' includes, firstly, the physical environment, secondly, the social environment, and thirdly, the values of a particular society. If our language influences our worldview, it allows us to distinguish more readily what language identifies and labels. Kewana's case is evidence of this. The term 'adoption' has no direct isiXhosa equivalent. In an intercultural environment, the lack of appropriate terminology makes it more difficult to access cultural values and the variants associated with those values. One's use of language tells others more about oneself than any other single characteristic. Meaning is not simply gleaned from analysing a series of works, it is inferred within the context of numerous social and psychological factors; and, even in exchanges between people of minimal cultural and social distance, confusions and misunderstandings often occur (Reichman, 1993:5).

Quite obviously, 'adoption' exists in isiXhosa-speaking society, as most of the witnesses, including the expert witnesses, pointed out. It is simply a difference in linguistic defini- tion or labelling, which causes confusion from a Western legal perspective. This point was exploited by the defence in an environment that operates essentially on Western ethics and principles. In this case, the highest court in the land attempted to mete out justice in an African setting where African customary law was more applicable than the regular statutes.

Societies throughout the world have rules concerning the way language should be used in interaction. These rules may differ from culture to culture. For this reason, a general awareness of these rules would be necessary if effective intercultural communication is to take place. There are many sources of cultural differences in communication. These become especially important in intercultural contacts for they can lead to "misinterpretation of intent, misunderstandings generally … negative stereotyping and so on" (Carbaugh, 1990:157). Carbaugh refers to interactional dynamics such as these as 'asynchrony'. It follows that there must be a measure of 'asynchrony' in an African and South African courtroom context. For this reason, it would be necessary for lawyers (who are in positions of control and power that afford them dominant participant status) to be aware of intercultural differences, some of which are highlighted here:

(i)    An isiXhosa-speaking person tends to avoid looking one in the eyes when speaking, as a sign of respect. In European culture, the converse is true. Thus, in a legal context, it is possible that a presiding officer may misconstrue a person's demeanour as untrustworthy, shifty or dishonest. In an interview, Chief Justice Beck from the Mthatha Supreme Court agreed that the body language of an accused or witness could influence his opinion of the character of a witness.

(ii)   Discourse behaviour within the English culture requires one to be succinct and to the point, whereas the isiXhosa tradition, with its strong oral and shorter literacy history, prefers behaviour that proceeds at a steady, measured and dignified pace. It would be rude to be precise and to the point. IsiXhosa greetings can serve as an example. As we have seen, it is not sufficient to simply bid someone a good morning or afternoon. We are expected to enquire about his or her health and the wellbeing of family members as well.

Such discourse behaviour can create problems. A witness may take a while to answer a question and the interpreter may interact at length with the witness; but eventually, the interpreter's statement or interpretation may amount to just a few words. A presiding officer will often ask, 'But what else did he say?', as we saw above in the case study of *A Reasonable Man.* In the words of one interpreter, "I may just be asking the witness for clarification, and I don't necessarily interpret this back to the bench". Surely the bench must be disadvantaged in such a scenario? A prominent Makhanda attorney and linguist, the late Mr A. Weakley, held the following view: "The interpreter often holds his own cross-examination, and this is bad. Although the interpreter is trying to save time and be helpful, he is in fact directing the accused, and the bench may miss aspects of demeanour and a cover-up of a witness may not be interpreted. I generally insist that these interactions be interpreted." Clearly, such discourse also makes for bad evidence in the legal context (Kaschula, 2021).

In view of factors such as those outlined above, if a person draws extensively on his or her own cultural background only when talking to and in interpreting the words of persons from a different background, communication breakdown(s) may result. When this does occur, and conversations between lawyers and clients (via interpreters) – indeed in any workplace environment – become stressful, it is rarely accounted for in sociological terms, but rather in psychological terms. According to Chick (1985:302), the one participant will therefore perceive the other as being "uncooperative, aggressive, callous, stupid, incompetent or having some other undesirable personal traits".

Regarding the question of language and culture, Kewana's case presents some interesting information. According to Professor Mqeke, *isondlo* (the payment made in an *ukondla* case) has no direct English equivalent, but the word 'maintenance' comes closest. In cross-examination, he maintained that *ukondla* and *ukukhulisa* mean the same thing, but he denied that these were the same as fostering. A witness, Mr J.M. Vuntu, verified this as follows:

> **Advocate Skweyiya:** … would there be an equivalent sort of terminology or concept for *isondlo* in English?
>
> **Vuntu:** … there is no direct equivalent.

Professor Bennett agreed that one of the major difficulties in this case was the lack of adequate terminology. He maintained, however, that he was left with the feeling that this was, in fact, a fostering. The defendants submitted that, on the evidence, the absence of an isiXhosa word for 'adoption' would indicate that adoption is not a recognised custom. They proposed that there is a real possibility that what is being confused is the custom of fostering and its isiXhosa equivalents, rather than an adoption. Furthermore, counsel for the defendant pointed out that Koyana (1980), in his glossary of African terms, does not refer to the alleged custom or to any word meaning 'adoption'.

The problem of terminology (or the lack thereof) and the problems stemming from an intercultural legal environment where an interpreter is used are illustrated in the analysis that follows. During the initial stages of the trial, the whole question of the ceremony of adoption was being explored. On more than one occasion, the interpreter seemed unable to interpret this event properly. This is highlighted in the following extract:

> **Advocate Skweyiya:** … with due respect the interpreter … he did not put the aspect which His Lordship is concentrating on, the presence of the public, was it important that there should be the presence of the public? That is what I understood His Lordship's question to be.

Beck CJ: Yes.

Advocate Skweyiya: And that aspect was missed by the interpreter, with due respect.

The interpreter had not emphasised the importance of the presence of the chief and the public at the ceremony, as expressed by the witness. This point was crucial to the plaintiff's case as the whole questions of adoption depended on the extent to which the ceremony was a public occasion. The presence of the public and the chief, as well as the slaughter of a goat, and not so much the lack of isiXhosa terminology associated with the concept of 'adoption', was crucial to the valid interpretation of what took place.

The question of terminological inconsistencies was further explored when the expert witness, Professor Mqeke, took the stand:

Advocate Dickson: ... You have *ukondla* and *ukukhulisa*?

Professor Mqeke: Ja ... we don't call them fostering ... you can actually raise someone else, but it isn't fostering as you (Europeans) know it.

Advocate Dickson: Yes, well, it is these grey areas between these terms that I am trying to clear up. And we are speaking English in court, but the terms used are isiXhosa terms.

At a later stage in the trial, Mr O. Kupe, a witness, responded to the question of whether a child could be rejected or 'chased away' by *ukukhulisa* parents if he or she misbehaved. Upon this, the following discourse took place:

Advocate Dickson: ... if the child turns out to be unsatisfactory, is it acceptable if the parents, who look after the child, chase the child away...?

Kupe: Yes, they do have a right to chase him away.

Advocate Dickson: ... then does the duty to maintain the child fall away...?

Kupe (via interpreter): If the child comes back and asks for a pardon, the adopting parent continues to maintain him.

Advocate Skweyiya: No, with respect, there was no question of the witness having used 'adopting', that comes from the interpreter .... The witness never spoke of 'adopting parent'.

Had the court accepted the interpretation of 'adopting parent', this could have had certain implications for the legal duties surrounding adoption, as an adoptive parent does not have legal right to force a child to leave as a result of misbehaviour. The point is made that there are certain cultural issues that are very difficult to put across in the other language, worse still if that language is an exoglossic language, such as English or Afrikaans (Mtuze, 1993:49-50). Mtuze points out that, for this reason, earlier language practitioners, especially in the legal profession, decided to borrow terms directly from the African language, for example, *ukuthwala* instead of 'abduction with intention to take as wife', or *lobola* instead of 'bride-price'. Mtuze further states that the cultural differences are discernible in the translations. According to the *Oxford Advanced Learner's Dictionary of Current English*, 'abduct' means "to take or lead ... away unlawfully, by force or fraud" (Hornby, 1974:2). With regard to the translation of 'abduction', Mtuze points out that "Unlawfulness is an essential element of abduction as evidenced by the definition, whereas *ukuthwala* is traditionally lawful. Sometimes the girl or woman's parents do give express permission that the girl be *thwala*ed" (Mtuze, 1993:50). A similar point is made about the difficulty's translators may face. Translators often have problems when they have to translate culture-specific words. These words very often do not have adequate translation equivalents in the target language (Smit, 1992:358).

The courtroom is often a confusing and hostile environment for the accused or the witness, both from a linguistic and a cultural point of view. The interpreter then presents the only key to the understanding of courtroom procedure and the language being used. The court interpreter is one of the most important participants in any particular case. Yet, in ordinary procedure, the original words of the accused or witness are not recorded. Only the interpretation is tape-recorded. The words of the witness or accused that encode the associated culture, worldview and personality linked to language, which are of outmost importance to a presiding officer in assessing character, honesty and so on, are lost. The witness or accused remains at a distance, unable to access the proceedings due to linguistic barriers. The witness or the accused is further disadvantaged where lawyers read from texts. The interpreters generally do not have texts before them, so they simply summarise what the lawyer is quoting; and sometimes it is not conveyed to the witness at all. The semantic gaps or blanks that become evident during the translation procedure are referred to by Dagut (1978:45) as 'semantic voids', which he defines as "the non-existence in one language of a one-word equivalent for a designatory terms found in another".

Dagut (1981:69) continues to point out that there are two types of semantic voids, namely referential and linguistic voids, which can be transferred by means of denotational and connotational equivalence. In relation to referential voids, he identifies two types: voids where the environment in which speech communities live is concerned; and cultural voids that denote customs peculiar to specific language communities. Clearly, Kewana's case is concerned with a semantic referential void related to the interpretation of a cultural concept of the notion of adoption. This case was arguably decided on a linguistic and cultural misunderstanding by a monolingual English-speaking judge.

In the case of *State* v *Van Breda,* the discrepancies were related to the evidence presented in Afrikaans and translated into English. Jansen (2017:122) notes that this forms part of the statement and relates to bad translation: "Post-mortem examinations conducted on the bodies of the three deceased shows [sic] … An axe and kitchen knife was [sic] recovered … There is expert medical opinion that the wounds are [sic] self-inflicted…." The singular forms relate to how an Afrikaans speaking person would express themselves in Afrikaans rather than the translated English version. These singular forms can again influence opinion about what happened. Henri van Breda, at some point, also disputes his translated statement. According to Jansen (2017:201), "Henri then avers that although his statement was not correct in all aspects, he did not want to sit around correcting the officers and reliving the trauma of the night before with another retelling of what had happened." In Henri's own words, he notes that:

> Although the gist of what was written down is correct, the statement does contain some inaccuracies and also does not contain all the detailed information that I conveyed to the officers. It also contains a number of grammatical errors, probably due to the fact that the statement is a paraphrased version by an Afrikaans-speaking officer (Jansen, 2017:251).

The lawyer, later in the trial, points out, "My client says it is definitely not the English he used" (Jansen, 2017:251). In a murder case such as this, every word is important, and any paraphrasing or loose translation can influence the outcome of the case.

Subsumed under the issues related to taboo and euphemism, as well as translation and interpreting across languages, is also the way in which we actually use words across different cultures. How much information are we expected to give and in what context? To what extent must this information be relevant, and so on? This information can be supported by taking into account the Gricean Maxims that relate to this sociolinguistic perspective. In a court of law, it is very important that information be relevant and to the point. This related to maxims that might differ across languages, more especially when it comes to African languages where more information is volunteered in a measured and dignified metaphorical way of speaking (Kaschula, 2021). However, such sociolinguistic underpinnings are generally lacking from any legislative framework, as shown above, even though the constitution does not allow for unfair discrimination on the basis of language, culture, sexual orientation or religion.

## Conclusions

Intercultural differences and awareness thereof in multilingual African societies, particularly in the workplace, need to be emphasised to avoid possible miscommunication in a situation where, for various reasons, including political reasons, the words 'language' and 'culture' are often seen as loaded terms. Exoglossic languages will remain important on the African continent, but space needs to be made for the use of regional languages in schools, universities, the government, and the public sector in order to truly empower the masses of African peoples to take part proactively in mainstream African economies, both as contributors and as beneficiaries within African economic systems.

This chapter began with extensive theoretical discussions on the constitutional, legislative, and sociolinguistic frameworks underpinning the various case law examples. The case law and additional case study highlight the contentious relationship between language, law, crime, power and culture in South African courtroom discourse. The chapter exposes the cultural and linguistic taboos in a monolingual legal system that prejudice witnesses and may result, in most instances, in unfair discrimination.

The chapter brings to the fore the linguistic challenges that have the potential of adversely affecting the outcome of rape and sexual assault cases, where loaded or culturally sensitive taboo terms present certain challenges during cross-examination.

What is needed is a more culturally and linguistically sensitised approach to cultural diversity in South African courtroom discourse. This would require linguistic and cultural training for legal practitioners and judicial officers.

## Acknowledgements

The financial and research assistance of the UWC Chair in Forensic Linguistics and Multilingualism and the National Institute for the Humanities and Social Sciences (NIHSS) is hereby acknowledged. Opinions expressed, however, remain those of the authors.

## References

Bruner, J.S., Goodnow, J. & Austin, G.A. 1956. *A study of thinking*. New York: Wiley. https://doi.org/10.2307/1292061

Carbaugh, D. (ed.). 1990. *Cultural communication and intercultural contact*. New Jersey: Lawrence Erlbaum Associates. https://doi.org/10.1515/semi.1990.80.1-2.15

Chandler, D. 1995. The Sapir-Whorf Hypothesis. Adapted from *The act of writing: A media theory approach*. http://visual-memory.co.uk/daniel/Documents/short/whorf.html [Accessed 21 October 2022].

Chick, J.K. 1985. The interactional accomplishment of discrimination in South Africa. *Language in Society*, 14(3):299-326. https://doi.org/10.1017/S0047404500011283

Dagut, M. 1978. *Hebrew-English translations. A linguistic analysis of some semantic problems*. Haifa: The University of Haifa.

Dagut, M. 1981. Semantic 'voids' as a problem in the translation process. *Poetics Today*, 2(4):61-71. https://doi.org/10.2307/1772486

Docrat, Z. & Kaschula, R.H. 2019. Monolingual language of record: A critique of South Africa's new policy directive. In: R.H. Kaschula, M.K. Ralarala & G. Heydon (eds.). *New frontiers in forensic linguistics: Themes and perspectives in language and the law in Africa and beyond*. Stellenbosch: African Sun Media. 71-88.

Docrat, Z., Kaschula, R.H. & Ralarala, M.K. 2017. The exclusion of South African sign language speakers in the criminal justice system: A case based approach. In: M.K. Ralarala, K. Barris & S. Siyepu (eds). *Interdisciplinary themes and perspectives in African language research in the 21st century*. Cape Town: Centre for Advanced Studies of African Societies. 261-278.

Docrat, Z., Kaschula, R.H. & Ralarala, M.K. 2020. South African cops need linguistic training – urgently. *The Conversation*, 5 July. https://theconversation.com/south-african-cops-need-linguistic-training-urgently-140075 [Accessed 21 October 2022].

Docrat, Z., Kaschula, R.H. & Ralarala, M.K. 2021. *A handbook on legal languages and the quest for linguistic equality in South Africa and beyond*. Stellenbosch: African Sun Media. https://doi.org/10.52779/9781991201270

Eades, D. 2005. *Aboriginal English and the law: Communicating with Aboriginal English speaking clients: A handbook for legal practitioners*. Brisbane: Queensland Law Society.

Eagleton, T. 1983. *Literary theory. An introduction*. Oxford: Blackwell.

Ehrlich, S. 2001. *Representing rape: Language and sexual consent*. London: Routledge.

Fromkin, V. & Rodman R. 1983. *An introduction to language*. 3rd Edition. New York: CBS College Publishing.

General Council of the Bar of South Africa. Legal Professional Ethics Code of Conduct: Uniform Rules of Professional Ethics of the General Bar Council of South Africa. https://www.johannesburgbar.co.za/wp-content/uploads/05-GCB-Uniform-Rules-of-Ethics-updated-2017-AGM.pdf [Accessed 21 October 2022].

Gibson, R. 2002. *Intercultural business communication: An introduction to the theory and practice of intercultural business communication for teachers, language trainers, and business people*. Oxford: Oxford University Press.

Grice, P. 1975. Logic and conversation. In: P. Cole & J.J. Morgan (eds). *Syntax and semantics 3: Speech acts*. New York, NY: Academic Press. 41-58. https://doi.org/10.1163/9789004368811_003

Hornby, A.S. 1974. *Oxford advanced learner's dictionary of current English*. London: Oxford University Press.

Jansen, J. 2017. *The De Zalze murders. The story behind the brutal axe attack*. Cape Town: Tafelberg.

Joubert, J.J. 2014. *Criminal procedure handbook*. 11th Edition. Cape Town: Juta.

Kaschula, R.H. 2021. *Languages, identities and intercultural communication in South Africa and beyond*. New York: Routledge. https://doi.org/10.4324/9780429345982

Kaschula, R.H. & Anthonissen, C. 1995. *Communicating across cultures in South Africa: Toward a critical language awareness*. Johannesburg: Wits Press.

Kaschula, R.H. & Maseko, P. 2012. Intercultural communication and vocational language learning in South Africa: Law and healthcare. In: C.B. Paulston & S. Kiesling (eds.), *Handbook of intercultural studies*. Wiley Blackwell: Oxford, UK; Malden, USA. https://doi.org/10.1002/9781118247273.ch16

Kaschula, R.H. & Ralarala, M. 2004. Language rights, intercultural communication and the law in South Africa. *South African Journal of African Languages*, 24(4):252-261. https://doi.org/10.1080/02572117.2004.10587242

Koyana, D. 1980. *Customary law in a changing society*. Cape Town: Juta & Co.

Langer, E. 1989. *Mindfulness*. Reading, MA: Addison-Wesley.

MacKinnon, C. 1988. *Feminism unmodified: Discourses on life and law*. Cambridge, MA: Harvard University Press. https://doi.org/10.2307/2070528

Majeke, A. 2002. Towards a culture-based foundation for indigenous knowledge systems in the custom and law. In: C.A. Odora Hoppers (ed.). *Indigenous knowledge and the integration of knowledge systems: Towards a philosophy of articulation.* Claremont: New Africa Books. 141-157.

Mbaya, M. 2002. Linguistic taboo in African marriage context: A study of the Oromo Laguu. *Nordic Journal of African Studies*, 11(2):224-235.

Mertz, E. 1994. Legal language: Pragmatics, poetics and social power. *Annual Review of Anthropology*, 23:435-455. https://doi.org/10.1146/annurev.an.23.100194.002251

Mtuze, P.T. 1993. The language practitioner in a multilingual South Africa. *South African Journal of African Languages*, 13(2):47-52. https://doi.org/10.1080/02572117.1993.105 86964

Reichman, A. 1993. Who is the witness? *Language Projects Review*, 8(1):22-35.

RSA (Republic of South Africa). 1996. *Constitution of the Republic of South Africa, 1996.* https://www.gov.za/documents/constitution/constitution-republic-south-africa-1996-1 [Accessed 21 October 2022].

RSA (Republic of South Africa). 1977. *Criminal Procedure Act 51 of 1977.* https://www.gov.za/sites/default/files/gcis_document/201503/act-51-1977s.pdf [Accessed 21 October 2022].

RSA SSA (Republic of South Africa. Statistics South Africa). 2011. 2011 Census. https://www.statssa.gov.za/?page_id=3839 [Accessed 21 October 2022].

RSA (Republic of South Africa). 2007. *Criminal Law (Sexual Offences and Related Matters) Amendment Act 32 of 2007).* nonstop://www.justice.gov.za/legislation/acts/2007-032.pdf [Accessed 21 October 2022].

Schwikkard, P.J. & Van der Merwe, S.E. (eds.). 2010. *Principles of evidence.* 3rd Edition. Cape Town: Juta Press.

Smit, M. 1992. Translating culture-bound words: A problem in bilingual lexicography. *Spil Plus*, 22(6):358-370. https://doi.org/10.5842/22-0-518

Ting-Toomey, S. 1999. *Communicating across cultures.* London: The Guilford Press.

Trudgill, P. 2000. *Sociolinguistics: An introduction to language and society.* 4th Edition. Oxford: Oxford University Press.

Wardhaugh, R. 2010. *An introduction to sociolinguistics.* 6th Edition. London: Wiley Blackwell.

Wolfsen, N. 1992. Intercultural communication and the analysis of conversation. In: J. Jansen (ed.). *Knowledge and power in South Africa.* Johannesburg: Skotaville.

## Case law:

*Kewana* v *Santam Insurance* (1990).

*State* v *Omotoso and Others* (2018) ZAECPEHC 81 (30 October 2018).

*State* v *Pistorius* (2014), *State* v *Van Breda* (2019).

*Afriforum* v *Julius Malema* (2022).

# RANKING OF DESCRIPTORS FOR COMPLAINANTS BASED ON PERCEIVED VICTIMHOOD

## A case of written opinions in the Tanzanian Court of Appeal

*Patricia Muraguri*
*Emmanuel Satia*

## Introduction

The crime of rape involves a violation of the person who experiences it. There has been a lot of interest in issues surrounding the adjudication of such cases. Of particular interest are the lexical terms used in referring to the persons who have experienced sexual assault, and even those referring to the perpetrators. The variations in observed descriptive terms reveal that the choice of terms is prompted by something more than just the purely legal facts of the case. Various studies have indicated that the terms reveal the existence of a hierarchy (Carrabine et al., 2009; Fohring, 2018; Jankowitz, 2018; Lawther, 2022; McAlinden, 2014). In the case of persons who have experienced sexual assault, there is a hierarchy of victimisation, while, in the case of the perpetrator, there is a hierarchy of guilt. Thus, the terms adopted when referring to the complainant and alleged perpetrator are often based on the user's perception of the person(s) in question.

The legal definition of rape,[1] in the Tanzania Penal Code, Cap. 16 R.E. 2019, considers rape to occur when a male person sexually assaults a woman; however, when a male sexually assaults another male, the act is regarded as an unnatural offence and is charged

---

130.- (1) It is an offence for a male person to rape a girl or a woman.

(2) A male person commits the offence of rape if he has sexual intercourse with a girl or a woman under circumstances falling under any of the following descriptions:

    (a)  not being his wife, or being his wife who is separated from him without her consenting to it at the time of the sexual intercourse;

    (b)  with her consent where the consent has been obtained by the use of force, threats or intimidation by putting her in fear of death or of hurt or while she is in unlawful detention;

    (c)  with her consent when her consent has been obtained at a time when she was of unsound mind or  was in a state of intoxication induced by any drugs, matter or thing, administered to her by the man or by some other person unless proved that there was prior consent between the two;

under section 154(1)(2) of the Penal Code. In the same vein, a sexual act on female family members, commonly referred to as 'incest', is also charged under a different section, namely 158(1)(2)(3). In this chapter, all forms of sexual assault committed on a male person, or a female person are regarded as rape. As such, the term 'rape' in this work is defined as follows: Rape is non-consensual sexual intercourse with a male or female where penetration of sexual organs occurs using another sexual body part or part of the body. Thus, any form of sexual assault, be it against a female or a male, is regarded as rape.

In the literature, women who have been raped are referred to by different terms. Some call them 'rape victims' while others refer to them as 'rape survivors' (Barefoot, 2014; Gardner, 2017). Golubovic (2017) argues that the utilisation of different terms when referring to women who have been raped has a profound influence on how people who have survived rape are perceived. Hockett and Saucier (2015) are of the opinion that the choice of terminology can be associated with the user's stand on oppression and their conceptualisation of women who have been raped.

In this study, the terms used to refer to the complainant in written judgments are referred to as 'descriptors'. The term is defined by *Merriam-Webster's Dictionary* (2022) as "something (such as a word or characteristic feature) that serves to describe or identify". The terms used to refer to the complainants are selected consciously or unconsciously to describe them. The term is considered most relevant since terms used to refer to the persons who have experienced sexual assault are not fixed and the term

---

(d) with her consent when the man knows that he is not her husband, and that her consent is given because she has been made to believe that she is another man to whom, she is, or believes herself to be, lawfully married;

(e) with or without her consent when she is under eighteen years of age, unless the woman is his wife who is fifteen or more years of age and is not separated from the man.

(3) Whoever –

(a) being a person in a position of authority, takes advantage of his official position, and commits rape on a girl or a woman in his official relationship or wrongfully restrains and commits rape on the girl or woman;

(b) being on the management or on the staff of a remand home or other place of custody, established by or under law, or of a women's or children's institution, takes advantage of his position and commits rape on any woman inmate of the remand home, place of custody or institution;

(c) being on the management or staff of a hospital, takes advantage of his position and commits rape on a girl or woman;

(d) being a traditional healer takes advantage of his position and commits rape on a girl or a woman who is his client for healing purposes;

(e) being a religious leader takes advantage of his position and commits rape on a girl or woman.

(4) For the purposes of proving the offence of rape –

(a) penetration however slight is sufficient to constitute the sexual intercourse necessary to the offence; and

(b) evidence of resistance such as physical injuries to the body is not necessary to prove that sexual intercourse took place without consent.

assigned depends on the conceptualisation of the facts of the case by the court. Thus, the descriptor describes the persons who have experienced sexual assault on a case-by-case basis. Since the descriptors are determined in this way, the court presupposes that there is either a continuum or a hierarchy of the terms used to describe these persons. The proposal is that these terms can be arranged in a hierarchy using the descriptors of those who are considered to have suffered the most harm at the higher end of the hierarchy, with those who are considered as having participated in their own victimisation falling on the lower end of the hierarchy. The existence of hierarchies for terms used to describe persons who have experienced sexual assault reveals that the status of persons who have experienced sexual assault is not fixed.

This study examines the judgments from the Tanzanian Court of Appeal. It is noted that some complainants who are presented by other courts as 'victims' may end up being viewed as 'liars', in the Court of Appeal's opinion. Further, the identities of these persons are constructed by the understanding that the court reaches regarding the facts of the case; but these identities are often heavily influenced by society. Differences in cultural backgrounds contribute to the dialogue on the types of victims and therefore the descriptors assigned. In Tanzania, a victim who has had previous sexual relations that are included as part of the facts of the case is less likely to be assigned the role of victim. Those who freely engage in sexual relations are regarded as adult; thus, it becomes more difficult for them to prove an assault since, when the facts are given, they may be suspected of complicity.

This chapter examines written judicial opinions from Tanzanian courts to identify descriptors used for persons who have allegedly been raped. It also aims to reveal how the judges' conceptualisation of these persons is revealed in the kinds of descriptors selected for use; and, ultimately, how the descriptors used reveal the position of the complainant in the hierarchy of victimhood. Sexual assault is assumed to be violent; therefore, those who suffer it are regarded as victims. However, due to the fact that the assault takes different forms and is committed on persons from different walks of life, the social evaluations of the circumstances of the assault lead to the crafting of different terminologies to name these persons both by the community and ultimately in the courts.

## Review of related literature and theoretical underpinnings

The manner in which a judge conceptualises the crime of rape determines the kinds of descriptors that he or she uses in the written decision to refer to the women who have allegedly been raped. Descriptors for the individuals who have experienced sexual assault or rape are selected according to various criteria, one of which is the field in which one is working. In counselling, the descriptors are likened to a journey metaphor (Young & Maguire, 2003), where the individual moves from one journey into another. The individuals begin as victims and, as they regain control of their lives, they become survivors. Tremble (2014) says that the term 'victim' is used at the coping phase of the sexual assault experience while the experience is still raw.

Among medical personnel, terms used to refer to individuals who have experienced rape are 'victim', 'survivor' and 'patient' (Gardner, 2017). Gardner (2017) conducted a study on how the Sexual Assault Nurse Examiner (SANE) programme curriculum addressed bias. She examined the keywords and phrases used when referring to individuals who had experienced sexual assault. The key descriptors were 'victim', 'survivor' and 'patient'; and she noted that there were patterns of meaning associated with these words. The term 'victim' was used in several circumstances. First, it was used when talking about the recipient of the violence in relation to the assailant. It was also used when referring to a negative aspect of their experience; and, finally, it was used when referring to the physical violence that the person had undergone, as a way of indicating that they did not have control over what had happened to them. The term 'victim' is also generally used when referring to children who have experienced sexual assault since, as she notes, "the child had no agency in their interaction with the assailant" (Gardner, 2017:8). The term 'patient' is used in the SANE curriculum, according to Gardner, to refer to a person who has experienced sexual assault in a medical context. The term is used to refer to the protocol in working as a SANE nurse. The term thus shows the power dynamic that exists between the person who has experienced sexual assault and the SANE nurse. She notes that the term 'patient' is more positive than 'victim', since 'patient' signals a relationship in which the nurse provides the 'victim' with care. 'Victim' highlights the negative aspects about the person's experience, while 'patient' signals a relationship of provision of care. The term 'survivor', according to Gardner, is used to refer to the situation when the person who has experienced sexual assault practises agency and choice in the situation. The term suggests the person's positivity.

In this study, the descriptors used by the judges for persons who have experienced sexual assault will be discussed in relation to Carrabine et al.'s (2009) concept of the existence of hierarchies of victimisation. Carrabine et al. (2004) argue that such "hierarchies of victimization" grade victims, with some victims enjoying a higher status in the crime discourse and their experiences of victimisation being taken more seriously than those of others. According to Carrabine et al. (2009), hierarchies of victimisation are generally shaped by the power and status of the victim, international politics, conditions of war, and stereotyping. Persons with low status and those who are powerless occupy the lower ends of the hierarchy of victimisation. Carrabine et al. (2009) note that the latter groups have to struggle to have their experience taken seriously. Stereotyping of victims, based on attitudes towards them by society, may also create hierarchies of victimisation. At the highest end of the hierarchy of victimisation, we have the 'ideal victims' who are typified as elderly women and children who are given the complete and legitimate status of being a victim (Christie, 1986).

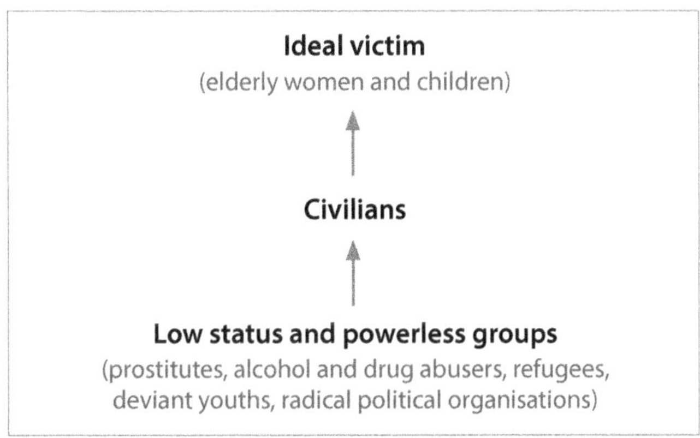


**FIGURE 7.1**   A diagrammatic representation of the hierarchy of victimisation, as proposed by Carrabine et al. (2009)

As seen in Figure 7.1, the 'ideal' victim occupies the highest place in the hierarchy and the lower end is occupied by those who are judged by society to be troublesome or distasteful.

This study focuses on persons who have been raped and it proposes that, in line with Carrabine et al. (2009), there are hierarchies that can be observed in written judgments in Tanzanian courts in the assignment of descriptors to persons who have experienced sexual assault or rape. Golubovic (2017) argues that the utilisation of different terms, when referring to women who have been raped, has a profound influence on how they are perceived. Hockett and Saucier (2015) argue that the choice of descriptors is associated with the researcher's or writer's stand on oppression and their conceptualisation of the women who have been raped. Therefore, the response of the criminal justice system (and, in this study, the conceptualisation in written judicial opinions), in terms of the choice of descriptors used in the written judgments, has great significance. The choice ultimately defines those complainants that society should consider victims, as well as others who, through their narratives, are either lying outright or telling some shade of truth. Thus, the use of a particular descriptor assigns a person a place in the hierarchy of victimisation, with the ideal victim occupying the highest position in the hierarchy. The judge's choice of a descriptor may reflect their assessment of the truthfulness of the accusations levelled against the accused and the perceived credibility of the women who have been raped, which, in turn, either makes the recipient of the alleged assault innocent or blameworthy. Carrabine et al. (2009) opine that, when a distinction is made between 'innocent' and 'blameworthy' victims, a decision is also concurrently being made about attacks that are justifiable in society and those that are not. Descriptors that are commonly used in the legal sector in written judgments include 'complainant', 'victim' and 'prosecution witness'. Other descriptors used are concocted from these terms, together with other novel ones designed to suit the nature of a case.

## Methodology

The data source for this study was written judicial decisions from Tanzania's Court of Appeal. A total of 30 judgments were collected online. Permission was sought and given from the court to study the judgments. Since some complainants' identities were already available online, they could not be concealed, but their names were used only when deemed completely necessary.

The judgments considered in the analysis are those where the decision was made after the amendment of the Sexual Offences Special Provision Act 1998, and where the primary count was rape. The parameter 'rape' was used to search for the judgments online. The judgments were gathered from the sites https:/www.judiciary.go.tz, https:// tanzlii.org and https://africanlii.org, after which purposive sampling was used to identify related judgments. 'Reported judgments that set precedents in the collected cases were also identified and included.'

Of the 30 decisions studied, 19 were made between 2016 and 2019, while eleven (11) were made between 2006 and 2010. Of the 30 written judgments gathered, eleven (11) of the appeals were dismissed and the judgment of the High Court was upheld, while fifteen (15) of the appeals were allowed and the conviction was quashed. Among the 30 judgments, four (4) were not considered for analysis since they dealt purely with matters of the law concerning a defective charge sheet and a defective notice of appeal, and the law on an appeal that had been summarily rejected by the High Court or reference to the person who experienced sexual assault was minimal. Some cases that had a defective charge sheet were considered for analysis where the reference to the person who experienced sexual assault was considered substantial. In the cases collected, all the appellants were male, while the complainants were both male (3) and female (27), as indicated in the definition of rape provided earlier. The charges of the 26 cases analysed are shown in Table 7.1:

**TABLE 7.1**   Charges of the cases

| Charge | Number of cases |
| --- | --- |
| Rape | 20 |
| Rape and unnatural offence | 1 |
| Unnatural offence | 3 |
| Gang rape | 1 |
| Incest | 1 |
| Total | 26 |

This study is qualitative; and, as Johnstone (2000:35) notes, qualitative studies focus on what forms are used by a writer, and how and why they are used. Johnstone argues that, in the courtroom, qualitative evidence is more demonstrable than quantitative evidence because it draws on language data. He (2000:60) further states that "qualitative results appeal to the non-mathematical but structured sense of probability held by judges and juries". The study further applied critical discourse analysis (CDA) as the theoretical and analytical framework (Fairclough, 1992).

The judgments were examined, and the kinds of terms used in referring to the complainants were noted for each judgment; then these terms were regarded as the descriptors, which were further grouped into legal descriptors and descriptors with social or moral connotations.

It is usually argued that appeal courts tend to focus on issues of law and do not include descriptions of an assault. In this study, Court of Appeal judgments were considered viable for study since they included descriptions of the assaults and the circumstances surrounding them, though they also dealt with issues of the law. Since the written judgments are the official reports of the events and observations made during the court proceedings, this study examines the patterns appearing in the descriptors used for the persons who experienced sexual assault. The analysis involves examination of the language used and is not an analysis of the judges who made or wrote the decisions.

## Analysis

In the judgments under study, it was important to note the ages of the persons who experienced rape. Complainants' ages ranged from the youngest at four (4) years to the oldest at sixty-five (65) years. The ages are significant in that most complainants were below 18 years of age. Of the 22 cases of persons below 18 years of age, three (3) appeals were allowed due to procedural issues in administration of the *voir dire* test to determine whether the child witnesses were capable of telling the truth; and, in three (3) other cases, the appeal was allowed due to a defective charge sheet.

**TABLE 7.2**   Ages of the complainants

| Age group | Number of complainants | Percentage |
|---|---|---|
| Below 10 years | 10 | 38 |
| Above 10 years but below 18 years | 12 | 46 |
| Above 18 years | 1 | 4 |
| Above 30 years | 1 | 4 |
| Age not stated | 2 | 8 |
| Total | 26 | 100 |

The analysis of the judgments was made within the framework of critical discourse analysis. It involved isolating the terms used to describe the persons who had experienced sexual assault, after which the circumstances of the usage of the term were critically explored in the judgments to determine whether the rape incident and its accompanying circumstances had influenced the choice of the descriptor(s) used.

There were two main groups of descriptors:

1. The legal descriptors that are found in the Penal Code, the Evidence Act and in the Criminal Procedures Act (and in other legal usages).

2. Those that had connotations of moral and or social censorship, those with social or moral connotations.

In the judgments under study, the descriptors identified were 'victim', 'complainant', 'witness', 'prosecution witness' (abbreviated 'PW'), 'alleged victim', 'alleged prosecutrix', 'prosecutrix', 'liar', 'proper names', 'small boy', 'little boy', and 'nursery school pupil'.

## Legal descriptors

These descriptors originate mainly from the Penal Code, Cap. 16, the Evidence Act, Cap. 6, the Criminal Procedures Act, Cap. 20, and other legal documents. Legal descriptors used include the proper names of the complainant, which were used when indicating the particulars of the charge. For instance, in *Alfeo Valentino* v *Republic*, the complainant is named as Grace d/o John. Another legal descriptor is an abbreviation(s) of the name(s) of the complainant used, for instance, in the case *Eliah Bariki* v *Republic*, the complainant is referred to as 'RF'; and in *Jamali Ally @Salum* v *Republic*, the complainant is referred to as 'BHD'.

Other legal ways of referring to these persons are in relation to their role in a case. They are referred to as 'prosecution witnesses', abbreviated as 'PW' and thereafter numbered. In most cases, the person who was raped is usually 'prosecution witness number one', abbreviated as 'PW1'. The other descriptors used include terms such as: 'prosecutrix', 'alleged prosecutrix', 'a child of tender age', 'complainant', 'prosecution witness', 'alleged victim', and 'victim'. Among these descriptors, the descriptor that reveals the age of the person who has experienced rape is 'child of tender years'.

The descriptor 'alleged victim' and 'victim' are used with reference to provision- on sexual harassment, incest by females and the heading of the provision is titled "effect of victim's consent on criminal responsibility for death or maiming." Therefore, the descriptors 'victim' and 'alleged victim' are sparingly used in the Penal Code and are not used at all with reference to rape itself. The term 'victim' is said to be defined generally as "a person who has been harmed as a result of the commission of an offence" (National Crime Victim Law Institute, 2014). The term 'victim' presents its own difficulties; and, as observed in the 2014 National Crime Victim Law Institute publication (NCVLI), it presumes the defendant's guilt. Fohring (2018) argues that the label 'victim' has both positive and negative consequences where the negative consequences involve victims being potrayed as being stereotypically weak, vulnerable, frail and fearful thus denying them agency. Others have proposed that the terms 'alleged victim' and 'complainant' be used as alternatives to the term 'victim'. They argue that the term 'complainant' is too broad and that the term 'alleged victim' does not clearly indicate whether the victim status has been determined. The NCVLI (2014) further claims that the modifier 'alleged' has synonyms which imply that the victim fabricated the charge and thus is not truly a victim.

In the judgments studied, the term 'victim' is used in nine (9) cases where the appeal was dismissed and in seven (7) cases where the appeal was allowed. The term 'alleged victim' is used in two cases where the appeal was dismissed. Therefore, the term 'victim' is used in sixteen (16) of the 26 cases studied. It is significant to note that, in eight (8) of the eleven (11) cases where the appeal was dismissed or denied, the descriptor 'victim' is used. In these eight cases, the persons are below eighteen years of age.

The term 'alleged victim' is used in three written judgments, indicating that it is not regularly preferred. This may be due to the associations that the word 'alleged' insinuates, as indicated above. The term is used a total of five (5) times in all three written judgments. In two of the written judgments where the term 'alleged victim' is used, the appeal is denied, whereas in the third written judgment, the appeal is allowed. In the case *Peter Abel Kirumi* v *Republic* where the appeal is allowed, the term 'alleged victim' is used twice when describing the case details. The term 'alleged victim' in this case carries undertones that the case was fabricated:

> The prosecution version was unfolded by two witnesses, namely, Nasma Said (PWl), the *alleged victim*, and Saida Khalid (PW2), who happens to be Nasma's mother. (p. 3)

> That would suffice to justify our intervention and take the unusual step of interfering with the concurrent findings of the two courts below on the reliability and sufficiency of the testimony of Nasma, *the alleged victim*. (p. 10)

Another term used is 'complainant'. A complainant is a person who experiences some wrong or feels they have been wronged and thus institutes a formal complaint in a court of law. Since the term is related to the action taken by the aggrieved person, it is mainly supposed to be a neutral way of referring to such persons. The term is used in eight (8) written judgments. In two (2) of these, the appeal is denied; in six (6), the appeal is allowed. The term is therefore preferred in judgments where the appeal is allowed because it is a way of referring to the person without overtly seeming to judge their character. In the cases where the appeal was denied, the term 'complainant' is repeatedly used, as in the case of *Galus Kitaya* v *Republic*. In this case, the person who was sexually assaulted had had sexual relations with the underage defendant for a period of about three years. The term 'complainant' is used 22 times in the judgment, while 'PW1' is used eight times. Since she had prolonged sexual relations with the defendant, there is preference for reference terms like 'complainant' and 'PW1' in the written judgment. Even though the term 'complainant' is supposed to be essentially neutral, its usage in the written judgment on the *Galus Kitaya* v *Republic* case is a way for the writers of the judgment and ultimately the court to distance themselves from the events of the case, especially where the person who experienced the assault seemed to have consented to the sexual relations. From the details of the case, the sexual relations between the accused and the complainant presuppose a consensual sexual relation. The accused was initially sentenced on his own admission of having had sexual relations with a minor. In this judgment, the complainant is referred to as a 'victim' only once when describing the admission of guilt by the appellant: "... the admission by the appellant that he had sexual intercourse with the *victim*..." (p. 7).

In other judgments, like those of *Imani Charles Chimango* v *Republic* and *Jackson Davis* v *Republic*, the term 'witness' is used. In *Imani Charles Chimango* v *Republic*, the complainant is referred to as a 'credible witness', whereas in *Jackson Davis* v *Republic*, he is referred to as a 'witness' six times. The term 'credible witness' is significant here, since it serves to justify further the complainant's claim to victimhood. In *Jackson Davis* v *Republic*, the term 'witness' serves to show that the complainant suffered the assault so reported.

The term 'prosecutrix' is used in one written judgment, *Godi Kasenegala* v *Republic*, where the appeal was allowed. The term 'alleged prosecutrix', on the other hand, is used in two judgments (*Godi Kasenegala* v *Republic* and *Shaban Amiri* v *Republic*); and in both cases, the appeal was allowed. The term 'prosecutrix' can be regarded as a neutral way of referring to the person who experienced sexual assault. The term is formed from the word 'prosecute', which is the action that is initiated when the person who suffered sexual assault reports the matter to authorities.

The use of proper names in these written judgments is observed in seventeen (17) of the written judgments. The extent of usage of the proper name varies: in six (6) of the judgments, the proper names are used once only, while in three (3) judgments, the proper names are used twice. In eight (8) of the judgments, the proper names are used more than twice, ranging from three times, as in the judgment *Edson Simon Mwombeki* v *Republic* where the complainant is referred to by her name three times, to the judgment *Peter Abel Kirumi* v *Republic*, where the complainant is referred to by her proper names 14 times. Proper names are used for three complainants who are 10 years old and younger; but it is noteworthy that, in these cases, the appeal was allowed, and the appellants were released. It is noted that, when the testimony of the complainant is regarded as untruthful, there is increased use of the proper name of the complainant. For instance, in the case *Peter Abel Kirumi* v *Republic*, the complainant's testimony was not regarded as reliable since she delayed in reporting the initial incident and her character is assessed as follows: "… it is beyond question that Nasma was not quite the salt of the earth in her account on the alleged episode" (p. 11).

The use of abbreviations to refer to the person who experienced the sexual assault is mainly done in two ways. First, the person who experienced sexual assault is commonly referred to using the abbreviation 'PW', considered to be a neutral way of referring to a 'prosecution witness'. In the 25 judgments studied, the complainants are referred to using the abbreviation 'PW' and the abbreviation is omitted in only one judgment (*Ludovick Kisanga* v *Republic*). Another form of abbreviation is the use of initials of the name of the person who experienced the assault. For instance, in the judgment *Jamal Ally @ Salum* v *Republic*, the girl who was sexually assaulted is referred to using the initials of her name 'BHD'. In other cases, arbitrary abbreviations are chosen to represent the persons who suffered assault. For instance, in the written judgment, *Kassim Twaha* v *Republic*, the complainant is referred to using the initials 'XYZ'. The use of abbreviations instead of names is not regulated by any legal requirement, so the decision to use them is at the discretion of the writer of the judicial opinion. Abbreviations instead of names are used in six judgments where the ages of the persons that experienced sexual assault range between six and 17 years. In other judgments, for instance, that of *Raphael Mhando* v *Republic*, the complainant is six years old but is referred to by her proper name (Beatrice d/o Isihaka) three times in the judgment, whereas in the case of *Dalali s/o Mwalongo* v *Republic*, the 17-year-old complainant is referred to using initials only.

## Social or morally based descriptors

Other terms used to refer to persons who suffered sexual assault have some social connotations. Terms like 'little boy', 'small boy', 'nursery school pupil' and 'five-year-old boy' will usually create a mental picture in the mind of the reader or hearer – that of a young child who should be safe and protected but is, instead, suffering abuse. The terms therefore elevate the complainant to the level of a victim. For instance, in the judgment in the *Jackson Davis* v *Republic* case, the complainant is referred to as 'little boy' and 'small boy'.

Other descriptions, e.g., "... not the salt of the earth ..." convey an overt moral judgment of the character of the complainant.

## Hierarchy of victimisation in the usage of terms

By examining these descriptors, one can observe an implicit ranking of the persons who have experienced rape. This rank places these persons on a certain level in the hierarchy. From the judgments, one can observe the expectations and criteria that need to be met for one to be considered a bona fide victim or 'ideal' victim by the society and the legal system. Though one may not meet all the implicitly set criteria, the closer one gets to meeting the criteria, the greater the possibility that one will be regarded as a victim. The criteria that one needs to meet if one is to be regarded as an ideal victim can be gleaned from the literature and from specific comments and phrases in the written judgments.

The ideal victim is a virtuous woman or girl who must prove her integrity and credibility. In the case of *Sprian Justine Tarimo* v *Republic*, the integrity and culpability of the complainant comes to light. The complainant is identified by her age (a 20-plus year old) and her status in society (a 'woman'). The identification of her age and the fact that her age qualifies her as a woman in society implies that she might have engaged in the sexual act as an adult. Her past is also brought into question when it is stated that she might have "had undisputed sex on several prior occasions with, to mention only one, the appellant". Thus, her claim of ideal victimhood is disputed and her status in the hierarchy, as a result of this opinion, diminishes. The implication is that, if there was any victimisation, the complainant participated in her victimization or was even responsible for her victimisation. Her age, her past and the moral expectations of society disqualify her from an ideal victim status. It is stated thus in the judgment:

> But even if the PF3 had been regularly received in evidence it would not have helped the prosecution in so far as the finding of the two courts below was predicated on the fact that PW1 had a **"ruptured hymen"**. What would one have expected from a 20-plus year old woman who had had undisputed sex on several prior occasions with, to mention only one, the appellant? (p. 10) (Original emphasis retained)

In a similar vein, in the case *Jackson Davis* v *Republic*, the observation is made that the trial court did not establish the credibility and truthfulness of the sexual assault allegations made by a nine-year-old boy. It is stated thus:

> … it is also apparent from the record that the trial magistrate made no specific findings on the credibility of the complainant. No reasons are reflected in the proceedings to establish that the trial court was satisfied the complainant was telling the truth…

The ideal victim is one who immediately reports sexual assault to authorities. This expectation is noticed in observations in the written judgments, such as in the case of *Alfeo Valentino* v *Republic*:

> One wonders why PW2, who is supposed to be a responsible mother, had to wait for four clear days before reporting the abhorrent "crime" of the appellant, if indeed this "rape" of PW1 took place. (p. 25) (Original punctuation)

In the same judgment, it is noted that: "PW1 was examined five days after the alleged incident" (p. 21); and "PW1 said she could not recall the day" (p. 22).

The same is noted in the judgment *Peter Abel Kirumi* v *Republic* where the complainant is faulted for late reporting of the incident:

> From the evidence of Nasma, it is beyond question that the young girl delayed to disclose the first incident for a good ten days and only did so in the aftermath of the aborted second occurrence.

The ideal victim is also expected to raise an alarm immediately after she is attacked and should continue to do so as the sexual assault is under way.

The ideal victim should be able to give every detail of the sexual assault, such as:

(a)   The date and time of the assault.

In the case *Shaban Amiri* v *Republic*, the complainant was not sure of the date and time when the sexual assault took place, especially when compared to her witnesses' evidence:

> As aptly argued by Mr Mzikila, the witnesses differ on the date when the offence was committed. Whereas PW1 vaguely or evasively testified that it was on a certain day in July 2001 at 6pm, PW3 and PW4 said it was in August 2001. Regarding the time, PW3 said it was at 7.30pm; while PW4 said it was at 8pm.
>
> The fact that she could not recall the exact day diminishes her credibility: "… if PW1 was telling the truth we have found no evidence to indicate as to why she did not recollect the exact day when she was allegedly raped" (p. 10).

(b)   Specific details of how the assault progressed, using words that are formally used in court to describe the nature of assault. This is required for every person who has experienced sexual assault, regardless of age. For instance, in the judgment *Alfeo Valentino* v *Republic*, the complainant, who was nine years old, described the act that was done to her as *matusi* (translated as 'insults').

> PW1 in a very incomprehensible manner told the trial court that one day they met the appellant who took them (herself and PW3) to his home, undressed her and then "*akanifanya matusi* (he did insults to me)" (p. 22).

In Tanzania, it is common for young children to refer to the act of sex as *matusi*. From the judgment, it is observed that no attempt was made by the trial court to find out and document what the witness meant by use of the word, *matusi*. Thus, since the Appeal Court could not find formal words giving specific details of the sexual act inflicted on the complainant, it was concluded that her account of events was 'incomprehensible' and that there was not an iota of evidence to support the claim that she had been raped. A witness for the complainant, PW3, who is also nine years old, also described the assault as *ujinga* ('foolishness').

Therefore, what determines whether one is a victim or not is not only the assault that he or she has undergone, but also society's assessment of the legitimacy to the claim of victimhood. The experience of the persons who have suffered sexual assault is gauged and they are then assigned a descriptor based on the assessed legitimacy of the assault and the truthfulness of their account. The descriptor is mainly based on how closely their account tallies with the court's expectations of the ideal victim.

Where the person who experiences assault by a stranger and immediately reports the incident, the claim to victimhood is greater and the individual is very likely to be referred to as a 'victim'. For instance, in the case, *Imani Charles Chimango* v *Republic*, the perpetrator of the assault was a stranger, as noted in the judgment:

> "… the learned counsel submitted that the *victim* (our emphasis) did not know the appellant prior to the incident."

In the same judgment, the complainant was able to give details of the assault and the circumstances that led to it: "She described graphically how the appellant received her. She explained also how she was cheated by the appellant at the bus stand …."

When the witness is not able to give graphic details, it lessens the gravity of the offence. The ability to remember and provide vivid details of the case, like dates and time, is expected of all complainants, regardless of age. In the case, *Alfeo Valentino* v *Republic*, the nine-year-old complainant was expected to have noted such details and no child talk was entertained. Very young children are subjected to the same rigors as older persons. The complainant's explanation is described as incomprehensible since she did not specify how the act was done to her but resorted to the use of euphemisms (*akanifanya matusi*) ("he did insults to me").

Therefore, in the hierarchy of victimisation, the term 'victim' occupies the highest end of the hierarchy. The term can only be superseded by the term 'ideal victim'; however, the latter term exists only in the expectations of the evaluators and is not used explicitly in judgments.

Next in the hierarchy is the term 'complainant'. In some judgments, like that of *Galus Kitaya* v *Republic*, the term is used in a way that allows the writer to avoid committing themselves to admitting that the person who was sexually assaulted also consented to sexual relations with the appellant, but then later went ahead and allowed him to be charged. The term allows the court to avoid using the term 'victim'.

The term 'prosecutrix' is next in the hierarchy. It is used in the judgments in the most neutral way to refer to the person who instituted the complaint that led to the case. It is followed by the terms 'alleged victim' and 'alleged prosecutrix'. The word 'alleged' does not clearly indicate whether victim status has been determined; and the modifier 'alleged' has synonyms, which imply that the person who experienced sexual assault fabricated the charge. At the lowest end of the hierarchy is the term 'liar', which is overtly used in judgments like that of *Shaban Amiri* v *Republic* where the complainant is described as a liar: "… worse still PW1 exposed herself as a liar in her evidence in court and by her conduct after the alleged incident of rape if ever it took place …".

In other judgments, like that of *Alfeo Valentino* v *Republic*, it is insinuated that the complainant is lying: "… there is no evidence on record, let alone credible evidence, to show that the appellant had sexual intercourse or even made an attempt to do so …."

Where there is doubt as to whether the person who is supposed to have experienced sexual assault consented to the act or not and the truthfulness of their allegations is questioned, the terms that are mainly preferred are 'PW1' and 'complainant'. Other terms like 'child', 'little boy', 'small boy' and 'nursery school pupil' are ways of elevating the nature of the offence by insinuating that, due to the age of the complainants, the act of the perpetrator breaks social norms.

In the judgments studied, the hierarchy of victimhood for persons who have experienced sexual assault can be presented diagrammatically as follows (the upward arrow represents increasing degrees of victimhood):

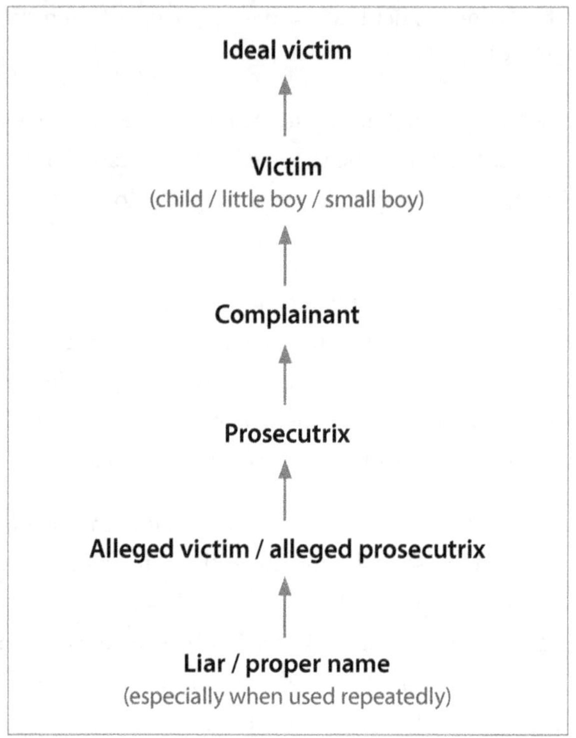


**FIGURE 7.2**   Hierarchy of victimisation (Research data, 2021)

## Discussion

Increasing degrees of victimhood can also be linked to the perceived agency of the person who experienced sexual assault in enabling, allowing, or encouraging the assault. The positions proposed above are not generally fixed, but the complainant status moves up or down the hierarchy based on a review of their cases by the Court of Appeal. The conceptualisation of the facts of the cases led to some complainants being regarded as outright liars. For instance, in the case *Peter Abel Kirumi* v *Republic*, the complainant delayed in reporting the assault and this led to a suspicion that she was lying and there was an insinuation of complicity.

There are social forces at work, which influence the descriptors used, such as in the case of *Sprian Justine Tarimo* v *Republic*, where the age and alleged previous sexual experience of the complainant is a factor in the judgment. The complainant does not fit the criteria of an innocent virgin, so her experiences are summarised as, "What would one have expected from a 20-plus year old woman who had had undisputed sex on several prior occasions with, to mention only one, the appellant?" When contesting for the victim's position, none of the complainants are exempted from society's expectations of an ideal victim and these expectations spill over into the courts. Even the very young must fulfil the stringent criteria set. The complainants are presented to the Court of Appeal as certain types of victims; but, on a determination based on the arguments made by the Court, they may retain their status, be elevated to higher levels, or have their status plummet to the lowest levels in the hierarchy. As the complainant moves lower in the hierarchy, victim blaming and secondary victimisation arise. The legitimacy of the complaint of the 9-year-old complainant in *Alfeo Valentino* v *Republic* is diminished by the fact that the complainant was not explicit in identification of the sexual organs and was too societally proper.

The court maintains a sense of propriety by minimising sexually explicit descriptions in the judgments; on the other hand, it requires the complainants to be as explicit as possible in their descriptions. This contradiction may confuse complainants, especially young children, and thus make them follow the leading of the court in maintaining social propriety, not realising that it is negatively affecting the legitimacy of their complaint.

## Conclusions

From the findings, we note that the complainants do not have power of choice on the kind of descriptor selected to describe them based on the sexual assault experienced, the court assigns it. The hierarchy that is noted in the use of the descriptors reveal the existence of implicit social forces that lead to decisions on the type of descriptor that can be assigned to a complainant. The decision can be influenced by the perceived extent of victimisation as you move higher in the hierarchy and as you go lower in the hierarchy by a determination of the extent of blameworthiness of the person who has experienced sexual assault. Lawther (2022:519) argues that the hierarchies of victimhood are created by competing political and social interests, which lead to demarcation of 'good' and 'bad' victims. The right to rise in the hierarchy of victimisation is determined by the complainant's ability to present him or herself as an ideal victim to the court. Even children who are considered to have a high position in the hierarchy of victimisation by Carrabine et al. (2009), are not guaranteed that position in rape case proceedings. Active resistance against the sexual assault and the ability to capture and retell details is key in contesting for victimhood in the court. From the findings, it is clear that there is a need for a re-examination of the descriptors used for the complainants and also of the language used in judgments to insure against victim blaming and re-victimisation of complainants.

## References

Barefoot, A. 2014. *Victim blaming, protests, and public space: News coverage of the Occupy Wall Street sexual assaults.* Master's thesis. Cornerstone: A Collection of Scholarly and Creative Works for Minnesota State University, Mankato. Mankato: Minnesota State University.

Carrabine, E., Cox, P., Lee, M., Plummer, K. & South, N. 2004. *Criminology: A sociological introduction*. New York: Routledge. https://doi.org/10.4324/9780203642955

Carrabine, E., Cox, P., Lee, M., Plummer, K. & South, N. 2009. *Criminology: A sociological introduction*. New York: Routledge. https://doi.org/10.4324/9780203884942

Christie, N. 1986. The ideal victim. In: E.A. Fattah (ed.). *From crime policy to victim policy*. Basingstoke: MacMillan. https://doi.org/10.1007/978-1-349-08305-3_2

Fairclough, N. 1992. *Discourse and Social Change*. London: Polity.

Fohring, S. 2018. Introduction to the special issue: Victim identities and hierarchies. *International Review of Victimology*, 24(2):147-149. https://doi.org/10.1177/0269758018755152

Gardner, S.D. 2017. Patient, victim, or survivor? An analysis of SANE Nursing Curriculum bias. Honor's thesis. Paper 458. Portland, OR: Portland State University.

Golubovic, N. 2017. Blame attribution in rape crimes: The effects of willing substance use, race, and rape myth acceptance. Thesis. Atlanta, GA: Georgia State University. http://scholarworks.gsu.edu/cps_diss/123

Hockett, J.M. & Saucier, D.A. 2015. A systematic literature review of "rape victims" versus "rape survivors": Implications for theory, research, and practice. *Aggression and Violent Behavior*, 25(A):1-14. https://doi.org/10.1016/j.avb.2015.07.003

Jankowitz, S. 2018. The 'Hierarchy of victims' in Northern Ireland: A framework for critical analysis. *International Journal of Transitional Justice*, 12:216-236.

Lawther, C. 2022. Heroes and hierarchies: The celebration and censure of victimhood in transitional justice. *The International Journal of Human Rights*, 26(3):518-540. https://doi.org/10.1080/13642987.2021.1946038

McAlinden, A.M. 2014. Deconstructing victim and offender identities in discourse in child sexual abuse: Hierarchies, blame and the good/evil dialectic. *British Journal of Criminology*, 54(2):180-198.

*Merriam-Webster Dictionary*. 2022. Descriptor. Springfield, MA: Merriam-Webster. https://www.merriamwebster.com/dictionary/descriptor [Accessed 26 October 2022].

NCVLI (National Crime Victim Law Institute). 2014. Use of the term "Victim" in criminal proceedings. *NCVLI News*, 1-6. 11th Edition (2009, updated in 2014). http://parliament.go.tz/polis/uploads/bills/acts/1457516075-ActNo-4-1998.pdf

Tremble, C.J. 2014. The counselor experience in counseling clients who have been sexually assaulted. PhD thesis. Kalamazoo, MI: Western Michigan University. http://scholarworks.wmich.edu/dissertations/316 [Accessed 26 October 2022].

Young, S.L. & Maguire, K.C. 2003. Talking about sexual violence. *Women and Language*, 26(2):40 ff.

## Statutes

Sexual Offences Special Provisions Act, 1998. http://parliament.go.tz/polis/uploads/bills/acts/1457516075-ActNo-4-1998.pdf [Accessed 8 November 2022]

Evidence Act Cap. 6

Penal Code, Cap. 16 R.E. 2019

Criminal Procedure Act Cap. 20

## Cases cited

*Alfeo Valentino* v *Republic* CA 92 Arusha (2006)

*Eliah Bariki* v *Republic* CA 321 Arusha (2016)

*Dalali s/o Mwalongo* v *Republic* CA 27 Mbeya (2017)

*Galus Kitaya* v *Republic* CA 196 Mbeya (2015)
*Godi Kasenegala* v *Republic* CA 10 Iringa (2008)
*Imani Charles Chimango* v *Republic* CA 382 Mtwara (2016)
*Jackson Davis* v *Republic* CA 127 Mtwara (2005)
*Jamali Ally @Salum* v *Republic* CA 52 Mtwara (2017)
*Kassim Twaha* v *Republic* CA 94 Dar es salaam (2017)
*Ludovick Kisanga* v *Republic* CA 278 Arusha (2006)
*Mwombeki* v *Republic* CA 94 Mtwara (2016)
*Peter Abel Kirumi* v *Republic* CA 25 Arusha (2016)
*Raphael Mhando* v *Republic* CA 54 Tanga (2017)
*Shaban Amiri* v *Republic* CA 64 Arusha (2003)
*Sprian Justine Tarimo* v *Republic* CA 226 Arusha (2007)

# LANGUAGE AND IDEOLOGY IN KURIA FEMALE GENITAL MUTILATION SONGS

*Boke Joyce Wambura*
*Emmanual Satia*

## Introduction

Violence against women is broadly perceived to be a deprivation of women's human rights and fundamental freedoms based on their gender. The Inter-American Convention on the Prevention, Punishment, and Eradication of Violence against Women (Organization of American States (OAS), 1994) defines violence against women as "any act or conduct based on gender that causes death, harm or physical, sexual or psychological suffering to women, both in the public and private spheres". Violence against women covers a wide range of cruel practices, such as domestic violence (moral, physical, sexual, psychological and property violence), sexual harassment, rape, genital mutilation, forced marriage, persecution, abortion or forced sterilisation, and feminicide, among others. This chapter focuses on Female Genital Mutilation (FGM) as a form of violence against women. Depending on the user's ideological standpoint regarding the practice, FGM is also known as Female Genital Cutting (FGC) or "incision" (WHO, 2019). The chapter examines how language is used among the Kuria of Kenya to legitimise violence against women by making FGM appear normal and acceptable, even good, thereby giving the victims no opportunity to resist.

### The Kuria people

The Kuria people, also called Abakuria, are a Bantu language group who live in both Kenyan and Tanzanian territories (Wambura, 2018). In Kenya, they live in the Kuria East and West districts in Migori County (the former Nyanza province); and in Tanzania they live in Serengeti, Tarime, Musoma, Bunda and some parts of the Mwanza district. The homeland of the Kuria is between River Migori to the east and the estuary of River Mara to the west. On the western side, the area stretches from the Migori district in South Nyanza to the Musoma district of Tanzania. To the south, the land borders the Transmara district on the Kenyan side and the Ngurueme region in Tanzania. To the north-west is Lake Victoria with a small corridor occupied by the Luo. The immediate neighbours of the Kuria people are the Abagusii, Maasai, Ngurueme, Zanaki, Ikoma,

Luo, Suba and Kalenjin. According to the 2009 Kenyan Population and Housing Census (KPHC), the Kuria people number slightly over 300 000 (Republic of Kenya (ROK), 2019), with three times this number living in Tanzania. They speak Kuria language or *Igikuria*, which has mutually understandable dialects.

Among the Kuria, there are several celebrated life ceremonies, such as birth, naming, circumcision, marriage and death ceremonies. In this chapter, we focus on the circumcision ceremony.

At the ages of 13 and 15 respectively, girls and boys start being taught how to be men and women. It is at this time that they are prepared for circumcision. Boys are therefore expected to build their huts (*ichisiiga*) and move out of their mother's hut, while girls stay in their mother's hut until marriage. Preparations for girls' circumcision start many weeks and months before D-day. Invitations to the ceremony are issued by their parents, older siblings, aunts, and other relatives. On the day of circumcision, girls are escorted by aunts, relatives and friends to the circumcision ground, during which there is a lot of singing. Once circumcised, those girls who are considered brave are escorted home amidst celebrations and singing and are received by friends and relatives, given gifts, and praised for their courage. Those who show fear or cry are left to walk home alone and are not rewarded; nor is there any singing.

Once home, they are secluded for two weeks to one month, to allow them to heal. During this period, they are fed well and prohibited from doing any physical work. They are taught how to be women in the community, how to respect their husbands, (once married) and how to take care of children. At the end of the healing period there is a graduation or 'coming out' ceremony (*omooroko*). This is a one-day ceremony where it is declared that they are ready to come out of seclusion, to interact with members of the other sex and are ready for marriage and family responsibilities.

## FGM songs

FGM songs are performed during FGM ceremonies. These songs perform socialising roles for community members; they express the experiences of the particular group that uses them, and they set social norms for the community (Baquedano-Lopez, 2001). FGM songs carry ideological discourses that describe the communities that use them. Such discourses legitimise unequal social positions, for instance, while affirming the subservient position of some women in relation to others.

Among the Kuria people, the songs are performed by women. It is argued (Shuker, 2013) that, by performing songs that assert a female subservient position of some women to other women, women reconstruct a discourse that promotes a sexist culture (a culture that promotes underlying discriminatory discourses against women in the guise of female empowerment) (Lazar, 2005). Consequently, through perpetuating hegemonic discourses, these women become accomplices in their own oppression. Circumcision songs, as a genre of folk songs, are therefore of interest because of their role as carriers of ideologies, as embodiments of institutional values, and as performances of identity construction. As social discourse, they construct and reproduce asymmetrical gendered relations among the Kuria people in both domestic and social spheres. They therefore provide a forum through which power and equality ideals can be scrutinised. Additionally, the songs comprise FGM-related vocabulary and are rich in sociocultural aspects. In this chapter, FGM songs are analysed in this chapter because they normalise and legitimise violence against women while legitimating the subservient position of some women in relation to others.

## Female genital mutilation (FGM)

At least 200 million girls and women have been cut in 31 countries, with representative data on prevalence (UNICEF, 2022). In the UK, 130 000 girls and women live with the consequences of FGM, while 60 000 are at risk of the most severe forms of FGM (Beckford & Manning, 2016). Every five minutes in Africa, a girl undergoes FGM; in Kenya, 28% of women and girls have undergone FGM (Oloo, Wanjiru & Newell-Jones, 2011) despite its illegal status. It is, however, encouraging that, in Kenya, "the practice of FGM has decreased significantly" (Sabetti, Traversity, Gentilhomme & Dean, 2021). This figure (28%) has since declined to "Twenty-one percent of women aged 15-49" (Kong'ani, Robert & Lawrence, 2015:331). Even so, roughly 475 022 girls are at risk of FGM in Kenya between 2022 and 2030, and 75% of girls undergo the cut between the ages of eight and 14 (Kimeu, 2022).

FGM has been approached from different perspectives. One notable work is by Thomas (2003), who examines FGM among the Meru of Kenya from a historical perspective. Situated at the height of the Mau Mau rebellion in Kenya, Thomas's study focuses on, among other issues, a ban of FGM by the *Njuri Ncheke* and how that ban precipitated a surge in FGM cases in defiance of the ban. She observed that the defiance took two forms: women and girls were circumcised in large numbers, and some performed 'self-circumcision'. According to Thomas, the practice was a rite of passage that transformed girls into young women and provided them with the opportunity to learn how to become young women and to behave as future wives and daughters-in-law. Accordingly, circumcised women in the community were privileged, while the uncircumcised were chided, abused and called names. A different scenario obtained for girls who were still in school: Thomas points out that, when girls returned to school after holidays, they were checked by a British doctor to establish whether they had undertaken the cut. If found to have taken the cut, the girls were segregated and mistreated.

Other than preparing girls to become young women, the rite of passage also demonstrated an underlying power struggle between those who had undergone the traditional cut and those who had undertaken circumcision on their own (*Ngaituni*). Those who had undertaken the traditional cut considered themselves superior and chided those who had performed self-circumcision.

Although Thomas links the cut to the Mau Mau rebellion, the link is not fully explored. Instead, she reports that women who had circumcised themselves openly presented themselves to the *Njuri Ncheke* to take punishment for defying the FGM ban. It was also apparent that the girls and women did not have much choice, since those who did not defy the ban would be subjected to untold cruelty if apprehended by the Mau Mau.

Thomas's work has a similar focus to this chapter's, as it reiterates some of the traditional attitudes towards FGM in a similar way. However, it differs from the current study in two ways. Firstly, Thomas is ambivalent towards the practice. She refers to the FGM act as 'incision', which constructs FGM act as a non-violent action. We are committed to values espoused in Critical Discourse Analysis (CDA) and therefore view FGM as a violent violation of a woman. Secondly, Thomas's perspective is historical, while ours is linguistic. Accordingly, we focus more on linguistic resources used in propagating the FGM ideology, particularly the legitimation, trivialisation, and normalisation of a violent act through language. This is different from Thomas's focus. Although there are several available works on FGM, the role of language in normalising and legitimising it has not been considered, yet the practice that is powered by culture is enshrined in language. In Kenya, efforts made to end the practice have included legislation through "The Prohibition of Female Genital Mutilation Act, No. 32 of 2011" (ROK, 2011) and awareness campaigns, but these have not borne fruit and the practice persists, with the ceremonies taking place in Kuria every two years.

The discussion in this chapter views FGM as an ideology and focuses on the discursive strategies used to propagate it against Kuria women.

## Ideology and language

Thompson (1984) provides one of the most comprehensive examinations of ideology. He reviews definitions of ideology, the limitations of each, then further proposes his own definition. For example, his review shows that ideology is regarded as a 'set of beliefs and attitudes', a 'system of thought', a 'system of thought and speech'. Thompson is critical of this position because it is too general and does not show the connection between ideology and language. He also finds that ideology is viewed as 'symbol systems', 'language variants' and 'elaborated codes'; but he criticises these views for delinking ideology from class domination, which is core in Marx's postulation of ideology. Accordingly, Thompson (1984:130-131) defines ideology as "the ways in which meaning (signification) serves to sustain relations of domination".

Fairclough (2003:9) contends that ideologies are representations of aspects of the worlds, which can be shown to contribute to establishing, maintaining and changing social relations of power, domination and exploitation, while Dijk (1995:21), working with a socio-cognitive approach to CDA, acknowledges that his socio-cognitive approach is at variance with classical and other contemporary approaches to ideology and so views ideologies as "very specific basic frameworks of social cognition, with specific internal structures, and specific cognitive and social functions." Social cognition here refers to socially shared knowledge, i.e., sociocultural knowledge, attitudes and beliefs shared by members of social groups, organisations or institutions. This is a more apt definition that is adopted in this chapter as it focuses on ways that make ideologies commonsensical or normalised truths.

There is consensus that ideologies are expressed through language (see Dijk, 1995, Fairclough, 1992, 2001, 2010; Hart, 2010; and Thompson, 1984). For example, Thompson (1984:85) contends that ideology is tied very closely to the medium of linguistic communication, while Fairclough (1992:89) states that "ideologies reside in texts". Ideologies therefore manifest in a wide range of linguistic forms including, but not limited to, lexical, phonological, pragmatic, presuppositional, grammatical and rhetorical choices. Accordingly, the discussion of data in this chapter will draw the reader's attention to relevant linguistic elements (lexical items, metaphors, and rhetorical devices) in which the FGM ideology is encoded.

## FGM and the law

Leye et al. (2007) argue that legislation has been used as the main intervention tool in Europe since Western governments became aware of FGM among immigrants. Sweden became the first country to introduce specific laws prohibiting FGM through the 1982 Act Prohibiting Female Genital Mutilation (Leye & Sabbe, 2009). Currently, there are laws prohibiting FGM in most Western countries. In Europe, about 45 criminal court cases on suspected FGM have been tried and many convictions obtained (Leye & Sabbe, 2009). The UK witnessed a court prosecution case relating to FGM in May 2014 to May 2015, which involved Doctor Dhanuson Dharmasena, a consultant, who was called to help deliver the baby of a woman who had been infibulated.[1] He

---

1   **Infibulation**: Narrowing of the vaginal orifice with a covering seal. The seal is formed by cutting and re-positioning the labia minora and/or the labia majora. This can take place with or without removal of the clitoris (UNFPA, 2022).

cut the woman to deliver the baby but re-infibulated her to stop the bleeding caused (she had undergone infibulation at the age of six years). He was charged in court for allegedly perpetuating FGM, although the mother did not want him prosecuted. He has since been acquitted (Eleftheriou-Smith, 2015). In 1996, the UK government passed legislation that established criminal penalties for cutting girls under the age of 18. At the same time, the American Medical Association denounced all medically unnecessary procedures to alter female genitalia. In Africa, 24 countries out of the 28 in which FGM is practised have passed legislation against it. For instance, in Senegal, a law passed in 1999 makes it a crime to carry out FGM or to encourage anybody else to do it (*The Economist,* 1999). In 2015, an act outlawing FGM was officially passed into law in Nigeria (Muganzi, 2015). In Tanzania and Mauritius, FGM is illegal when performed on minors (Shell-Duncan & Hernlund, 2013). In Eritrea, Ethiopia and Togo, fines are levied, not only against practitioners, but also against anyone knowing about the practice and failing to report it (Shell-Duncan & Hernlund, 2013). In 1996 in Egypt, human rights advocates and women's groups successfully pressured the Egyptian government to issue regulations that prohibited ritual surgery on female genitals. Even with these legislative measures, UNICEF has emphasised that there is little research on the process and type of legislative reform needed in different contexts: "The role that legislation plays in promoting behaviour change in FGM/C is an area that is particularly complex, under-researched and not fully understood" (UNICEF, 2010:3).

### The Kenya Anti-FGM Act (2001, 2011)

In 2011, efforts to end FGM came into full force again when parliament passed a second Anti-FGM Act (2011), which prohibited FGM (Wangari, 2011). This Act was signed into law on 6 October 2011 after being drafted by the Kenya Women Parliamentary Association (KEWOPA), with support from the parliamentary council and UNFPA/ UNICEF's joint programme (Humphres, Abdi, Njue & Askew, 2007). Key aspects of the Act include a definition of FGM, the establishment of the Anti-FGM Board, an outline of its functions, the identification of FGM offences, and a stipulation of penalties for the offences contemplated in the Act. Accordingly, the Act criminalises all forms of FGM performed on anyone, regardless of age and status, and bans the stigmatisation of women who have not undergone FGM. It also makes it illegal to aid someone in performing FGM, taking them abroad to have the procedure done, and/or failing to report to the authorities if the individual was aware that FGM had taken place. The penalties for those violating this Act are severe: they include three to seven years' imprisonment or, in cases where the victim dies, life imprisonment for causing death by performing FGM; the penalty also includes a fine of up to one million Kenya shillings.

In addition to the Act, there are several constitutional provisions that indirectly outlaw FGM. Three of these are cited here:

*Article 44 (3)*

A person shall not compel another person to perform, observe or undergo *any cultural practice or rite.*

*Article 53 (1) (d)*

Every child has the right – to be protected from abuse, neglect, *harmful cultural practices, all forms of violence, inhuman treatment* and punishment, and hazardous or exploitative labour.

*Article 55 (d)*

The state shall take measures, including affirmative action programmes, to ensure that the youth – ... (d) are *protected from harmful cultural practices* and exploitation (ROK, 2010).

In each article, the constitution protects individuals from harmful practices such as female genital mutilation.

Additionally, Articles 2 (5) and (6) of the Constitution of Kenya, 2010 (ROK, 2010), provide that "the general rules of international law shall form part of the law of Kenya" and that "Any treaty or convention ratified by Kenya shall form part of the law of Kenya under this Constitution". Accordingly, all international human rights conventions signed by Kenya and which provide a strong basis for characterisation of FGM as a violation of human rights, such as the Convention on the Elimination of Discrimination Against Women (CEDAW); Convention on the Rights of the Child (CRC); International Convention on Economic, Social and Cultural Rights (ICESCR); Maputo Protocol to the African Charter on Human and People's Rights on the Rights of Women in Africa (The Maputo Protocol), and the African Charter on Human and People's Rights (The Banjul Charter) (UN Women, 2011) are part of Kenyan law. The African Union (AU) declared the years 2010-2020 to be the decade for African Women; and Kenya, which is a member, is expected to continue its commitment to promote and to protect the rights of women.

Finally, before The Kenya Children's Act 2001 (ILO, 2001) came into force, the second president of the Republic of Kenya, Daniel Moi, issued two presidential decrees banning FGM and prohibiting government-controlled hospitals from performing FGM (MYWO, 1992). In 1999, The Ministry of Health launched the National Plan of Action for the elimination of FGM in Kenya. This detailed the government's commitment to ending the practice (MOH, 1999). This was later revised as Sessional Paper No 3 of 2019 in order to align it with the Constitution of Kenya, 2010 (ROK, 2019). The National Plan of Action for the elimination of FGM in Kenya (1999) was followed by the passing of the Children's Act (ILO, 2001). This came into full force in 2002 and made FGM illegal for girls under 18 years. The penalties under the Act include 12 months' imprisonment and/or a fine of up to fifty thousand Kenya shillings (approximately $500). There were cases of court charges after this Act, but the efforts were hindered by widespread criticism that the Act offered inadequate protection and did not apply to adult women who were also being subjected to the practice. The Act was said to have failed to curb FGM because it was poorly implemented (Oloo et al., 2011).

To date, there have been several successful prosecutions under the 2011 Act (see Wangari, 2011; *Pauline Robi Ngariba v Republic* Criminal Law Appeal No 6 of 2014). Although FGM has been declared illegal in Kenya, there is a clash between subscription to international norms and local socio-political allegiances. The commitment to protect community interests and minority rights and the protection and promotion of cultural aspects as outlined in the Kenyan Constitution (2010), have been used by practitioners to fight the government's efforts to end the practice. For fear of being demonised by these minority communities, the government is ambivalent: it positions itself in the middle, both with and against the international community.

However, this ambivalence has since been resolved in the ruling of the Constitutional Petition No. 244 of 2019. In the *Tatu Kamau* v *Attorney General & 2 others, Equality Now & 9 others (Interested Parties), Katiba Institute & another Constitutional Petition 244 of 2019*, Dr Tatu Kamau (a medical doctor), challenged the constitutionality of the Prohibition of Female Genital Mutilation Act, No. 32 of 2011 (ROK, 2011) and the Anti-Female Genital Mutilation Board formed thereunder (hereinafter 'the Act' and 'the Board' respectively). The appellant pleaded that Sections 2, 5, 19, 20 and 21 of the Act contravene Articles 19, 27, 32 and 44 of the Constitution of Kenya (ROK, 2010) by limiting women's choice and right to uphold and respect their culture, ethnic identity, religion, and beliefs, and by discriminating between men and women. One of the questions that the court set out to determine was whether it was constitutional to prohibit an adult woman from freely choosing to undergo FGM under the hand of a trained and licensed medical practitioner. The court dismissed the petition, arguing that it was not persuaded that one can choose to undergo a harmful practice.

## Methodology

This chapter is derived from research conducted in Kuria, Kenya, in 2015 (Wambura, 2015). Data constituted 25 FGM songs and interview responses. For data collection, a multi-method approach involving three methods was adopted: audio recording, interviewing, and observation/taking field notes. The researcher participated in the FGM ceremonies as an observer and recorded FGM songs as and while they were being performed. She also conducted interviews for women and men involved in the ceremonies that season. A total of 25 songs were collected. Of these 12 were sampled for analysis if it "illuminated some features or process in which we are interested (Silverman 1993:387). In our case, a song was sampled if it focused on the FGM act, praised the initiates and women who have undergone the practice, if it spelt out the consequences of not undertaking the FGM act bravely, if it minimised or trivialised the FGM act or expressed the community's attitude towards uncircumcised women. On the basis of the last criterion, metaphors and lexical items were also sampled.

The target linguistic features were analysed using Fairclough's Textually Oriented Discourse Analysis. The identified features enabled the analyst to answer the question, 'Which lexical items and metaphors are employed in legitimating FGM?' From the analysis, it was possible to show how categories of women were differentiated through the words chosen to describe and label them; and, through this naming and labelling process, violence against one group of women was propagated by another group of women.

Following critical discourse analysis principles, analysis began with identifying the most dominant items and working through to the least dominant while numbering accordingly. Of importance was how women (circumcised and uncircumcised) were positioned in relation to each other, and the lexical items used to represent them through references to their roles and behavioural expectations.

Two tables list identified lexical items and metaphors that were relevant in addressing the issue at hand. The tables have two sections, each with lexical items and metaphors representing circumcised and uncircumcised women. See Table 8.1 for lexical items:

**TABLE 8.1**   Selected lexical items in the circumcision songs and their frequencies (the number in brackets indicates the frequency of the word in the songs)

| Circumcised women | Uncircumcised women |
|---|---|
| Attributive nouns | Attributive nouns |
| Rock (17) | Uncircumcised (7) |
| Server (4) | Dog (1) |
| Water fetcher (4) | |
| Soda (3) | |
| Solar (3) | |
| Ship (2) | |
| Bomb (2) | |
| Tree (2) | |
| Chicken (1) | |

| Circumcised women | Uncircumcised women |
|---|---|
| **Descriptive nouns** | |
| Her beauty lies in her: | |
| Teeth (5) | |
| Necklaces (3) | |
| Beads (3) | |
| Beautiful hair (2) | |
| Belts (2) | |
| Earrings (2) | |
| **Verbs** | **Verbs** |
| Spreads (7) | Embarrasses (4) |
| Serves (5) | Touches the circumciser (2) |
| Closes the gate (4) | |
| Opens the gate (4) | |
| Gives birth (3) | |
| Laughs (3) | |
| Cooks (2) | |
| Adorns (2) | |
| Entices (2) | |

Focus was on how the identified linguistic features (lexical items) contributed to maintaining unequal power relations, legitimising, or reifying the state of affairs, and how the lexical items represented and positioned circumcised women as more powerful than the uncircumcised. The study examined whether uncircumcised women were being repeatedly denigrated and trivialised or positioned in subordinate (or dominant) roles (as suggested by Alemu, 2007) compared to their circumcised counterparts. Recurring lexical items, as well as those appearing once only, were considered, bearing in mind that lexis relates to ideology because the meanings of words and wordings of meanings are matters that are socially variable and socially contested as they are facets of a wider social and cultural process (Fairclough, 1992). Fairclough (2010) stresses that words are not neutral, and choices can be used to normalise the power of particular groups over others (see also Wodak & Meyer, 2016) and to advance certain ideologies. The choice of words to describe a particular circumcised or uncircumcised woman indicates the Kuria society's interest, attitude, and feelings towards the women. Table 8.2 shows a list of metaphors used for the circumcised and uncircumcised women.

During the interviews, interviewees' opinions were obtained on different aspects of FGM and violence against women in order to corroborate insights derived from our analysis of the songs. These two methods were also triangulated, with data derived from observation of FGM ceremonies in which the researchers participated.

**TABLE 8.2**   Metaphors in the female circumcision songs and their frequencies

| Circumcised women | Uncircumcised women |
| --- | --- |
| Rock (17) | Dog (1) |
| Soda (3) | |
| Solar (3) | |
| Earrings (2) | |
| Bomb (2) | |
| Ship (2) | |
| Tree (2) | |
| Chicken (1) | |

# Theoretical framework

This chapter makes use of Critical Discourse Analysis (CDA) in describing how language works. CDA speaks to, and also intervenes in, social and political issues, problems and controversies in the world and is committed to social critique, "critical social analysis" (Fairclough 2013:9).

Critical Discourse Analysis (CDA) has a "starting point in social issues and problems" (Fairclough, 2001:229), such as violence against women. It does not begin with texts and interactions but with issues that preoccupy sociologists, political scientists and/ or educationists (Fairclough, ibid.). CDA is therefore theoretically well placed to seek, identify, and explain the workings of discourses and the discursive legitimation of violence against women. Using CDA presupposes a power discrepancy, that is, that one group is relatively marginalised within asymmetrical power relations.

Conducting a critical discourse analysis on the topic of violence against women is important in the development of an understanding of the underlying ideologies, power struggles and mitigating factors underlying the practice of FGM at local, national, and international levels. A focus on Kenya, and particularly Kuria, is appropriate because, despite anti-FGM campaigns and efforts made to end the practice, it persists and is publicly conducted.

Methodologically, this chapter is based on a version of CDA by Norman Fairclough's (2001) textually oriented discourse analysis. This framework includes three stages of analysis: description, interpretation, and explanation. In the description stage, we identify lexical items and metaphorical structures used in the songs and relating to FGM. In the interpretation stage, we explore intertextuality (how songs draw on the context of Kuria society), and interdiscursivity (looking at the order of discourses and how some discourses shore up others). In the explanation stage, we examine the effect of the linguistic representations on normalisation and perpetuation of FGM and violence against women. It is worth noting that Fairclough's approach is appropriate for this kind of analysis due to its focus on power inequalities because, where there are inequalities, some groups suffer. In this case, girls' rights are violated. Sunderland (2004:28) argues that discourses are not always recognised easily; they "are not simply out there waiting to be spotted". Instead, as Baker (2008:95) argues, "what is there are linguistic features: 'marks on the page', words spoken or even people's memories of previous conversations, which, if sufficient and coherent, may suggest that they are 'traces' of a particular discourse." The focus here is on discourses that legitimate violence.

To be effective, discourses must have the characteristic of repetition (Baker, 2008), although single instances (and absences) are also considered. An analyst does not only consider repetition but also the articulation of a discourse by a powerful speaker and how accessible the discourse is to a large number of people. In the case under discussion, discourses of violence are articulated in a subtle manner by older women; and, since these women are considered to be knowers with a powerful position in the asymmetrical relations that characterise women in Kuria, they are not challenged. This work sets out to challenge this status quo.

Once a discourse has been identified and named, it is important to look at its social significance, and to find out how it positions social actors, for instance, women and men, boys and girls. This is because any discourse is not just a concept but also a social and constitutive process. Particular discourses construct women, men, girls, and boys in unequal ways, and such positions are taken up as the norm and not challenged.

Different discourses do not simply reflect different realities but play an active role in creating realities, identities and relationships by constructing and maintaining ideologies that shore them up. Potentially, there is an infinite number of available discourses. Certain discourses have evolved throughout history into dominant discourses, whilst others have become marginalised. The knowledges, behaviours and meanings embodied in dominant discourses are those that emerge as permissible or desirable in a particular society. In this way, they develop into culturally dominant discourses about what kinds of knowledges are valid and what behaviours and meanings are permissible (Sauntson, 2012). Dominant discourses accrue power, making them difficult to challenge. The less they are challenged, the more they become normalised: they take on the appearance of being naturally occurring, stable and inevitable. Beneath these overt discourses is a form of power that is not explicit to everyone, but which plays a role in the normalisation process.

Dominant discourses, such as the FGM discourses, promote the idea that there is one absolute truth. This is relevant in this chapter because dominant discourses about violence against women in the African society have been normalised through the naturalisation process so that, among the Kuria, for example, it appears natural and true that circumcised women should exhibit behaviour and knowledge that is perceived as superior, while uncircumcised women should exhibit behaviour that is perceived as inferior. These dominant discourses put ideological constraints upon what is socially and culturally acceptable as power-filled and powerless behaviour. The effect of this normalisation process is that, if one group behaves in a way that is not considered 'normal' within dominant discourses in that context, members of that group are perceived as behaving unnaturally and constructed as socially deviant in terms of their identity. In African contexts, they are labelled, criticised and punished.

## Discussion

FGM songs that were the subject of this chapter are a discursive structure that communicates and perpetuates the community's ideology (what Dijk (1995:18) refers to as "socially shared attitudes").

Three ideologies are evident in the songs: FGM as beautification; FGM as a rite of passage, and FGM as an easy undertaking, as will be illustrated next.

### FGM as a rite of passage

The songs suggest that FGM has a transformative role: a role that transforms a Kuria girl into a Kuria woman. This is evident in Song No. 9, which is sung after women have been circumcised. The persona explains:

> Song 9
>
> Today she has become a rock
> Our child has become
> Has become a *woman* like others
> She has become a soda, she has become a solar, she has become a rock
> Our child has become a *woman* like others

This excerpt suggests that, by undergoing FGM, a Kuria girl transforms in four different ways: she becomes a 'rock' (line 1), a 'woman' (line 2), a 'soda' and a 'solar' (line 34). Each of these transformations is significant. Excerpt 2 suggests that the word 'rock' has different meanings:

> Song 3
>
> Our sons dance slowly
> A small rock of a woman was born

Song 9
She has become a rock
She has become a rock
*Eye ee eye*
Our child has become
She has become a woman like others
She has become a rock

The word 'rock' has three meanings and interpretations: the two types of rocks used in the songs are *akagena* (small rock) and *irigena* (normal rock). A small rock (*akagena*) is used for a girl who is being prepared to be circumcised; it is therefore commonly included in the songs that are performed during preparation and the day before circumcision. That she has accepted and is ready to undergo FGM makes her a 'small rock', meaning that she is prepared to withstand any pain and/or can bear it, just like the grinding stone does. Once she is circumcised, she becomes a rock (*irigena*). The word 'rock' normally refers to a man – a firstborn son is described as the 'rock of the family'; and any man who has been successful is also described as a 'rock'. Therefore, once circumcised, the woman becomes a 'rock': she becomes dependable (one of the characteristics ideologically associated with men) by virtue of the fact that she has borne the pain.

The circumcised woman also becomes a proper member of society by being initiated into womanhood. As a woman, she can be married at any time and, most importantly, she can bear children. Therefore, with FGM comes an elevation of a woman's low status from childhood to being marriageable. FGM therefore positions circumcised women as being in a higher marriageable position than those who are not circumcised.

The 'soda' and 'solar' metaphors are used together to refer to circumcised women. Asked about why they said ("she has become a soda"), the response was that, before circumcision, she could not be 'eaten', literally meaning that she could not give in to sexual relations (read 'marriage'), but now she has a right to 'be taken' like a soda. She is now sweet for men to drink from her 'source'. This means that, with FGM, a girl is free to engage sexually with any man who wishes to seek her hand in marriage in the same way a soda is available for anyone who can afford it. On the other hand, the solar metaphor is used to mean she can illuminate herself and attract men towards her since she is ready for marriage. Solar panels are a recent phenomenon in Kuria. Only a few homesteads that are considerably rich can afford them. They are considered expensive but of great value, compared to the usual cloth lamp (*ekoroboi*), or tin lamp (*etara*) whose light is not as bright as that of a solar-charged battery. Without light there is darkness, so the use of the 'solar metaphor' for circumcised women shows their value compared to the uncircumcised whose use is short-lived. Circumcised women are ideologically perceived to be a bright light that can be seen from a distance, which attracts many suitors, just like a bright light attracts many insects. The metaphor also suggests that, as solar lights last longer, the women will perpetuate the continuity of the family line of the men who marry them. This underpins the expected role and behaviour of a Kuria woman once married. The two metaphors are only used with reference to the circumcised women, so one who is not circumcised lacks these qualities.

## FGM as an easy undertaking

In the songs, FGM is presented as a painless activity, a normal and natural thing to go through, and as an easy task to undertake. This normalisation of FGM and the trivialisation of the pain serves to make it expectable of and acceptable to those who have not gone through it. The pain associated with the FGM act is diminished through euphemisms like, 'prick', 'pick', 'touch' and 'nothing' to describe it. The first of these three carry connotations of less pain, unlike 'cut', which conjures up images of more intense pain; and the last totally removes the possibility of any pain resulting from the FGM cut when the woman bears the pain, as expressed in Song 12: "When you bear it, it is nothing". Similarly, diminished pain is suggested in wording chosen to explain the duration of the FGM cut. In Song 21, the persona indicates how quickly the act takes place: "She just touches twice, and she is up"; "It is only twice she touches and gets up"; and in Song 13: "She only bends twice, and she gets up". The minimisers "just" and "only" used in the descriptions suggest that the FGM act happens within seconds. It is presumed that such a quick act cannot be painful.

The FGM act is also, discursively, presented as a playful act as exemplified in the apparent play with words: 'touch', 'pick', and 'prick' in Song 23:

> **Song 23**
>
> If she is *touching* let her *touch*
>
> …
>
> If she is *picking* let her *pick*
>
> …
>
> If she is *pricking* let her *prick*

These ways of talking about the FGM act make it seem a painless, normal, and natural process to undertake. This therefore entices the Kuria women to undergo the FGM cut.

The FGM act is also trivialised and presented as a normal, everyday activity to which the girls are accustomed and which they find enjoyable, such as grinding millet or stirring porridge. In Song 12, the persona talks about what she witnessed:

> **Song 12**
>
> When I saw her (the circumciser) kneeling I thought she was *grinding*
> I thought she was *grinding* so I could *stir* for her (our emphasis)

Using verbs that portray everyday actions, such as "grinding" and "stir", which the girls are used to, and which they find easy and enjoyable, is a discursive strategy employed by the songs' producers to portray FGM as normal as any other activities they undertake every day.

Because of this trivialisation, it is expected that the women will undergo the FGM cut. However, when this does not work, threats of banishment are issued instead. For example, in Songs 1, 3 and 13, the uncircumcised woman is threatened with banishment.

### Song 1

If you *embarrass* us in broad daylight
**Go** and be circumcised in Luo land
With those who circumcised teeth, feet and finger nails

### Song 3

And we are telling you to bear it, to be strong
If you *embarrass* us go that way
**Go** to the uncircumcised the Luo
Those who circumcise teeth and umbilical spots

### Song 13

When you *embarrass* us go that way/ don't come back
Go to the uncircumcised, the Luo
and
If you *embarrass* us go far (our emphasis)

This threat to strip these women of their identity as Kuria woman serves to instil fear of loss of their name and sense of belonging among their people, thereby compelling young girls to give in to the demands.

"Failing to bear the pain appropriately", "embarrassing" and "going to the Luo" are discursively repeated in Songs 12, 13 and 14, with the girl being admonished against touching the circumciser's hand since that is taboo. Note that one who touches the circumciser's hand (Song 12) or pulls her stomach up (Song 14) (traditionally interpreted as signs of fear) is equated to the one who is not circumcised at all and she is therefore not a proper woman, even if she has been cut. Such girls are ostracised and cast away to the Luo community because they are considered to belong among those who do not 'circumcise properly'. The Luo rite of passage, which, traditionally entails the removal of teeth, is derogated as that of those who "circumcise teeth, feet, fingernails and umbilical spots". Incidentally, this threat to banish persons who express fear during circumcision is not peculiar to the Kuria. Sure and Satia (2017:29) find a similar threat issued to Bukusu boys being escorted to face the circumciser. They are warned: *Omusinde oterema kaachia Ebunyolo* (Bukusu language) meaning, 'the initiate who trembles should go to *Ebunyolo*, the land of the Luo'.

Additionally, not being circumcised also strips a woman of her dignity. This is evident in Song 23 where the persona states:

Song 23

The one with dry legs please crow
So, I can be taken off this bad uncircumcised state
The state that has made me not be greeted *Nyamwita*
The state that has made me called a dog

In this example, the girl reminisces about her state as an uncircumcised woman: "The state that has made me be called a dog" and "the state that has made me not be greeted *Nyamwita*". *Nyamwita* is a respectable title given to women who have given birth to a firstborn son and named him Mwita. It therefore literally means 'one of Mwita' or 'one with Mwita'. A Kuria lady is only allowed to give birth and name a child after undergoing FGM. So, in order to vacate that unpleasant status, she is fired up for the FGM act and desires that she undergoes it as fast as possible. She therefore says, "Someone give me a sisal rope so that I can cane the night with it to dawn fast" and calls on "The one with dry legs [the cockerel], please crow so that I can be taken off this bad uncircumcised state".

## FGM as beautification

In addition to the transformations already discussed, it is evident that FGM is also viewed as an act of beautification and this is what, additionally, makes the circumcised Kuria woman marriageable. In Song 7, the persona, talking about how the FGM act is conducted, states that the circumciser "touches like it is a *beauty cut*", while in Song 21, the same act is referred to as a *"beauty prick"* (our emphasis). Beauty is regarded as a useful attribute for a woman who intends to be married because it is what attracts wealthy suitors. In Song 14, it is apparent that women deliberately adorn themselves to attract the attention of potential suitors:

Song 14

Women will collect the beads and adorn themselves
They will walk around enticing men
They will entice men so that their fathers can get cattle
Those that are brown and black

Such suitors pay the bride price in the form of cows. The songs show that, where a suitor has no cows of his own, he will raid neighbouring communities to steal them. This is revealed in Song 8, where a male voice in the song states:

Song 8

Our women are like earrings
Those that we see and run fast
We go to get cattle from our enemies
We get the enemies' cattle by force and bring them home.

Given that marriage takes place after circumcision, it seems that it is only after circumcision that a woman becomes sweet and attractive and marriageable. This view tends to reinforce the discourse that the 'woman's body needs readjustment'.

In addition to beautification, FGM confers positive attributes on the Kuria woman. This is why such a woman is compared to Hillary Clinton, one of America's most powerful women. The persona in Song 23, while reminiscing over with what she can compare a woman preparing to undergo FGM, says:

> Song 23
>
> My sister, what can I compare you to?
> You are like Clinton the boisterous one.

The fact that Clinton vied for presidency constructs her as a strong, courageous, and powerful woman – and this is how the circumcised woman is viewed among the Kuria. This is not surprising because the circumcised woman among the Kuria is elevated to the level of men. Wambura (2016) finds that the Kuria society has three levels of hierarchy: men, circumcised women, uncircumcised women. The comparison of a circumcised woman to Clinton, therefore, confers power, strength and courage on the circumcised woman. In contrast, the persona makes no mention of any positive attributes associated with the uncircumcised woman. This elision, which is a subtle construction of the 'other', implies that the uncircumcised woman is unattractive and can therefore not be associated with Clinton's positive attributes.

## Conclusions

This chapter has sought to examine FGM as an ideology that has been normalised among the Kuria and has focused on the discursive strategies used to propagate the ideology. It has been demonstrated that the FGM ideology is perpetuated in subtle ways: FGM is portrayed as a necessary rite of passage, as an easy undertaking, and as a beautification process. Consequently, women who undergo the FGM cut are hailed, while those who are uncircumcised, or do not undergo it 'properly', are devalued and derogated by being threatened with banishment, being stripped of their identity and by being admonished and despised. However, these are overt strategies. At the discursive level, the FGM ideology is perpetuated through using metaphors with positive connotations, such as 'rock', 'solar' and 'soda', and through minimisers and euphemisms. Minimisers ensure that the pain associated with FGM is trivialised and therefore normalised. More subtle discursive strategies included the use of repetition, for example, repeatedly warning women not to 'embarrass' them, or that, if they do not endure the pain, they should go to 'Luoland'. The same repetition is noted in the play on words such as "pick" and "picking" (Song 23).

Although the discourses around FGM tend to reinforce the ideology, thereby making it difficult to eradicate the vice, a two-pronged approach is required in this fight. First, clarity about FGM-related laws is required. Towards this end, it is commendable that the Constitutional Court has pronounced itself on the question of constitutionality of practising FGM in view of constitutional provisions in the Bill of rights. The next strategy should now target a change in discourses on FGM so as to portray FGM as a violent practice that dehumanises women.

# References


Alemu, A. 2007. Oral narrative as an ideological weapon for the subordinating of women: A case of Jimma Oromo. *Journal of African Cultural Studies*, 19(1):55-79. https://doi.org/10.1080/13696810701485934

Baquedano-Lopez, P. 2001. Creating social identities through Doctrina narratives. In: E. Duranti (ed.). *Linguistic anthropology: A reader.* Malden: Blackwell. 343-358.

Beckford, M. & Manning, S. 2016. MPs condemn FGM in Britain as 'a national scandal' but official NHS figures say fewer than five have been carried out in the UK. *Mail Online (The Mail on Sunday),* 2 April. https://www.dailymail.co.uk/news/article-3520730/MPs-condem-FGM-Britain-national-scandal-official-NHS-figures-say-fewer-five-carried-UK.html [Accessed 30 November 2022].

Dijk, T.A. 1995. Discourse analysis as ideology analysis. In: C. Schäffner & A. Wenden (eds.). *Language and peace.* Aldershot: Dartmouth Publishing. 17-33.

*Economist.* 1999. Female genital mutilation: is it a crime or culture?. 11 February. https://www.economist.com/international/1999/02/11/is-it-crime-or-culture [Accessed 25 December 2022].

Eleftheriou-Smith, L.M. 2015. FGM: What is female genital mutilation and why was the first doctor to stand trial in the UK acquitted? *Independent*, 5 February. http://www.independent.co.uk/news/uk/crime/fgm-what-is-female-genital-mutilation-and-why-was-the-first-doctor-to-stand-trial-in-the-uk-10027205.html [Accessed 30 November 2022].

Fairclough, N. 1992. *Discourse and social change.* Cambridge: Polity Press.

Fairclough, N. 2001. *Language and power.* 2nd Edition. London: Longman Group.

Fairclough, N. 2003. *Analysing discourse: Textual analysis for social research.* London: Routledge. https://doi.org/10.4324/9780203697078

Fairclough, N. 2010. *Critical discourse analysis: The critical study of language.* 2nd Edition. London: Routledge.

Fairclough, N. 2013. Critical discourse analysis. In: J.P. Gee & M. Handford. *The Routledge handbook of discourse analysis.* London: Routledge. 9-20.

Hart, C. 2010. *Critical discourse analysis and cognitive science: New perspectives on immigration discourse.* Houndmills, Basingstoke, UK: Palgrave Macmillan.

Humphres, E., Abdi, M.S., Njue, C. & Askew, A. 2007. *Contributing towards efforts to abandon female genital mutilation/cutting in Kenya: A situational analysis.* Nairobi, Kenya: Ministry of Gender, Sports, Culture and Social Services.

ILO (International Labour Organization). 2001. Children's Act. *Official Gazette, No. 8 of 2001, Kenya.* Nairobi, Kenya. 493-680. NATLEX (Database of national labour, social security and related human rights legislation). http://www.ilo.org/dyn/natlex/natlex4.detail?p_lang=en&p_isn=61290 [Accessed 30 November 2022].

Kimeu, C. 2022. 'Every chemist has a backroom': the rise of secret FGM in Kenya. *The Guardian.* 15 December. https://www.theguardian.com/society/2022/dec/15/every-chemist-has-a-backroom-how-medicalised-fgm-risks-gains-made-in-kenya# [Accessed 30 December 2022].

Kong'ani, R.U.K., Robert, C.B.B. & Lawrence, I. 2015. Female genital cutting in Kenya. In: *Kenya demographic and health survey.* Kenya National Bureau of Statistics: Nairobi. 331-349. https://www.dhsprogram.com/publications/publication-fr308-dhs-final-reports.cfm [Accessed 30 January 2023].

Lazar, M.M. (ed.). 2005. *Feminist critical discourse analysis: Gender, ideology and power in discourse.* Basingstoke, UK: Palgrave Macmillan. https://doi.org.10.1057/97802 30599901

Leye, E., Deblonde, J., Garcia-Anon, J. & Johnsdotter, S. 2007. An analysis of the implementation of laws with regard to female genital mutilation in Europe. *Crime, Law and Social Change,* 47(1):1-31. https://doi.org/10.1007/s10611-007-9055-7

Leye, E. & Sabbe, A. 2009 *Overview of legislation in the European Union to address female genital mutilation, challenges and recommendations for the implementation of laws.* Addis Ababa, Ethiopia: UN.

Muganzi, R. 2015. Female genital mutilation outlawed in Nigeria. *Kuchu Times,* 8 June. https://www.kuchutimes.com/2015/06/female-genital-mutilation-outlawed-in-nigeria/ [Accessed 30 November 2022].

MOH (Ministry of Health, Kenya). 1999. *National Plan of Action for Elimination of Female Genital Mutilation.* Nairobi: MOH.

MYWO (Maendeleo ya Wanawake Organization). 1992. *Traditional practices that affect the Health of Women and Children.* Nairobi: Maendeleo ya Wanawake Publications. https://sussex.primo.exlibrisgroup.com/permalink/44SUS_INST/iv463q/alma993 28911902461 [Accessed 30 January 2023].

Oloo, H., Wanjiru M. & Newell-Jones, K. 2011. *Female genital mutilation practices in Kenya: The role of alternative rites of passage: A case study of Kisii and Kuria districts.* London: Feed the Minds. https://doi.org/10.31899/rh2.1075

Organization of American States (OAS). 1994. Inter-American Convention on the Prevention, Punishment, and Eradication of Violence against Women ("Convention of Belem do Para"). https://www.refworld.org/docid/3ae6b38b1c.html [Accessed 30 November 2022].

ROK (Republic of Kenya). 2010. *The Constitution of Kenya, 2010.* Nairobi: Government Printers. http://kenyalaw.org/kl/index.php?id=398 [Accessed 30 November 2022].

ROK (Republic of Kenya). 2011. *Prohibition of Female Genital Mutilation Act, No. 32 of 2011.* Nairobi: National Council for Law Reporting. http://kenyalaw.org:8181/exist/kenyalex/actview.xql?actid=No.%2032%20of%202011 [Accessed 1 December 2022].

ROK (Republic of Kenya). 2019a. *2019 Kenya Population and Housing Census Vol IV: Distribution of Population by Socio-Economic Characteristics.* Nairobi: Kenya National Bureau of Statistics. https://bit.ly/391hUjb [Accessed 15 September 2021].

ROK (Republic of Kenya) 2019b. Sessional paper no. 3 of 2019 on national policy for the eradication of female genital mutilation towards a society free from harmful cultural practices.

Sauntson, H. 2012. *Approaches to gender and spoken classroom discourse.* London: Palgrave Macmillan. https://doi.org/10.1057/9780230343580

Shell-Duncan, B. & Hernlund, Y. 2013. Legislating change? Responses to criminalising female genital mutilation. *Law and Society Review,* 47(4):803-835. https://doi.org/10.1111/lasr.12044

Shuker, R. 2013. *Understanding popular music.* 4th Edition. London: Routledge. https://doi.org/10.4324/9780203188019

Silverman, D. 1993. *Interpreting qualitative data: Methods for analysis of talk, text and interaction.* 3rd Edition. London: Sage.

Sunderland, J. 2004. *Gendered discourses.* Basingstoke: Palgrave. https://doi.org/10.1057/9780230505582

Sure, K.E. & Satia, E. 2017. Language crimes: language and grammar of hate speech in Kenya. *Journal of the Department of Swahili & Other African Languages, Moi University,* 1(1):21-37.

Thomas, M.L. 2003. *Politics of the womb: Women, reproduction and the state in Kenya.* Berkeley, CA: University of California Press. https://doi.org/10.1525/9780520936645

Thompson, J.B. 1984. *Studies in the theory of ideology.* Berkeley, CA: University of California Press.

UN Women (United Nations Women). 2011. *Sources of international human rights law on female genital mutilation.* https://www.endvawnow.org/en/articles/645-sources-of-international-human-rights-law-on-female-genital-mutilation.html [Accessed 30 January 2023].

UNFPA (United Nations Population Fund). 2022. *Female genital mutilation (FGM) questions.* https://www.unfpa.org/resources/female-genital-mutilation-fgm-frequently-asked-questions [Accessed 10 January 2023].

UNICEF (United Nations Children's Fund). 2010. *The dynamics of social change: Towards the abandonment of female genital mutilation/cutting in five African countries.* Report. Florence, Italy: UNICEF Innocenti Research Centre. https://data.unicef.org/resources/the-dynamics-of-social-change-towards-the-abandonment-of-female-genital-mutilationcutting-in-five-african-countries/ [Accessed 30 November 2022].

UNICEF (United Nations Children's Fund). 2022. *Female genital mutilation (FGM).* https://data.unicef.org/topic/child-protection/female-genital-mutilation/ [Accessed 1 February 2023].

Wambura, J.B. 2015. The shields and the earrings: Challenging female genital mutilation (FGM) practices in Kenya through critical linguistic analysis. A paper presented at the *British Association for Applied Linguistics (BAAL) Conference.* Aston University, Birmingham. 3-5 September.

Wambura J.B. 2018. Gender and language practices in female circumcision ceremonies in Kuria, Kenya. PhD thesis. Leeds, UK: University of Leeds.

Wangari, F. 2011. Cultural rite. Daily nation special report. *Daily Nation,* 14 August. 18-19.

WHO (World Health Organization). 2019. *Female genital mutilation.* https://www.who.int/news-room/factsheets/detail/female-genital-mutilation [Accessed 10 December 2021].

Wodak, R. 1997. *Gender and discourse.* London: Sage. https://doi.org/10.4135/9781446250204

Wodak, R. & Meyer, M. 2016. Critical discourse studies: History, agenda, theory and methodology. In: R. Wodak & M. Meyer (eds.). *Methods of critical discourse analysis.* 3rd Edition. London: Sage. 1-22.

## Case Law

*Pauline Robi Ngariba* v *Republic* Criminal Law Appeal No 6 of 2014. http://kenyalaw.org/caselaw/cases/view/101111/ [Accessed 31 January 2023].

*Tatu Kamau* v *Attorney General & 2 others, Equality Now & 9 others (Interested Parties), Katiba Institute & another.* Constitutional Petition 244 of 2019 (Formerly Machakos High Court Petition 8 of 2017).[2] http://kenyalaw.org/caselaw/cases/view/209223/ [Accessed 31 January 2023].

---

2   This case had many interested parties listed below:
    Tatu Kamau (Petitioner)
    and
    The Hon. Attorney General (1st Respondent)
    Anti-Female Genital Mutilation Board (2nd Respondent)
    The Director of Public Prosecutions (3rd Respondent)
    and
    Equality Now (Interested Party)
    Equality Commission (Interested Party)
    Federation of Women Lawyers (FIDA-K) (Interested Party)
    Samburu Girls Foundation (Interested Party)
    Msichana Empowerment Kuria (Interested Party).

# FUELLING THE FEAR FACTORY

## A rhetorical criticism of selected South African television news reports on violence against women and children

*Sisanda Nkoala*

## Introduction

Crime is one of the most dominant issues that societies grapple with, because it affects us individually, as we worry about our safety, and it also influences public policy by informing what governments prioritise. In South Africa, where the level of crime, particularly violent contact crimes, such as murder and rape, is significantly higher than in many other countries around the world (United Nations Office of Drugs and Crime, 2018), this is a problem uppermost in people's minds. Moreover, there seems to be a discrepancy between laws on paper aimed at mitigating crime problems and actual laws that do not reduce crime rates in this context (Newham, 2005; Plessis & Louw, 2005; Deane, 2018; Chitsamatanga & Rembe, 2020). This has implications for how crime and justice, as notions, are understood (Pelser & Rauch, 2001). This study undertakes a rhetorical criticism of selected mass news reports on the criminal justice system in South Africa, with a particular focus on news reports aired over the 16 Days of Activism for No Violence against Women and Children from 25 November to 10 December 2020. The question the study sought to answer is: How did selected South African television news reports during the 16 Days of Activism for No Violence against Women and Children use language to depict these crimes? There do not appear to have been any recent studies that have looked at news media coverage of the 16 Days of Activism campaign in South Africa in the last 15 years, which is one of the imperatives for this particular study.

The 16 Days of Activism against Gender-Based Violence is described here:

> ... an annual international campaign that kicks off on November 25, the International Day for the Elimination of Violence against Women, and runs until December 10, Human Rights Day. It was started by activists at the inaugural Women's Global Leadership Institute in 1991 and continues to be coordinated each year by the Center for Women's Global Leadership. It is used as an organizing strategy by individuals and organizations around the world to call for the prevention and elimination of violence against women and girls. (United Nations Women, 2021)

Every year, a global theme is declared, and countries around the world participate in observing the campaign in different ways. During this period, the news media coverage of violence against women and children increases (Harries & Bird, 2005). However, as well-intentioned as this may be, studies have exposed several shortcomings in news coverage, which they find undermine what the noble campaign aims to achieve. Buthelezi's (2006) work shows how, by using language and visuals that perpetuate gender stereotypes, isiZulu newspaper reports published during the campaign tend to disempower the very victims for whom they are purportedly advocating. Meanwhile, Harries and Bird's (2005) study of over 36 South African radio, television, and print news reports concludes that these reports limit the extent to which survivors of abuse can shape the discourse on the violence they experience because news publications do not give them sufficient space to tell their own stories.

This study builds on this earlier work and undertakes a rhetorical criticism of South African television news reports on violent crimes against women and children. Here rhetoric is defined as, "the use of language as a symbolic means of inducing cooperation in beings that by nature respond to symbols" (Burke, 1969:43). Central to this view of rhetoric is that language can be used as a tool to make people do things physically, or think about things in a certain way, as expressed in his conceptualisation of language as symbolic action. The view of the use of language in news reports as symbolic action is relevant for this study because it directs the analysis to how those who craft news media texts use language to "identify symbolically their perspectives as they attempt to define situations, create orientations or attitudes and shape an individual's view of reality" (Foss, 2017:74). Words "shape our relations with our fellows. They prepare us for some functions and against others, for or against the persons representing these functions. [They] go further, they suggest how you shall be for or against" (Burke, 1984:4).

## Literature review and theoretical underpinnings

The news reports considered in this study, namely those related to the 16 Days of Activism for No Violence against Women and Children in 2020, form part of the broader topic of news coverage of women, which the scholarship overwhelmingly finds to be a "product of a male perspective that perpetuates stereotypes and myths about women while ridiculing and trivialising their needs and concerns" (Meyers, 1996:3) (see also Geertsema-Sligh, 2019; Liwag-Lomibao, 2020; Thomas et al., 2021). These texts have a direct impact on how society functions. Through the words used, women are told what is good and evil, what behaviour is, or is not, acceptable and, ultimately, who or what is behind the violence perpetrated against them daily. With language and visuals that place the gaze primarily on them as objects, highlighting what has happened to them and their relationship to the male perpetrators, the deviance is often attributed to them and their choices (e.g., either to have stayed with an abusive man, or to have been out and about).

Research on the factors that shape opinions on the criminal justice system argues that most people's views are not primarily based on personal encounters with the system (Sacco, 1982; Dorfman & Schiraldi, 2001). Instead, perspectives are communicated primarily by seeing, reading, or hearing from secondary sources, such as mainstream news media (Gies, 2007). Legal scholar and former judge, Antoine Garapon, asserts that, "for millions of people, the television has become ... the main, not to say the sole, source of information, culture, and entertainment ... and therefore, for many, the only contact they have with the law" (Garapon, 1996:231). It was recognition of just how media-saturated the world has become that gave rise to research into a notion called 'popular legal culture', which is based on the hypothesis that, because "the extent of programming and coverage [by the media] is so vast ... it must have an influence on how people view and understand the law (Robson & Schulz, 2016:2).

Popular legal culture is premised on the fact that media are an important platform for depicting and enacting a society's criminal justice system. These depictions and enactments provide a perspective on how this system works and why it works as it does (Riccio, 2007). Thus, popular legal culture is different from traditional legal culture based on individuals and institutions' actual performance in the criminal justice system. Studies in popular legal culture shift the focus from the letter of the law, which can seem cold and disconnected from other aspects of society, to focus on the context in which the law is lived out, namely in everyday life. Ewick and Silbey explain it by noting that legality "is not solely sustained by the formal law of the Constitution, legislative statutes, court decisions, or explicit demonstrations of state power, such as executions. Rather, legality is enduring, because it relies on and invokes commonplace schemas of everyday life" (Ewick & Silbey, 1998:17). Gies (2003:19) terms this the "paradox of distance and familiarity". Given the mass reach and appeal of media and its role in popular culture, these platforms are essential channels for shaping public perspectives and providing a window through which we observe the criminal justice system in everyday life. Through the daily news reports on court and crime matters, as well as the plethora of legal dramas and films, audiences are exposed to matters of law, giving them a sense of familiarity with procedures they otherwise might not know of, making media coverage an essential aspect of how people make meaning of legal matters (Robson, 2006). Gies (2007:1) goes as far as to term this influence, "the mass media's iron grip on the popular legal imagination". This, in turn, influences people's perceptions of the criminal justice system, as Thompson, Young and Burns (2000:409-410) argue: "What people believe about crime and criminals influences ...[c]ourt decisions, criminal justice policies, the election of public leaders, and the routine activities of the public."

Many attitudes and beliefs about crime and criminals are shaped and influenced by media representations of crime. Consequently, while the study's analysis is at the level of the text only, this is done with the view that, in understanding how the text is constructed to influence, we can then understand how society is being influenced and ultimately postulate on the consequences of this influence. It is important to note that television news reports are shaped by more than just the mere whims of a particular journalist or even the editorial policies of specific newsrooms: they are shaped by the political, legal and economic contexts in which news content is produced, the universally accepted news values (Harcup & O'Neill, 2017; Parks, 2019; Al-Rawi, Al-Musalli & Fakida, 2021), and the context in which journalists are socialised. Thus, in critiquing the use of language and visuals at the level of the texts, one can draw inferences of the values of the whole media ecosystem, and the items become more than just isolated reports about discrete incidents but, instead, are understood as products of the whole system that ascribes to certain values.

Television has been chosen as the medium for consideration primarily because of its place in popular culture. Despite the proliferation of other media forms, such as digital media, this medium remains among the most widely consumed in the South African context. A 2019 survey conducted by the Broadcast Research Council of South Africa (BRCSA) found that not only does television reach more South Africans than the internet (96% of the population compared to 61% respectively), but television also has double the viewing time that mobile devices connected to the internet have (BRCSA, 2019). Thus, when analysing how audio-visual news media constructs reality on any given issue, televised news reports still carry considerably more clout in this context because they reach more people than the digitised counterparts.

With specific reference to persuasion, the view in this study aligns with that of Adoni, Cohen, and Mane (1984:34), namely that, for television, the "symbolic representation of reality is based on selection and editing of material derived from reality, and thus depicts only a certain part of reality and portrays it from a specific point of view." This "certain part of reality" and the "specific point of view" articulated by the reports are what the analysis in my study is most interested in, since analysing which "certain part of reality" and "specific point of view" are advanced by the coverage, may help us understand the communicative work these reports are engaged in.

## Conceptual framework

This study uses two concepts to undertake a rhetorical criticism of South African television news report on the 16 Days of Activism for No Violence against Women and Children, and how these texts use language to depict reality: Kenneth Burke's (1966a) notion of language as symbolic action and Pumla Gqola's (2021) concept of the Female Fear Factory.

## Language as symbolic action

As discussed above, Burke's theory of language as symbolic action is an interpretive communication studies theory that considers language beyond linguistic perspectives and views it as a tool through which reality is socially constructed. It is rooted in a view of man as a "symbol-using (symbol-making, symbol-misusing) animal" (Burke, 1966a:16). In his conceptualisation of language, Burke describes it as a mechanism for exchanging ideas and as an instrument to do things in the world. He views language as "a species of action, symbolic action – and its nature is such that it can be used as a tool" (Burke, 1966a:15). This symbolic action is contrasted to practical action through an example of chopping down a tree. Burke states that chopping down a tree is practical action, while talking about chopping down a tree is a symbolic action. Both are activities where someone is doing something. In considering rhetorical criticism from Burke's perspective, one seeks to consider what kind of symbolic action is being done when people use language, and aims to answer the question that he poses: "[w]hat is involved when we say what people are doing and why they are doing it?" (Burke, 1969:xv).

To operationalise the concept, Burke introduces the idea of "terministic screens", which he describes as the way we use language as filters or screens through which we view reality (Burke, 1966). He supports this notion of terministic screens by explaining the use of these screens is a form of symbolic action, wherein "terms direct the attention to one field rather than to another" (Burke, 1966b:46). Our interpretation of what a particular news event means is therefore informed by the language and visuals used to describe it. In line with Pumla Gqola's notion of the Female Fear Factory, this chapter argues that the televised news reports that are the filter or screen through which audiences are steered to view reality is instrumental in the manufacture of female fear.

## Female Fear Factory

The Female Fear Factory is a notion used by Gqola to explain the manufacture of female fear in public spaces and in mediated form through language (Gqola, 2015:n.p.). Describing it as both theatrical and spectacular, Gqola states: "By theatrical, I allude to its exaggerated performance in front of an audience in terms that are immediately understood. It is spectacular in its reliance on visible, audible, and recognisable cues to transmit fear and control." Initially used in discussing its role in propping up rape as the language to express patriarchal violence, Gqola (2012) argues that "[t]he Female Fear Factory travels through respectability and through shame, and is normalised through repetition so that we no longer recognise it for what it is, consequently taking it for granted as 'life'."

In considering the role of television news in the functioning of the Female Fear Factory, one can look at three sites. The first is news media entities that use theatrical and spectacular content to attract viewers and thus increase profits due to the political economy that drives these companies. The second relates to news media production approaches, including newsgathering practices and the notion of news values, which socialise journalists to consider violence against women from a male perspective. The third relates to the news media reports as texts in their own right, constructed to be read in particular ways by audiences. The first two sites are where practical action is at play. In contrast, the third site, namely news media texts, is the realm of Burke's symbolic action and is thus the focus of this discussion on the fear-laden 'reality' depicted through the language used in South African television news reports on the 16 Days of Activism for No Violence against Women and Children campaign.

## Methodology

### Data collection

This qualitative study employed terministic screens to analyse the symbolic action being undertaken in how language is used in the news reports considered. The data collected were 32 English-language prime-time news bulletins aired on SABC 3 and eTV between 25 November and 10 December 2020, both dates inclusive. These dates coincided with the start and end of the 16 Days of Activism for No Violence against Women and Children campaign. SABC 3 and eTV were chosen because, combined, they are the most significant television news broadcasters in South Africa in terms of viewership (Nkolala, 2019; Nkoala, 2021). The decision to consider reports from both channels was to ascertain whether the reportage differed depending on the broadcaster, or if there were generalisable trends across the two. The prime-time news bulletins were selected because they are deemed the most important news bulletins of the day (Grindstaff & Turow, 2006). The recorded bulletins were transcribed and analysed. A total of 16 hours of audio-visual footage was transcribed by a transcriptionist, comprising sixteen, 30-minute bulletins from each broadcaster.[1]

### Data analysis

This study makes use of a Burkean approach to rhetorical criticism called 'cluster criticism'. This is an analytical approach that allows the researcher to examine key terms used in a text to develop unique insights into the nature and intentions of the people who constructed those key terms by considering the frequency and intensity of their use. The view is that, even though producing a text is a deliberate process, the author is not conscious of the clusters they are producing, and the criticism is thus geared at examining what is being communicated at a level where the author inadvertently reveals "who they are, the subjects about which they are engrossed, and the meanings

---

1    The categorised transcriptions are available on: https://doi.org/10.6084/m9.figshare.20919970.

they have for those subjects" (Burke, 1973:20). Burke (ibid.) explains this as follows: "the work of every writer contains a set of implicit equations. He uses 'associational clusters – what kind of acts and images and personalities and situations go with his notions of heroism, villainy, consolation, despair, etc." Littlefield and Quenette (2007:32) argue that cluster criticism "derives from the idea that the words any author or speaker chooses reveal the person's true nature, character, and motivation". Cluster criticism allows one to analyse the worldview and meaning advanced by the language used in a particular text (Foss, 2017).

For this study, two sets of key terms were considered: those that related to descriptions of men and those that related to descriptions of women. Table 9.2 on page 188 provides some examples of terms that clustered around descriptions of men and women respectively.

## Findings and discussion

Table 9.1 below provides the headlines of the stories broadcast on SABC 3 and eTV regarding gender-based violence in the period considered. Next to each headline is an indication of where the story featured in the bulletin (i.e., 'Story 1' means this was the first story, 'Story 3' means it was the third story, etc.). 'None' means there was no relevant report. These headlines tell us which developments the news reporters deemed most important to report on during the campaign. They also give us an idea of how language is used to foreground the aspects of the developments that were made most salient in the texts.

The two broadcasters aired 27 individual news reports on violence against women and children over the 16 days. These focused on a range of developments, including crimes committed, pronouncements by the government on the issue, stories from survivors, civil society demonstrations, and reports on court cases. Due to the scope of this study, only some of the reports are considered because an in-depth analysis of 27 reports, using cluster criticism, would result in an extremely long analysis. The specific reports considered are those highlighted in bold in Table 9.1.

**TABLE 9.1**  News stories featured between 25 November 2020 and 10 December 2020 on SABC 3 and eTV

| Date | SABC | eTV |
| --- | --- | --- |
| 25 November 2020 | Story 1: Presidential dialogue on gender-based violence & femicide<br>Story 2: Tackling gender violence at Delft in the WC | Story 1: A story of survival and hope<br>Story 2: How to fight gender-based violence<br>Story 3: Rape-accused ANC member reinstated<br>Story 4: Bushiri alleged victims speak out |
| 26 November 2020 | Story 1: Three stories: Women and five children killed by her lover<br>Story 1: Man allegedly killed his partner and child<br>Story 2: Female chief killed and set alight | Story 4: Woman and five children murdered |
| 27 November 2020 | None | Story 5: We won't forget her<br>Story 6: Family murder suspect arrested<br>Story 7: Mpumalanga ANC makes u-turn |
| 28 November 2020 | Story 2: Youth march to ConCourt to raise awareness of GBV | Story 1: Women prepared to fight back<br>Story 2: Ukhuthwala must end<br>Story 3: Young men need to take accountability<br>Story 4: UCT partners with rape crisis organisation |
| 29 November 2020 | None | None |
| 30 November 2020 | Story 2: Man accused of killing his wife and kids<br>Story 3: Mpumalanga's legislature committed to empowering women to fight against GBV | Story 5: Former police captain accused of sexual abuse<br>Story 6: Family of six murdered |
| 1 December 2020 | Story 4: Northern Cape families seek justice for teenage rape survivors | None |
| 2 December 2020 | Story 4: Family accuses police of not arresting rapist | None |
| 3 December 2020 | None | None |
| 4 December 2020 | None | Story 7: Palsea Madiba's murderer found guilty |
| 5 December 2020 | None | Story 7: AmaZulu King protect women and children |
| 6 December 2020 | Story 4: A family of six laid to rest | None |

| Date | SABC | eTV |
|---|---|---|
| 7 December 2020 | **Story 5**: Activists want rapists of minors to be charged with attempt murder too | **Story 5**: Miguel Louw murder accused found guilty<br>**Story 6**: Viral rape abandons jail |
| 8 December 2020 | None | None |
| 9 December 2020 | None | None |
| 10 December 2020 | None | None |

Table 9.2 provides examples of terms that clustered around descriptions of men and descriptions of women, respectively. From this, one firstly observes that there was an inclination to use language that foregrounded men through references to their positions as leaders than women (e.g., President Cyril Ramaphosa, former police captain, AmaZulu King Goodwill Zwelithini). Conversely, they are described as perpetrators, or suspects, or the accused. In each of these instances, the terms afford the men agency as characters who act rather than as subjects who are acted upon, as is the case with the terms that cluster around the references to the women. Secondly, the terms that cluster around references to the women are inclined to employ language that views the women in relation to other people (e.g., partner, mother, sister). This speaks to whose words shape stories versus about whom the stories are told and how language can be used to empower some, while disempowering others.

The two tables give a broad overview of the types of stories that received coverage and the overall approach in the language used in these reports. In the next section, the chapter engages in a more in-depth discussion of the ideologically laden meanings being conveyed through the words used in these reports. It starts by considering the male and female characters in these stories and the differences in the language used concerning women. It then considers the use of language in reference to the crime.

**TABLE 9.2**  Cluster criticism of terms describing men and women in the news reports considered

| SABC | eNCA |
|---|---|
| **Description of Men** | |
| **November 25**<br>• President Cyril Ramaphosa<br>• Blue Downs Cluster Commander<br>• Head: Anti-Gang Unit | **November 25**<br>• Rape-accused ANC member<br>• A senior ANC member<br>• Party's provincial spokesperson<br>• ANC Mpumalanga Spokesperson<br>• The pastor<br>• PSL Chairman |
| **November 26**<br>• Her partner<br>• The man<br>• Father | **November 26**<br>• Her boyfriend |
| **November 30**<br>• Man accused of killing his wife and kids<br>• 32-year-old Nowa Makula<br>• NPA Spokesman<br>• The accused | **November 27**<br>• Sole accused Muzikayise Malephane<br>• Lawyer<br>• Son of Juliet Dakada<br>• Little Mala's rapist<br>• Family murder suspect arrested<br>• A 32-year-old man<br>• Mhlanti's boyfriend<br>• The suspect<br>• An alleged rapist |
| **December 1**<br>• Perpetrators<br>• A man who allegedly robbed, dragged her to a veld and raped her<br>• 17-year-old teen's father | **November 28**<br>• Perpetrators<br>• Perpetrators of gender-based<br>• Her partner<br>• Young men<br>• Sports, Arts and Culture Minister Nathi Mthethwa<br>• Former police captain<br>• Alleged sexual abuse survivor<br>• A former commander of a Cape Town police station<br>• The 39-year-old's father<br>• Your dad<br>• A 32-year-old man<br>• Nowa Makula, a Zimbabwean national |
| **December 2**<br>• Rapists<br>• Her rapists<br>• Alleged rapists<br>• Alleged perpetrators<br>• Teenage boys she knows, who are between the ages of 16 and 18<br>• Police spokesman | **December 4**<br>• Palesa Madiba's killer<br>• Her killer<br>• 36-year-old Dumisani Mkhwanazi<br>• Judge Prince Manyathi |

| SABC | eNCA |
| --- | --- |
| **Description of Men** | |
| December 6<br>• The mother's 34-year-old partner<br>• Daddy<br>• Minister of Police<br>• MEC for Education | December 5<br>• AmaZulu King Goodwill Zwelithini |
| December 7<br>• Miguel Louw's killer<br>• Mohammed Ebrahim<br>• 44-year-old Ebrahim<br>• The boy<br>• Rapists of minors<br>• 45-year-old man accused of raping two minors<br>• Bikers Against Child Abuse<br>• #NOTINMYNAME | December 7<br>• Miguel Louw murder accused<br>• The man accused of his kidnapping and murder<br>• A man accused of raping two minors<br>• The accused<br>• The 45-year-old<br>• Bikers against GBV<br>• #NotInMyName<br>• Schoolboy |
| December 9<br>• Tshegofatso Pule murder suspect<br>• Muzikayise Malephane, the man accused of killing 28-year-old Tshegofatso Pule | |
| **Description of Women** | |
| November 25<br>• Western Cape Police Commissioner, General Yolisa Matakata<br>• Victim<br>• Women of all ages | November 25<br>• Survivor and Activist<br>• Our women<br>• Nuraan Osman, Director for the Ihata Shelter for Abused Women and Children in Montague<br>• Bushiri's alleged victims<br>• His wife, Mary<br>• Alleged rape victim |
| November 26<br>• Mother and her five children<br>• Woman and her five children killed<br>• Their daughter and her five children<br>• His partner | November 26<br>• A 42-year-old Eastern Cape woman and her five children<br>• His mother, Nomzamo Mhlanti<br>• Mother<br>• Youngest sister |
| November 30<br>• His partner<br>• 42-year-old Nomzamo Mhlanti and her five children<br>• 25-year-old Baliswa Sikhundwana<br>• Her sister and her children<br>• ANC Women's League<br>• ATM<br>• Rural women<br>• Multiparty Women Caucus<br>• DA Member of Legislature<br>• Gender-based violence survivor | November 27<br>• Young heavily pregnant woman<br>• The 8-year-old autistic girl<br>• An Eastern Cape woman and her five children<br>• Nomzamo Mhlanti |

| SABC | eNCA |
|---|---|
| **Description of Women** | |
| December 1<br>• Teenage rape survivors<br>• Two pupils<br>• 17-year-old<br>• 18-year-old daughter<br>• Grade 11 pupil | November 28<br>• Gender-based violence protesters<br>• Protesters<br>• Anne Insam<br>• One of thousands of women allegedly beaten up.<br>• Gender-based violence survivor<br>• Rape Survivor<br>• UN under-secretary and Executive Director of Women, Phumzile Mlambo-Ngcuka<br>• Professor Loretta Feris<br>• University of Cape Town<br>• Survivors of gender-based violence |
| December 2<br>• A 15-year-old learner from Khayelitsha in Cape Town<br>• Girl | November 30<br>• Nomzamo Mhlanti and her five children |
| December 4<br>• WOSA<br>• ANC Women's League<br>• JSE CFO<br>• ANC NEC<br>• Director: Wise4Africa<br>• Minister of Women | December 4<br>• University of Johannesburg student, Palesa Madiba |
| December 6<br>• A mother<br>• ANC Women's League: Amathole Region<br>• For vulnerable children who are victims of neglect, physical and mental abuse<br>• Noupoort Drop-In Centre<br>• Head of Social Work: Red Cross Memorial Children's Hospital<br>• Isibindi Technical Advisor<br>• Noupoort Wind Farm | December 5<br>• Victims<br>• Victim<br>• Mercy and Peace Foundation |
| December 7<br>• 9-year-old Miguel Louw<br>• An 11- and a 13-year-old<br>• EFF | December 7<br>• Jaqueline Hendricks<br>• Two minors<br>• The girls<br>• Two girls aged 11 and 13 |
| December 9<br>• 28-year-old Tshegofatso Pule<br>• Tshegofatso Pule, who was eight months' pregnant | |

## The characters

On 27 November 2020, eTV aired a news report titled, "We won't forget her", highlighting three ongoing court cases where a woman or a child was raped or killed or both. The introduction to this news report follows:

> **Anchor**: While the war on South Africa's women rages on, countless families are waging their own battles in court. Today we bring updates on the cases of gender-based violence that shook Gauteng in 2020. And in all three, the judgment is still not within reach.

The report recapped three high-profile cases where men raped and/or murdered women and children in Gauteng. The circumstances of each of the victims were different: one was a pregnant woman, another an older woman, and the third an autistic child:

> **Reporter**: We won't forget Tshegofatso Pule … The body of the young heavily pregnant woman was found hanging from a tree in Roodepoort in June … We won't forget Juliet Dakada. The Soweto gogo was brutally raped, beaten, and killed at her family's Dobsonville home in July … And we won't forget the little girl we call Mala. The 8-year-old autistic girl was raped in Thokoza in October.

The way the report is written focuses on the circumstances of the victims, namely a pregnant woman, an elderly woman (whom the report affectionately calls "Gogo") and an autistic girl. This has an instructive undertone that infers that, if "these" women can be brutalised, no one is safe. On the other hand, the men involved are mentioned in passing through references to the status of their respective trials:

> **Reporter**: Today, her family is still waiting for the sole accused, Muzikayise Malephane, to finally stand trial … There's no bail for the two men arrested for the crimes. They return to court next month …. Little Mala's rapist still walks the streets apparently due to outstanding evidence. (eTV, 27 November 2021)

This approach is contrary to the approach that the literature says is adopted by the news media in Western contexts, like America and Britain, where the reportage tends to depict the perpetrators as monsters or sex-fiends to "paint [violence against women] as the domain of psychopaths and 'monsters' only" (Caputi, 1993:12). Here we see the focus is on the women and their surprising circumstances. The approach is the same in the report on the murder of the mother and her five children.

The symbolic action being performed in choosing to foreground the victims in this context is a demonstrative and an instructive one that perpetuates male supremacy by placing the gaze on women as victims, while simultaneously removing it from men as perpetrators. It first demonstrates that who is raped is of greater concern than who is raping in South African society. It then advances a version of reality that instructs that, in our focus on who gets raped, those with 'unusual' circumstances (as arbitrarily decided on by those who produce news) should get greater priority. This plays right into the news media's role as an instrument of the Female Fear Factory because, as Gqola (2021) argues:

> ... the language, names and stories that societies tell about gender power and crises are not innocent. While it goes without saying that some rape cases will receive more attention than others, it is important to note that studying such prominent cases often illuminates a society's anxieties about gender power and women's lives, on the one hand, and the systems through which values and fear circulate.

The inclination not to name men as perpetrators of abuse can also be observed in how the reports focus on women as the abused, rather than men as the abusers. In a report broadcast on eTV on 5 December 2020, the news story is headlined, "AmaZulu King: Protect women and children". The anchor's introduction to the story is:

> **Anchor**: Stop protecting women and children abusers ... that is the strong call from AmaZulu King Goodwill Zwelithini. He was speaking at a dialogue to discuss gender-based violence in Durban this weekend. It was hosted by the Mercy and Peace Foundation, which has brought together various stakeholders to address the scourge.

Here, the abusers are not explicitly identified as men, but the victims are directly identified as women and children. This silence, read together with the super, "Protect women and children", begs the question, 'Protect them from whom?' Throughout this story, the proverbial elephant in the room, namely the source of the abuse, is spoken around and never directly addressed as such. The language used is such that the focus is on everything else except for the social, political, and cultural factors that create an environment where misogyny and patriarchy fuel the violence meted out by men against women in this context.

Another way in which there are disparities in the characterisation of men versus women in these reports is in how language can be used to blame women for their victimisation while downplaying the actual victimisers, the men. In a report on SABC on 1 December 2021, two families are relaying their experiences after their teenage daughters were allegedly raped. A sound bite from one of the girls' fathers was articulated as follows:

> I don't know what happened because we have been trying to protect our child by stopping her from roaming the streets at night or going to taverns. We wanted a bright future for our child, but a stranger came from nowhere to try and destroy our child's future.

Meyers (1996) comments that the language used in the news media's portrayal of violence can be a means of social control, showing women what is and is not acceptable for them to do; and, in media depictions:

> … the vulnerability of women is a given and, linked to questions of complicity, remains lurking in the shadows of representation. Was she where she shouldn't have been? Did she fail to take precautions to lock a door, to arrange for security? Did she do something to provoke the attack? (Meyers, 1996:9)

In this case, this sound bite articulates a commonly employed approach of victim shaming (Gqola, 2021). Gqola (2021:n.p.) argues:

> … the Female Fear Factory requires many bodies, minds and numerous components to ensure that the conveyor belt moves through successive stations without interruption. These stations alter the product of the conveyor belt slightly, but are part of the same process of repetition and product modification.

In this case, a father who, at face value, is expressing outrage and heartbreak at what has happened to his daughter, provides an example of how a news report can perpetuate victim shaming, acting as part of the conveyor belt that drives the Female Fear Factory. In this sound bite, the father advances a view that children who roam the street at night or visit taverns can expect something like being raped to happen to them, because they are not protected. Yet, as his child's experience, and most of those of the others reported on during this period show, including the rape of the autistic girl and the rape of the elderly woman, where women go is not the determining factor of their vulnerability to being raped.

Through this father's words, the report advances a view that, if his daughter had been roaming the street or going to taverns, then her rape would have been explicable, and probably inevitable, articulating a version of reality where an incident of rape is viewed in light of what the woman did, rather than what was done to her. The reality is that violence against women is ubiquitous in South Africa. The various incidents reported during the 16 Days of Activism campaign show that. The news reports highlight incidents, like the experiences of these two girls, based on the news values of novelty and timeliness when, in fact, they are common. They highlight them because, based on the prevailing view in this context, the rape of 'good girls' who were on their way from school *should* be an anomaly, whereas the rape of women who are out at night and in taverns should not. In fact, in this context, it is not about where women are but about the societal conditions that are conducive enough for men to rape women, irrespective of the environment and conditions.

The chapter will now discuss the type of language used about the violent crimes committed against women and children in these reports by focusing on one specific case that received prominent coverage in 2020.

## The crime

> **Anchor**: It's day 2 of the annual 16 Days of No Violence against Women and Children campaign. But despite the spotlight on these crimes, a 42-year-old Eastern Cape woman and her five children have been hacked to death, one of them a 6-month-old baby. Police believe her boyfriend can shed light on the brutal murders. (eTV, 26 November 2020)

This is how an eTV news report began on a particular case of gender-based violence that would dominate news reports over the 16 days. The incident was broadcast as the day's top story on SABC and eTV on 26 November 2020. It was about a woman and her five children who were allegedly hacked to death by the woman's partner in a rural village called Xhora in the Eastern Cape. In the SABC report, sound bites from four people were featured. The first was of the victim's father relaying how the bodies were discovered. The second was of the victim's mother lamenting the economic implications of the incident in terms of the costs they expected to incur to bury the six people. The third sound bite was of a neighbour who remarked how unusual the case was, and reinforced the mother's statements on burial costs, even appealing to the government for financial assistance. The final sound bite was of the police spokesperson appealing to the public for information that could lead them to the suspect.

The eTV report began with a sound bite of the victim's surviving son detailing how he discovered his deceased family members. It was followed by the woman's mother lamenting how she would struggle to cover the costs of burying the six victims. The final sound bite was of the victim's sister talking about the abusive relationship, highlighting that her deceased sister had spoken to her about planning to leave her abusive partner. The visuals used across both reports were extreme wide shots of the area and a wide shot of the informal structure that the woman was using as a home. SABC included visuals of some community members seated inside a building in a posture of mourning. eTV included still images of the deceased woman and some photos that featured the children.

The women's sound bites are used to convey the horror and devastation for the woman's family, while the men are featured in less emotional postures, primarily relaying information about the incident.

In particular, the victim's mother spoke about being heartbroken about the deaths and the fact that the family would be forced to incur unaffordable funeral expenses because of this incident. In a voiceover translation by the SABC, the victim's mother states:

> It hurts so much. In this home, we live on social grant money. Our children are unemployed. I don't even have food to give to the people who come and mourn with us. He took the children's SASSA card. He then cut their birth certificates and ID documents into pieces. We didn't find the SASSA card in the house. (SABC, 26 November 2020)

In the eTV report, the victim's mother says:

> I am devastated. I haven't eaten since yesterday. I can't eat. How will I bury so many people? (eTV, 26 November 2020)

The men, including the woman's surviving son, are featured speaking more objectively:

> **Balungile Mhlanti** (victim's son): I opened the door, and I saw the bed full of blood and that baby was stabbed. I ran back to alert my grandmother. (eTV, 26 November 2020)

> **Pepela Skhundwana** (victim's father): My daughter stayed with someone. But on Tuesday night, a family member who came from watching soccer at a neighbour's house came and knocked. But my daughter's partner said they would not open at that time of the night. Then on Wednesday morning, he went there again to prepare for school. He knocked and the door opened by itself. He saw the bodies lying in a pool of blood. They were all beheaded and hacked. He then came and told us. We went there, but we did not find her partner. (SABC, 26 November 2020)

The narrative in both reports laments the gruesome nature of this incident:

> **Anchor**: A 42-year-old Eastern Cape woman and her five children have been hacked to death, one of them a 6-month-old baby.

> **Reporter**: He walked in to find his mother's lifeless body and the bodies of his five young siblings … According to police, the bodies were found with stab wounds on the head, throat, and face. It is also believed an axe was found at the scene. (eTV, 26 November 2020)

The focus on the gruesome nature of the crime may be a combination of two related things. Firstly, it is due to news values that commonly prioritise incidents deemed unusual. In this case, the killing of six people in such a violent manner, namely by hacking them to death with an axe, and the fact that one of the victims is a six-month-old child, speaks to the unusual element. Linked to this, in the SABC report, there is mention that some of the children whom the alleged perpetrator killed were his biological children. Without explicitly stating it, the reports suggest that it is unusual for a man to do this. Yet, in reality, in 2020, "47 000 women and girls worldwide were killed by their intimate partners or other family members", with a considerable number of these occurring in South Africa (UNODOC, 2021).

News reports on violence against women and children are inclined to use language that highlights the most gruesome aspects of this societal issue prompting audiences to focus on the abhorrent nature of the crime rather than the societal and systemic issues that give rise to it (Carll, 2005). The minimal references to the abuse and systemic conditions that enabled the violence to fester to this point, where a woman and her five children are killed, is typically not brought to the fore, partly because of the inclination of news reports to focus on specific and discrete issues, rather than on broad and generalisable factors (Wouters, 2015). Here language and visuals are not primarily about foregrounding systemic issues but instead shine the light on the shock value of these incidents. The symbolic action performed through the reportage is akin to a collective gasping at how unbelievable *this* story is.

In his description of the incident, the SABC journalist calls it "another senseless killing where a woman and her children are the victims at the hands of a man"; but describing it as a "senseless killing" suggests that the factors that give rise to these crimes are not well understood, which is not the case. The journalist also states, "The brutal attack comes a week after the Safety Department has urged people not to tolerate any kind of assault from their partners". Here there is an element of victim-blaming as the notion of tolerating any assault from their partners suggests that victims, such as this woman, have the resources that enable them to decide whether or not to tolerate the abuse.

## Conclusions

This chapter has analysed the use of language in selected South African television news reports broadcast by eTV and SABC on the 2020 campaign of 16 Days of Activism for No Violence against Women and Children to consider how the language in these reports depicts the crimes committed. The analysis was undertaken using two frameworks, namely Kenneth Burke's (1966) language as symbolic action, and Pumla Gqola's (2021) Female Fear Factory. Gqola notes that "fear is fostered through exaggerated visual performances, audible cues, and other coded signs, all of which are repeated until the target audiences have mastered the form of communication and have started to take fear for granted, as something inevitable." This 'factory' is supported by structures and institutions to keep women living in fear, and news media reports are an element of how society "communicates both to the target and to the audience the possibility of being the victim, and teaches and enshrines power in patriarchal society" (Gqola, 2021:n.p.). Concerning the news, Gqola states: "The cases that make the headlines are all instructive: there is no safety" (Gqola, 2021).

The chapter found that the news reports considered were, firstly, inclined to use language that empowers men by affording them the status of agents in the stories, while women are prone to be depicted as subjects who are acted upon. The study also found an inclination not to name men directly as perpetrators of abuse, thus invisibilising their complicity in this societal issue. It also argued that there is an inclination to focus on the most horrendous crimes to portray violence against women in discrete and exceptional terms rather than dealing with its pervasiveness in contexts like South Africa. From this, the conclusion is that these news reports employ language to engage in the symbolic action of fuelling the Female Fear Factory that causes women to live in fear due to the emphasis on the gruesome and pervasive violence they are at risk of daily. Instead of directly addressing the perpetrators of these crimes, the reports shy away from calling out men and instead portray a version of reality where violence against women and children is portrayed as an inexplicable phenomenon perpetrated by some unnamed 'other'. These reports offer a distorted version of reality that masks the pervasiveness of violence against women and children and the complicity of men in this.

# References


Adoni, H., Cohen, A.A. & Mane, S. 1984. Social reality and television news: Perceptual dimensions of social conflicts in selected life areas. *Journal of Broadcasting & Electronic Media*, 28(1):33-49. https://doi.org/10.1080/08838158409386513

Al-Rawi, A., Al-Musalli, A.A.-M. & Fakida, A.F. 2021. News values on Instagram: A comparative study of international news. *Journalism and Media*, 22:305-320. https://doi.org/10.3390/journalmedia2020018

Borchers, T. 2012. *Persuasion in the media age.* 3rd Edition. Long Grove: Waveland Press.

BRCSA (Broadcast Research Council of South Africa). 2019. *The establishment survey: March 2019.* Johannesburg: Broadcast Research Council of South Africa. https://brcsa.org.za/establishment-survey-march-2019-release/ [Accessed 5 November 2021].

Burke, K. 1966. *Language as symbolic action: Essays on life, literature, and method.* Los Angeles, CA: University of California Press. https://doi.org/10.1525/9780520340664

Burke, K. 1969a. *A grammar of motives.* Los Angeles, CA: University of California Press.

Burke, K. 1969b. *A rhetoric of motives.* Los Angeles, CA: University of California Press.

Buthelezi, T. 2006. 16 Days of Activism and gender stereotypes in *Ilanga, Isolezwe* and *UmAfrika* newspapers. *Southern African Linguistics and Applied Language Studies*, 24(4):497-509. https://doi.org/10.2989/16073610609486437

Caputi, J. 1993. Sexual Politics of murder. In: P.B. Bart & E.G. Moran (eds.). *From violence against women: The bloody footprints.* London: Sage. 5-28.

Carll, E.K. 2005. Violence and women: News coverage of victims and perpetrators. In: E.E. Cole & J.H. Daniel (eds.). *Featuring females: Feminist analyses of media.* Washington, DC: American Psychological Association. 143-153. https://doi.org/10.1037/11213-010

Chitsamatanga, B.B. & Rembe, N.S. 2020. School related gender-based violence as a violation of children's rights to education in South Africa: Manifestations, consequences and possible solutions. *Journal of Human Ecology*, 69(1-3):65-80. https://doi.org/10.31901/24566608.2020/69.1-3.3203

Deane, T. 2018. Sexual violence and the limits of laws' powers to alter behaviour: The case of South Africa. *Journal of International Women's Studies*, 19(2):84-103. https://vc.bridgew.edu/cgi/viewcontent.cgi?article=2005&context=jiws [Accessed 2 September 2022].

Dorfman, L. & Schiraldi, V. 2001. *Off balance: Youth, race & crime in the news.* Building Blocks for Youth. http://www.bmsg.org/sites/default/files/bmsg_other_publication_off_balance.pdf [Accessed 26 January 2022].

Ewick, P. & Silbey, S.S. 1998. *The common place of law: Stories from everyday life.* Chicago, IL: University of Chicago Press. https://doi.org/10.7208/chicago/97802 26212708.001.0001

Foss, S.K. 2017. *Rhetorical criticism: Exploration and practice.* Long Grove, IL: Waveland Press.

Garapon, A. 1996. Justice out of court: The dangers of trial by media. In: D. Nelken (ed.). *Law as communication.* Aldershot, UK: Dartmouth Publishing. 231-245.

Geertsema-Sligh, M. 2019. Gender issues in news coverage. *The International Encyclopedia of Journalism Studies*, 1-8. https://doi.org/10.1002/97811188415 70.iejs0162

Gies, L. 2003. Explaining the absence of the media in stories of law and legal consciousness. *Entertainment Law*, 21:19-54. https://heinonline.org/HOL/P?h=hein. journals/entersport2&i=19 [Accessed 26 January 2022].

Gies, L. 2007. *Law and the media: The future of an uneasy relationship.* London: Routledge-Cavendish. http://ndl.ethernet.edu.et/bitstream/123456789/58695/1/ 15pdf.pdf [Accessed 26 January 2022].

Gqola, P.D. 2015. *Rape: A South African nightmare.* Auckland Park: Melinda Ferguson Books. https://search-ebscohost-com.ezproxy.uct.ac.za/login.aspx?direct=true&db= nlebk&AN=1240044&site=ehost-live [Accessed 4 November 2021].

Gqola, P.D. 2021. *Female Fear Factory.* Cape Town: Melinda Ferguson Books. https:// search-ebscohost-com.ezproxy.uct.ac.za/login.aspx?direct=true&db=nlebk&AN=295 5656&site=ehost-live [Accessed 4 November 2021].

Grindstaff, L. & Turow, J.T. 2006. Video cultures: Television sociology in the "new TV" age. *Annual Review of Sociology*, 32:103-125. https://doi.org/10.1146/annurev. soc.32.061604.143122

Harcup, T. & O'Neill, D. 2017. What is news? News values revisited (again). *Journalism Studies*, 18(12):1470-1488. https://doi.org/10.1080/1461670X.2016.1150193

Harries, G. & Bird, W.B. 2005. Keeping an eye on the campaign: Monitoring media coverage of the 16 Days of Activism: No Violence Against Women and Children campaign. *Agenda*, 19(66):90-96.

Littlefield, R.S. & Quenette, A.M. 2007. Crisis leadership and Hurricane Katrina: The portrayal of authority by the media in natural disasters. *Journal of Applied Communication Research*, 35(1):26-47. https://doi.org/10.1080/00909880601065664

Liwag-Lomibao, M.A. 2020. A tale of three women: Framing as a patriarchal practice in the news coverage of women in distress. *Plaridel*, 18(1):1-24. https://doi.org/10.52 518/2020-03lmibao

Meyers, M. 1996. *News coverage of violence against women: Engendering blame.* Thousand Oaks, CA: Sage. https://doi.org/10.4135/9781452243832

Newham, G. 2005. *A decade of crime prevention in South Africa: From a national strategy to a local challenge.* Research report for the Centre for the Study of Violence and Reconciliation (CSVR). http://www.csvr.org.za/docs/policing/ decadeofcrimeprevention.pdf [Accessed 2 September 2022].

Nkoala, S. 2021. Persuasion across platforms: A rhetorical analysis of televised and digitised news reports on economic matters. In: G. Motsaathebe & S.H. Chiumbu (eds.). *Television in Africa in the digital age*. London: Palgrave Macmillan. 127-144. https://doi.org/10.1007/978-3-030-68854-7_7

Nkolala, S. 2019. Internal affairs: An Aristotelian perspective on SABC 3 news. *African Journal of Rhetoric*, 11(1):224-243. https://journals.co.za/doi/pdf/10.10520/EJC-1ae3312c23 [Accessed 24 February 2021].

Parks, P. 2019. Textbook news values: Stable concepts, changing choices. *Journalism & Mass Communication Quarterly*, 96(3):784-810. https://doi.org/10.1177/10776 99018805212

Pelser, E. & Rauch, J. 2001. South Africa's criminal justice system: Policy and priorities. *South African Sociological Association SASA Annual Congress on Globalisation, Inequality and Identity*. 1-4. https://help.csvr.org.za/wpcontent/uploads/2001/07/southafricascriminal.pdf [Accessed 25 January 2022].

Plessis, A. & Louw, A.L. 2005. Crime and crime prevention in South Africa: 10 years after. *Canadian Journal of Criminology and Criminal Justice*, 47(2):427-446. https://doi.org/10.3138/cjccj.47.2.427

Riccio, V. 2007. Media, images of justice, and Brazilian reality television. *Observatorio*, 1(2):147-166. https://doi.org/10.15847/obsOBS12200784

Robson, P. 2006. Lawyers and the legal system on TV: The British experience. *International Journal of Law in Context*, 2(4):333-362. https://doi.org/10.1017/S1744552306004010

Robson, P. & Schulz, J.L. 2016. A transnational study of law and justice on TV: Introduction. In: P. Robson & J.L. Schulz (eds.). *A transnational study of law and justice on TV*. London: Bloomsbury Publishing. 1-6. https://doi.org/10.2139/ssrn.2845383

Sacco, V.F. 1982. The effects of mass media on perceptions of crime: A reanalysis of the issues. *Pacific Sociological Review*, 25(4):475-493. https://doi.org/10.2307/1388925

Smith, C.R. 1977. Television news as rhetoric. *Western Journal of Communication*, 41(3): 147-159. https://doi.org/10.1080/10570317709389608

Thomas, M., Harell, A., Rijkhoff, S.A. & Gosselin, T. 2021. Gendered news coverage and women as heads of government. *Political Communication*, 38(4):388-406. https://doi.org/10.1080/10584609.2020.1784326

Thompson, C.Y., Young, R.L. & Burns, R.B. 2000. Representing gangs in the news: Media constructions of criminal gangs. *Sociological Spectrum*, 20(4):409-432.

United Nations Women. 2021. *16 Days of Activism against Gender-Based Violence*. https://www.unwomen.org/en/what-we-do/ending-violence-against-women/take-action/16-days-of-activism [Accessed 21 January 2022].

UNODOC (United Nations Office of Drugs and Crime). 2018. *DATAUNODC: Violent & Sexual Crime*. https://dataunodc.un.org/dp-crime-victims-sexual-violence [Accessed 24 January 2022].

UNODOC (United Nations Office on Drugs and Crime). 2021. *Killings of women and girls by their intimate partners or other family members: Global estimates 2020*. https://www.unodc.org/documents/data-and-analysis/statistics/crime/UN_BriefFem_251121.pdf [Accessed 26 January 2022].

Van Dijk, T.A. 1998. *News analysis: Case studies of international and national news in the press*. Hillsdale, NJ: Lawrence Erlbaum.

Wouters, R. 2015. Reporting demonstrations: On episodic and thematic coverage of protest events in Belgian television news. *Political Communication*, 32(3):475-496. https://doi.org/10.1080/10584609.2014.958257

# PART III

## Language and crime

# TERRORISM THREAT NOTES AS CRIMINAL SPEECH ACTS

## A corpus-based approach


*Gilbert Francis Odhiambo*
*Daniel Ochieng Orwenjo*


## Introduction

Terrorism is the greatest challenge in the world today. The Heritage Foundation (2017) reports that from 1970 to 2014 there were 141 966 terrorist incidents worldwide. In 2014 alone, 13 463 terrorist attacks occurred around the world, causing at least 32 700 deaths and more than 34 700 injuries. 9/11 stands out as the day about 3 000 people in the US lost their lives in the single biggest terror attack. The upsurge in terrorism has affected even countries, such as Kenya and Tanzania, leaving in its wake massive destruction and loss of life. On 7 August 1998, two US embassies in East Africa were bombed almost simultaneously, leaving 224 dead and more than 4 500 wounded (A&E Television Networks, LLC, 2017). Later, between 15 June and 17 June 2014, there was an attack in Mpeketoni area at the Kenyan coast in which more than 60 people were killed. Again, on 2 April 2015, an attack on Garissa University College, Kenya, killed 148 people.

The few terrorist incidents highlighted above clearly indicate a wave of terror. The rise in terrorist attacks should engender research interest. Applied linguistics should pursue a deeper understanding of terrorism with the goal of seeking solutions. Of importance is that many terrorism attacks are accompanied by terrorist messages. At a time when terrorism is on the rise, the meaning in these messages could provide opportunities for addressing terrorism.

Terrorism messages are delivered before, during or after the attacks. The communication before a terrorist attack is often a threat. During the attack, the communication has hitherto been short, such as an utterance of some religious phrase like *Allah u wakbar!* or a pronouncement of death to those being attacked. Yet lately, terrorist attacks have taken longer time, and with the communications environment being in continuous change (Russel, 2019), communication during an attack has become long and protracted. After a terrorist attack, the author's intention is usually to claim responsibility for the attack, gloat about its perceived success and, often, warn of future attacks unless certain preconditions are met (Golder & Williams, 2004).

The pre-attack messages are the focus of this study. As mentioned, communication prior to a terrorist attack is often a threat, thus the name 'terrorism threat notes'. A few weeks before the 9/11 attacks, the then leader of al-Qaeda, Osama bin Laden, issued a chilling message entailing a 'plan' that would make big news and in which he also exhorted God to grant "our brother's success" (Withnall, 2015:43). In the Garissa University incident (in Kenya, 3 April 2015), the terrorism threat note, which read, "Kenyan cities will run red with blood" (Torchia & Odula, 2015), was available to security personnel way before the attack: a few days prior, an SMS warning of an impending attack was widely circulated, even among the university students. According to Bosh (5 April 2015), a few days before the attack, there was a ragged piece of paper on the students' noticeboard, whose message was clear in communicating that a terrorist attack would happen soon on the campus.

Apparently vital pre-attack communication was available in both the 9/11 and Garissa University attacks. Unfortunately, the significance of the threat communication in both cases was not sufficiently and effectively grasped, leading to a lack of appropriate response. The threat notes were not adequately analysed and utilised for purposes of lessening the impact of the attacks or avoiding them altogether. Had there been more understanding of the threat communication, there could have been better preparation for and an improved response to the attacks. Therefore, there is need to pay enough attention to these messages and comprehend them adequately because only then can the realisability of the threats be determined and appropriate preparation and action be taken.

Threats, which can range from mild warnings to death threats and are a part of our daily lives, have received considerably less attention compared to the attention given to police investigations and court proceedings (Gibbons, 2003) and other legal notes. Even so, work on threats (Gibbons, 2003; Grant, 2008; Olsson, 2008, 2012; Shuy, 2014) only provides general discussion, without a specific framework and methodology for analysis. Because of this inadequacy, linguistic evidence on threats has been subjected to criticism and deemed inadmissible in court (Van den Berg & Surmon, 2019). This points to the need for more research on threat texts, including terrorism threat notes, to understand the language of threats, as well as to provide a framework for analysis.

Jacobsen (2010), Salgueiro (2010) and Kravchenko (2017a, 2017 b) have studied threats from the perspective of general linguistics. A few scholars, such as Salguero (2010), and Van den Berg and Surmon (2019), have applied Speech Act Theory (SAT) to an analysis of threats in a forensic linguistics context; yet the three do not focus on terrorism threat notes. The current study examines terrorism threat texts using the lens of SAT and essentially responds to the need for more research in the area. Further, since Van den Berg and Surmon's (2019) threat continuum only ranges from mild warnings to death threats, and Gibbons (2003), Olsson (2008, 2012), and Olsson and Luchjenbroers (2013) only mention certain genres of written textual threats (hate mail, bribes and blackmail, ransom notes and hate speech), this study extends the threat continuum to include terrorism threats and its related genre, terrorism threat notes.

## Theoretical issues

The analysis of the texts was informed by the tenets arising from SAT (Austin, 1962; Searle, 1975). As will be clarified later, SAT forms the basis for the explanation of what constitutes a terrorism threat. According to Austin (1962), within SAT, a statement describes a situation, states some facts, and, crucially, performs a certain kind of action by itself. He shifts focus: from the long-held assumption that the main function of language is to give a true or false description of objective reality, to the performance of language acts, such as making requests, promises and threats. He highlights the 'use' or 'utterance-as-action' aspect of language.

SAT (Austin, 1962; Searle, 1975) assumes that the minimal unit of communication is not a sentence or other expression, but the performance of a language act. Austin calls actions performed via utterances 'speech acts'. He estimates that a good dictionary contains ten thousand verbs, which he calls 'performatives', the uttering of which is action itself; and, without the utterance, the action is not done. He emphasises that such words will never be true or false, but can turn out to be felicitous or infelicitous: that is, the success or failure of such utterances depends on the appropriateness of the circumstance of the speech event. Further, Austin (1962) opines that, in uttering a sentence, three kinds of acts are simultaneously performed: a) a locutionary act (the utterance and its literal meaning); b) an illocutionary act (the meaning intended in the utterance), and c) a perlocutionary act (the effect or consequence of the utterance).

Searle (1994) improves on Austin's work and sheds more light on the issue of speech acts, which he defines as, "the basic or minimal units of linguistic communication" (1994:21). He says that "speaking a language is performing speech acts" (1994:21). He further draws a distinction between a particular speech act and the words used in some language to express it, and notes that every speech act can be expressed in many ways. According to Searle, the production of speech acts is governed by "certain rules for the use of linguistic elements" (1994:23). He calls these rules 'constitutive rules' and distinguishes them from 'regulative rules'. A basic distinction between the two is that constitutive rules constitute, while regulative rules regulate. Taken further, however, constitutive rules "create or define new types of behavior" (Searle, 1969:33). They create the very possibility of engaging in certain kinds of conduct (Searle, 1969:33). For Searle, the formal way of thinking about constitutive rules is the following: "X counts as Y in context C" (Searle, 1969:35). On the other hand, regulative rules regulate antecedent or independently existing forms of behaviour (Searle, 1969:33). They require, or permit, certain acts and characteristically take the form of: "Do X" or "If C do X" (Searle, 1969:35). This distinction is relevant in the present study since we view the speech act of threatening, as contained in terrorist threat notes, as creating the possibility of engaging in terrorist acts, and therefore making those notes worthy of analysis and comprehension if such acts are to be avoided.

Despite its widely acclaimed explanatory prowess as a theoretical paradigm, SAT has been criticised as being speaker-centred and not easily admitting that meaning of acts is negotiated or conceptualised (Yoshitake, 2004). Yoshitake argues that SAT downplays the assimilated dialogical nature of communication, especially the listener's place, to derive meaning and the prospect of multiple interpretations. Yet, it is partly for this very criticism of being speaker-centred that SAT is appropriate for the current study. Terrorism threats are speaker-centred and hardly dialogical. They are monologues that admit little, if any, negotiation of meaning between the threatener and the threatened.

This study proposes that the application of the principles of SAT to terrorism threat notes can help clarify the language of terrorists, that is, how they use language and why. The study explains the concept of a threat in relation to Austin's (1962) performatives and felicity conditions. It further analyses the terrorist threat notes in relation to Searle's (1975) categories of performatives and indirect speech acts. According to Searle (1999:25), indirect speech acts are "cases in which one illocutionary act is performed indirectly by way of performing another". In analysing specific terrorism texts, the question that is asked is whether there are instances like these:

> ...[where] the speaker communicates to the hearer more than he actually says by way of relying on their mutually shared background information, both linguistic and non-linguistic, together with the general powers of rationality and inference on the part of the hearer. (Searle, 1975:60)

## Terrorism threat notes as criminal speech acts

The talk of language-based crimes is, understandably, surprising to an ordinary language user or a criminal law practitioner. This is because, in ordinary circumstances, criminal acts involve physical violence, such as assault and battery, rape, robbery, theft or homicide, and it is rarely the case (though not unusual) for criminal acts to be committed by speech or writing. The term "language crime" was originally put forth by Shuy (1993:1). He defines "language crimes" as any statement whose illocutionary force is that which constitutes the commission of a crime, for example, bribery, extortion, acceptance of a bribe, perjury, drug deals, or other illegal transactions. To this list can be added 'threats' of whichever form and, specifically, terrorist threats.

It is a basic legal assumption in many jurisdictions worldwide that, as a necessary and sufficient ingredient for the commission of a crime, the criminal is required to have committed a certain type of wrongful act (*actus reus*) while having a particular mental state (*mens rea*). This chapter focuses on a crime committed primarily by means of language, that is, terrorists using threat notes to accomplish the act of threatening.

As already pointed out in the theoretical section, speech acts involve using language to perform certain types of actions. Some of the acts ordinarily performed by speech are promising, questioning, threatening, lying, soliciting, and agreeing. Some of these are illegal in specific circumstances. SAT is relevant, not just to criminal law, but also to certain areas of civil law, such as contracts.

In line with Austin (1962), in uttering a language crime, just like other sentences, the three kinds of acts are simultaneously performed. First is the utterance itself, the locutionary force. Then there is the intended meaning, the illocutionary act. All language crimes focus on the actor's intent. As noted, for a criminal to execute a crime, he or she must have the intention to do so. Then there is the consequence of the utterance, perlocutionary act. Other language crimes also concern themselves with the perlocutionary effect of the act. Specifically, for the language crime of threatening, both the illocutionary and the perlocutionary acts must come into play, because a statement that does not leave the recipient feeling intimidated is not a threat, whatever the intent.

## The speech act of threatening

Under Speech Act Theory, a threat is a performative utterance that does not lend itself to the true or false dichotomy but can instead be judged in terms of the appropriateness of the situation of utterance, that is, it is deemed felicitous or infelicitous according to a set of conditions Yule (1996). The term, 'felicity conditions' (also called 'presuppositions') refers to the conditions that must be met and the criteria that must be fulfilled for a speech act to achieve its purpose. By definition, felicity conditions are a state when the utterances made have met the appropriate conditions, such as appropriate context, conventional existence, authority, and also speaker sincerity. These kinds of utterance are only validly recognised as felicitous speech acts if the speaker (S) meets the required condition of being able to validate the context. Searle (1969) proceeds to offer more concerning felicity condition for each illocutionary act. He argues that several conditions, such as psychological ones and the beliefs of S or hearer (H), have to be fulfilled for an utterance to be felicitous. These rules include prepositional content, preparatory condition, sincerity condition, and essential conditions. Because the speech act of threatening deals with a state of affairs that is likely to happen in the future, threats are similar to warnings and predictions. Threats must therefore be carefully distinguished from other futuristic speech acts (Fraser, 1998). The important distinction is that a person who makes a threat expresses an intention to bring about, or cause, the event or state of affairs. Thus, one pragmatic ingredient for a threat is that S must state or imply that he will cause something to happen in the future.

Another necessary ingredient for a threat to pass as one is that the threat issuer must believe that the future event or state of affairs that constitutes the threat will be bad for the addressee. To this end, threats are like warnings, which also refer to a bad future state of affairs. The difference is that warnings are typically aimed at protecting someone from a potential harm caused by natural forces or by someone else (Tiersma, 2002). The third necessary ingredient is that S must intend (*mens rea*) his utterance or statement to intimidate the addressee. A final ingredient for the speech act of threatening, which is also common to many speech acts, is that a threat must appear to be sincere. It is important, however, to emphasise that, to make a threat, S does not, in fact, have to be sincere but need only to appear sincere. To be more exact, S must intend the addressee to believe that S intends to carry out the threatened act. This ingredient is made explicit in New Jersey's statute (The New Jersey Code of Criminal Justice, 2C:12-3), which makes it a crime to threaten to kill another person:

> A person is guilty of a crime of the third degree if he threatens to kill another with the purpose to put him in imminent fear of death under circumstances reasonably causing the victim to believe the immediacy of the threat and the likelihood that it will be carried out. (Justia US Law, 2021)

In summary, within the framework of SAT, a threat is a performative utterance, which can be judged only in terms of the doctrine of infelicities, that is, things that can be wrong and go wrong on the occasion of such an utterance. The following are the felicity conditions for a threat (see next paragraph for meaning of 'S', 'H' and 'A'):

   i.   S promises H to do A

   ii.   S believes H does not want A done

   iii.   S is able to do A

   iv.   S is willing to do A

   v.   A has not already been done. (Searle, 1969:66-67)

Regarding the texts that were analysed in this study, '**S**' refers to the different terrorist groups (al-Qaeda, ISIS, Boko Haram and al-Shabaab) who authored the texts; '**A**' represents the injurious act that the terrorists threaten to do; and '**H**' represents the people for whom the messages are meant (the Nigerian, Kenyan and American governments and their peoples). The language that the terrorist groups use in communicating their threats is deemed to be understandable by the objects of their threats. Even in instances where S uses a language (for example, Arabic), which is unfamiliar to H (such as the Kenyan government and its people), it is taken that the message can be translated and interpreted.

## Methodology

As suggested by the chapter title, the study presented in this chapter adopted a corpus-based approach in gathering the data on terrorism threat notes. A corpus is defined as the compilation of texts that has been gathered for a specific reason (Cheng, 2011), or a collection of naturally occurring instances of language use stored electronically (Tognini-Bonelli, 2001). Corpus-based studies typically use corpus data to gain insights into naturally occurring instances of language use in order to explore a theory or a hypothesis, aiming to validate it, refute it or refine it. It is thus claimed that the corpus itself embodies a theory of language (Tognini-Bonelli, 2001:84-85). The approach accommodates the full evidence from the corpus and analyses this with the aim of finding "probabilities, trends, patterns, co-occurrences of elements, features or groupings of features" (Teubert & Krishnamurthy, 2007:6) and arrives at generalisations about language phenomena.

In the present study, a corpus of terrorism threat notes was downloaded, compiled, and saved in a computer. The notes were then analysed with a view to identifying the various speech acts of threatening within the notes.

The target population for the study was terrorist threat notes available on the internet. Any text that possessed the desired characteristics of a terrorist threat note, and which was found on the websites of terrorist organisations, was considered. The researcher considered the following characteristics for inclusion: the message is from a well-known terrorist organisation; the message explicitly or implicitly expresses a threat; the action that is threatened is injurious, unfavourable, or detrimental to the person(s) at whom it is directed; and the threat action is yet to be executed (it is posed as a future event). The messages that were considered for inclusion in the study were retrieved from the websites of al-Qaeda, al-Shabaab, ISIS and Boko Haram. These four terrorist groups were selected because they are among those considered the most dangerous terrorist organisations and thus their names appear most frequently in the news (*The Independent*, 2019).

The study adopted a stratified purposive sampling technique to obtain sample cases that would best help the researchers to comprehend terrorist threat notes. According to Saunders, Lewis, and Thornhill (2012), purposive sampling (also referred to as 'judge-mental', 'selective' or 'subjective' sampling) relies on the judgment of the researcher when it comes to selecting data to be studied. They note that the use of purposive sampling is appropriate where the sample is quite small, as opposed to probability sampling, which is appropriate where the data sample being studied is large. Despite the small sample, purposive sampling ensures that a wide variety of ideas in line with the subject of the study is captured (Lund, 2012). Using purposive sampling, the researcher selected texts with good prospects for providing the required information. Since the exact number of terrorist threat notes available on the internet cannot be established, the intention of purposive sampling was to maximise the value of data by gathering data rich enough for the study.

In this study, the researchers only considered texts that constituted a terrorist threat note as they had the desired characteristics. Two adult postgraduate students in applied linguistics (who had been thoroughly trained in qualitative analytic research methods and the procedure for conducting a document analysis) assisted the researcher to select the units for study.

Patton (1990) opines that purposeful samples can be stratified by selecting particular units or cases that vary according to a key dimension. In this study, terrorist threat notes were purposefully sampled, and were stratified by their text format (written, audio or audio-visual) and author/source of the text (such as Boko Haram, ISIS, al-Shabaab and al-Qaeda). A total of 39 texts were mined and stratified (see Table 10.1 below).

Qualitative analysis procedures for document analysis were used to analyse the data. Document analysis is a systematic procedure for reviewing or evaluating printed and electronic (computer-based and internet-transmitted) material. The aim of document analysis is to examine and interpret data in order to elicit meaning, gain understanding, and develop empirical knowledge (Corbin & Strauss, 2008; see also Rapley, 2007). Documents typically constitute text (words) and images that have been recorded without a researcher's intervention.

The data was analysed descriptively. The aspect of meaning that was analysed was the meaning of a threat, an aspect of language that can be discussed at length by description. To explain the nature of a threat within SAT, the concept was explained in relation to Austin's performatives and felicity conditions. The notes were also qualitatively analysed in relation to Searle's (1975) categories of performatives called 'commissives' and 'indirect speech acts'. Searl's (1975) categories were used because threats fall within the commissives category in the Searlean performatives paradigm; moreover, terrorism threats may not necessarily be overt.

**TABLE 10.1**   Population stratified by source of text

| | Source | | | | Total |
|---|---|---|---|---|---|
| | Boko Haram | ISIS | al-Shabaab | al-Qaeda | |
| Population | 33 | 3 | 1 | 2 | 39 |
| Sample | 16 | 2 | 1 | 1 | 20 |

Of the 39 texts, using proportional stratification, 20 texts were selected for the study. Since out of the entire study population there was only one audio-visual text and one Twitter text, the researchers ensured that these two texts were included in the sample. The sample thus comprised one audio-visual and 19 written texts. The threat notes were from Boko Haram (16), ISIS (2), al-Shabaab (1) and al-Qaeda (1). For ease of reference, the 21 texts were numbered from T1 to T20 (where 'T' stands for text). The study used a stratified purposive sampling approach to lend credibility to the study as it is known that there are text-form-related characteristics that may influence how the phenomenon of terrorist threat messages manifests. The threat notes in written, audio and audio-visual formats were purposively sampled with the expectation that each would provide unique, rich and valuable information for the study. The significance of purposive sampling is that emphasis is on obtaining a comprehensive understanding from the selected sample until no new substantive information is acquired. Therefore, it was important to include written, audio, and audio-visual formats in the sample.

The study preferred a small and specialised corpus of data, based on the understanding that there is still a place for such corpora (Cameron & Deignan 2003; Flowerdew, 2004). This is in line with Sandelowski's (1995) principle that a suitable sample size in qualitative research is such that it results in a novel and rich understanding of knowledge and permits qualitative inquiry's deep, case-orientated analysis. Further, the size of the sample was dictated by the data saturation point. Faulkner and Trotter (2017) note that data saturation is the point in the research process when no new information is discovered in data analysis, and this redundancy signals to researchers that data collection may cease. A researcher can then be reasonably assured that further data collection would yield similar results and serve to confirm emerging themes and conclusions. This saturation point also signals the completion of the study when the judgment of diminishing returns is reached, and there is little need for more sampling.

## Findings

### The threat in terrorism threat notes

We have already seen how a threat constitutes a language-based crime. Accordingly, to establish that terrorism threat notes constitute criminal speech acts, it is essential that the 'act of threatening' in terrorism threat notes be established. This study considered two definitions of terrorism threat notes, otherwise referred to as 'threatening communication'. The first definition describes it as "a verbalized, written, or electronically transmitted statement that states or suggests that some event will occur that will negatively affect the recipient, someone or something associated with him/her, or specified or non-specified" (Fitzgerald, 2007:1). This definition is significant for pointing out the various formats that threatening communication takes. Such communication can be oral and delivered in a face-to-face encounter, or in a voice or audio-visual recording. It can also be in written format like letters, emails, cards, notes, Facebook posts, blogs, tweets, or text messages written to individuals or a group. With today's digitised media, such communication is often posted on the internet or sent via mobile phones and computers, television, radio, etc. The data for this study included one audio-visual note (transcribed and translated for purposes of the study) and written texts mined from the internet.

The second definition considered in this study is from The California State Penal Code Section 422. This definition states that a threat is as a wilful act, where a person or group:

> ...threatens to commit a crime which will result in death or great bodily injury to another person, with the specific intent that the statement, made verbally, in writing, or by means of an electronic communication device, is to be taken as a threat, even if there is no intent of actually carrying it out, which, on its face and under the circumstances in which it is made, is so unequivocal, unconditional, immediate, and specific as to convey to the person threatened, a gravity of purpose and an immediate prospect of execution of the threat, and thereby causes that person reasonably to be in sustained fear for his or her own safety or for his or her immediate family's safety... (Justia US Law, 2019).

This definition is elaborate and brings to the fore certain salient features of a threatening communication:

1. The threat is made by a person or group, known or unknown;
2. The act is wilful;
3. The future act contained in the threat is a crime;
4. The threat message is to be taken as a threat act (even if there is no intention to carry it out).

In the texts under study, the acts that the terrorists promise are varied. They include threats where an attack is not explicitly stated [T1, T2, T4, T5, T6, T7, T8, T10, T11, T16, T18, T20], unspecific attacks [T1, T2, T3. T11], war or *jihad* [T5, T9, T13, T16], killing [T3, T12, T14], action against authority [T3, T5, T17], demolition of buildings [T18] and bombing [T14]. Table 10.2 summarises the terrorist acts contained in the terrorist threat notes:

**TABLE 10.2**   Summary of terrorist acts in the threat notes

| Terrorist acts | Text |
| --- | --- |
| Unstated attacks | T1, T2, T4, T5, T6, T7, T8, T10, T11, T16, T18, T20 |
| Unspecific attacks | T1, T2, T3, T11 |
| War or *jihad* | T5, T9, T13, T16 |
| Killing | T3, T12, T14 |
| Action against authority | T3, T5, T17 |
| Demolition of buildings | T18 |
| Bombing | T14 |

From the data, the majority of texts are those that express unspecified attacks and those without a stated act that is threatened. Regarding the latter category, although there are no explicit threats, the presence of the terrorists in the lands in question would, by itself, constitute a threat. In T1, the terrorists only announce their presence by saying "We are in your cities. We are in your streets. You are our goals anywhere". In T2, the threat note only says that ISIS "will pass from here soon". That these texts have been authored by well-known terrorist groups with demonstrable ability to carry out their threats itself points to them being threat messages. Indeed, some terrorist groups are so infamous that a message of greeting from them in certain contexts should be considered a threat. Furthermore, when terrorists do not specify an action, they intend to give themselves more options and to raise their chances of executing their threat as the security personnel will have an additional unknown to crack.

As indicated in earlier sections, a speech act must meet certain felicity conditions to pass as a threat. In the texts studied, the terrorists promised several future actions that had not already happened. Further, these promised actions were understood to be injurious to H. The unspecified attacks are understood to be injurious within the contexts of the respective texts. None of the acts would be beneficial to H, but they would be unfavourable and detrimental.

Regarding the condition that S must be sincere for a threat to be felicitous, the circumstances of the release of the texts studied reveals a level of sincerity. The level of commitment by S can be seen in a number of lexical and grammatical stance markers. For example, the use of the word "promise" [T18, T19] suggests an intention to fulfil the promise. Secondly, the absence of the if-clause in the texts suggests severe danger to the threatened. Thirdly, S's intentionality and commitment can be seen in the detailed and commanding forms in the texts. Rugala and Fitzgerald (2003) comment that the more detailed the threat, the more committed the threatener is. The use of adverbs ("immediately" [T7]), verbs ("chop", "hack", "sever", "kill" [T3], "eliminate" [T15]) and contemptuous and offensive term ("Kaffir" [T3]) that convey harmful intentions can form part of the detail or can, in themselves, be indicative of the threatener's dedication and obligation to carry out the threat. In the case of terrorist threat notes, by the public nature in which the threats are communicated, S is also seen to be sincere. Often threats are given in 'public', with the messages recorded before being sent to H, using a medium that S feels is appropriate.

Finally, ordinarily, no one is under obligation to carry out the acts specified in the threats, on or against anybody; but once a threat is uttered, S, the threatener, changes the act, which hitherto was a non-obligation, to an obligation.

The foregoing discussion on felicity conditions leaves no doubt that all the texts that were the subject of this study were threats. This is despite the fact that the performative verb 'threaten' was used in none of them and that, in two cases, the performative verb "promise" was used.

## Categories of speech acts

Searle (1976) classifies speech acts as direct and indirect. An utterance is seen as a direct speech act when there is a direct relationship between the structure and the communicative function of the utterance. On the other hand, he defines an indirect speech act as one that is performed by means of another, thereby implying an indirect relationship between the form and the function of the utterance and requiring H to do more in processing the intended meaning of the utterance. The terrorism threat notes analysed in this study exhibited both direct and indirect speech acts, as presented next.

- *Direct speech acts*

Searle (1976) identifies direct speech acts as 'declaratives', 'commissives', 'directives', 'expressives', and 'representatives'. Declaratives are utterances that impose immediate changes in the institutional affairs. They declare something to be so, and they may be used to assign a name or role. Examples are baptism and pronouncing a couple husband and wife. In the terrorism threat notes that comprised the data of this research, no declarative was noted.

Directives are acts that cause H to do something as a response. In other words, directives are used to get H do what S wants H to do. Examples are requests, commands, advice, questions, and invitations. In the terrorism threat notes studied, there are several directives in the form of advice, commands, and invitations. In T3, Al-Shabaab advises H to be prepared ("Shabaab [al-Shabaab] we are coming be prepared!"); in T6 and T16, Boko Haram gives an order ("...all those arrested should be released immediately..."); in T20, Boko Haram warns Sahara ("... So we are warning them to stop making their site an avenue for attacking Islam, otherwise we will find a way of attacking them"). The directive here is that Sahara should stop being a conduit for attacks on Islam, otherwise there will be dire consequences. In addition, they give the following advice: "Your salvation will only come in your withdrawal from our land, in stopping the robbing of our oil and resources, and in stopping your support for the corrupt and corrupting leaders."

An expressive is an event or act (A) that expresses S's emotion, that is, it articulates S's psychological state to H expressing pleasure, pain, like, dislike, and regret. Examples are when S thanks, apologises, or welcomes H. The terrorism threat notes that were studied exhibited expressives, such as in T5 and T6, where anger is expressed.

Searle's category of representatives expresses propositions and states S believes in, things that can be evaluated to be true or false. Yule (1996) says these are utterances that state what S believes to be the case, or not. Examples are pronouncements of fact, assertion, conclusion, and prediction. The terrorism threat notes studied in this research show an extensive use of representatives. A few examples will suffice: in T4, Boko Haram says: "... the present police commissioner, director state security service (dsss) and ward heads have jointly started arresting our members in your state ...".; in T5, the following is said: "We want to reiterate that we are warriors who are carrying out *jihad* [religious war] in Nigeria and our struggle is based on the traditions of the holy prophet...".; and, in T6, Boko Haram says: "... This is almost 11 yrs. Our members are being killed!"

A commissive speech act occurs when S commits to a future action. Common commissive acts are promises and threats, oaths, offers, vows and volunteering. According to Van den Berg and Surmon (2019), commissive speech acts are the most common utterances in threat acts, and this should apply to terrorism threat notes. Essentially, the main purpose of a terrorism threat note is to express the message that S would perform some action in the future. The greatest concern of a person who has been threatened by a terrorist should be the act that the terrorist commits himself to doing. Secondly, a commissive is an essential part of a threat. In other words, a threat must include S's commitment to a future action. As has been highlighted, this future action can be in the form of a threat expressed, explicitly or implicitly, as a warning or a promise. In that case, warning and promising are acts that closely relate to threatening and, together, form the most common acts in terrorism threat notes. They therefore require sharper focus.

■   *Indirect speech acts*

Searle (1999:25) defines indirect speech acts as "cases in which one illocutionary act is performed indirectly by way of performing another". Threats are intentional acts in which language is used to send a message "which conveys an intention to perform an act viewed by the addressee as unfavourable as well as an intention to intimidate the addressee". Three categories of indirect speech acts of threatening were identified, namely promising, warning, and where no overt performative utterance is used.

- *Indirect speech acts with no overt performative utterance*

Threats perform both commissive acts and other speech/pragmatic acts such as representative (informing, asserting, stating); directive (ordering/commanding); and declarative (making pronouncements). There are also those threats and promises in which the main objective of the utterance is not commissive, that is, not intended to commit S conditionally or unconditionally to do something, but are directive, meant to get H to do something (Salgueiro, 2010:215). Thus, there is the distinction between commissive-conditional promises or threats and directive-commissive conditional promises or threats. In the former, S's future action is conditional on the satisfaction of some condition, yet the intent of the promise or threat is not to get H to bring about the satisfaction of that condition. Typically, threats are understood to be a type of commissive-conditional promise, yet within the context of terrorism, where there is an underlying perceived cultural and historical reasons and perceived victimisation and, therefore, terrorism and religious extremism are viewed as a revenge act, the main objective of the promise or threat is not to get H to bring about the satisfaction of a condition. Indeed, such a condition rarely exists in the context of terrorism as a revenge act. If it exists, then obviously the condition is beyond the fulfilment of H. Text T13 below alludes to this unfulfillable condition:

> **T13**: For the first time since the killing of Mallam Mohammed Yusuf, our leader, we hereby make the following statements: That we have started a *Jihad* in Nigeria which no force on earth can stop...

In revenge terrorism, and as is exemplified in T13 above, terror threats adopt a new meaning and new pragmatic structures where S does not necessarily anticipate the performance of certain conditions. The threats appear like simple commissive acts where S commits to perform a future A, which is deemed detrimental to H. In such a case, the threats or warnings are communicated like an unconditional promise; and the execution of the threat is considered as retribution for a perceived injustice, or denial of some rights.

Traditionally, threats have been presented as conditionals or disjunctions, that is, the structure has had the conditional "if you do ..., I'll do ..." form, or with a disjunction, "you do ... or I'll do ..."); yet this does not appear to be the case with terrorism threat notes. The apparent lack of conditions in the threats and the fact that the threats often appear like a commissive promise, or a mere provision of information of a predetermined future action, often leaves H or the reader wondering what to do to avoid the threatened consequence. Indeed, terrorism threats simply declare intentions to harm or kill without offering any option or condition to the one threatened. This, according to Salgueiro (2010), is what makes the acts count as threats, whose primary objective is to intimidate the person threatened. This is in line with the contention of Storey (1995), who posits that a threat is not a threat until the threatened interprets or accepts it to be so.

Where the terrorist feels there is need to enlighten the threatened on the former's ability, the terrorist can provide relevant information. In T3, al-Shabaab refers to their exploits by mentioning their stranglehold on Somalia and enumerating places they have previously attacked, such as Mpeketoni, Lamu and Mombasa. For the group, the lesson on who they are has already been learnt, as can be seen in this note:

> T14: They say, [t]hey know who we are, we have given them a good example on how we shoot hot bullets.

Attempts at self-introduction on the part of the terrorists also appear to be significant as they often leave a stamp of identity in their threat messages. Consider the following:

> #AmessagefromISIStoUS [T1],
>
> Soldiers of the Islamic state of Iraq and Syria [T2],
>
> Shabaab [T3],
>
> …we are warriors who are carrying out *Jihad* [religious war] in Nigeria [T5],
>
> …Mallam Mohammed Yusuf, our leader… [T13].

In T1, the tweet carries the hashtag that indicates the message is from ISIS. T2 leaves little to the imagination as to who the author is. In T3, Shabaab [al-Shabaab] proclaims loudly that they are not in the mood for jokes. In T5, Boko Haram also reveals their identity by stating who they are: "We are warriors who are carrying out *Jihad* [religious war] in Nigeria". This is also the case when they mention their slain leader, Mallam Mohammed Yusuf, in T13. Self-introduction helps with the effectiveness of the threats because it is the intention of the threatener to intimidate and instil fear. This end is achieved when they make it clear who they are, as they are terrorist groups with well-known, intimidating reputations.

## Warning

Threats, like any other pragmatic or commissive acts, depend on the illocutionary force of the utterance. Threats and promises are the same in the sense that they both perform directive-commissive acts (Salgueiro, 2010:214), yet differ in that threatening is an "intrinsically hostile act" (Fraser, 1998), while promising is not.

According to Searle (1989), a warning is given when H has reason to believe that a future event or state will occur and that this event is not in his best interests. Also, the event's occurrence is not obvious to either S or H. S also believes that the event is not in H's or the listener's best interests. In this way, warning is like advising rather than requesting. In the two texts, S makes it clear that H or his agents are doing something that is not pleasing to S and so advises that the offensive actions should be stopped.

> **T4**: Having got the clear picture of what happened, it has come to our notice that the present police commissioner, director state security service (dsss) and ward heads have jointly started arresting our members in your state (Kano) known to you or not, a situation which we will not take lightly by the grace of Allah. (Boko Haram)

> **T6**: This is almost 11 yrs. Our members are being killed! Anything people want to say or do, we say enough is enough! (Boko Haram)

In T4, S is warning H that an event noxious to H will occur and is advising him against allowing or sending his agents to arrest members of Boko Haram. In T6, S is advising H against killing the members of Boko Haram.

## Promising

An act of promise must be predicated on S and cannot be a past A (Searle, 1989). S cannot promise A that someone else will do; S cannot promise A that has already been done. S may promise to do something, may promise to do something repeatedly or sequentially, or may promise to be, or remain, in the same state or condition. An utterance is considered a promise if it is a pledge to do something for you, not to you. What is promised must be something that S wants to do, and H wants it done. Both S and H consider what is promised to be in the interests of H and would prefer it being done rather than not. Searle (1969) adds that the essential feature of a promise is that it is undertaking an obligation to perform a certain favourable act.

Fraser (1998) provides three conditions that are indicative of a threat, as opposed to a promise or warning: S (threatener) expresses intent to commit, or be responsible for committing A; S's belief that A will result in an unfavourable state of the world for H; and S's intent to intimidate H through S's awareness of the intention. Besides these conditions, it is also clear that in terrorism threats to the reputation of S have an important role in whether the threat will be effective in its intention to intimidate and instil fear. So, the reputation of the threatener is a significant indicator. Terrorist groups, such as ISIS, al-Shabaab, and Boko Haram are known for their ruthlessness and brutality, so it would be superfluous to demand knowledge of them from H for their threats to be taken seriously. Acquaintance with these terror groups is widespread.

While promising, warning and threatening have been distinguished as different types of commissive acts (Fraser, 1998), in terrorism discourse threats frequently appear as promises; and indeed, the word 'promise' is usually used. Despite this, the message remains a threat in both content and structure, as illustrated in these two examples:

**T18**: We promise the West and Southern Nigeria, a horrible pastime….

**T19**: We promise to demolish 500 buildings for any one of our houses that the government destroys.

These examples also illustrate Searle's (1969) assertion that most communicative encounters are indirectly realised.

## Conclusions

At a time of organised crimes and international terrorism, the field of forensic linguistics inevitably becomes increasingly significant. It is on this basis that the need arises to investigate legally valuable texts, such as terrorism threat messages. This study has focused on linguistic evidence in terrorism threat notes that would lead to determining their realisability, clarifying what exactly they entail and establishing their textual resources.

Situating terrorist threat notes within speech acts, the study has revealed that all the texts had neither the performative verb 'threaten' nor the word 'hereby'; yet a threat, which is the focus of the present study, falls under performatives. Despite the absence of the performative verb 'threaten' and the appearance of the performative verb 'promise' in the texts studied, all the texts were threats and, as such, fulfilled Austin's (1962) felicity conditions. This is in line with Fraser (1998), who states that direct (verbal) threats, unlike other speech acts, are not made using a performative verb. He says that indirect threats are implied, and it behoves the threatened to infer the unfavourable act to be performed and determine if a threat has actually been made. Fraser adds that even an interrogative may be perceived as a threat.

The study then analysed the terrorism threat notes within the provisions of felicity conditions, basically to assess the appropriateness of their use or utterance, to determine if the texts satisfy the criteria of a threat so that they achieve their purpose. From the scrutiny of the terrorism threat notes, it was found that all the texts met the felicity conditions for a threat. The terrorist groups (al-Qaeda, ISIS, Boko Haram and al-Shabaab) promise the people for whom the messages are meant (the Nigerian, Kenyan, and American governments and their agents and peoples) to carry out unspecified and unstated attacks, war or *jihad*, killing, action against authority, demolition of buildings, and bombing – all acts both unfavourable and detrimental. Secondly, the terrorists believe that those that they threaten would not want the said acts to be carried out. Thirdly, going by their past records, the terrorists are clearly capable of these acts. Fourthly, they are willing to carry out those acts. Their intention to carry out the acts is abundantly apparent from their use of the word "promise", the absence of the if-clause in the texts, the detailed and commanding forms in the texts, the use of adverbs such as "immediately", the use of harsh verbs like "chop", "hack", "sever", "kill" and "eliminate", and the use of the contemptuous and offensive term "kaffir". Fifth, it is clear that the said acts have not already been carried out.

This study was a response to one of the challenges of the present world, terrorism, and how linguistic knowledge can be used to help understand it. For deeper understanding of terrorist communication, we recommend that further research be done to cover other modes of presentation. Considering that in the present research multi-modality was not explored, it would be interesting to find out what a multi-modal investigation would unearth.

## References


A&E Television Networks, LLC. 2017. US Embassies in East Africa bombed. *A&E Television Networks*. 1 May. http://www.history.com/this-day-in-history/u-s-embassies-in-east-africa-bombed [Accessed 4 November 2020].

Austin, J. 1962. *How to do things with words*. Oxford: Clarendon Press.

Cameron, L. & Deignan, A. 2003. Combining large and small corpora to investigate tuning devices around metaphor in spoken discourse. *Metaphor and Symbol*, 18(3):149-160. https://doi.org/10.1207/S15327868MS1803_02

Cheng, W.L. 2011. *Exploring corpus linguistics: Language in action*. Milton Park, Oxfordshire: Taylor & Francis.

Corbin, J. & Strauss, A. 2008. Basics of qualitative research: Techniques and procedures for developing grounded theory. 3rd Edition. Thousand Oaks, CA: Sage. https://doi.org/10.4135/9781452230153

Faulkner, S.L. & Trotter, S.P. 2017. Data saturation. In: J. Matthes, C.S. Davis & R.F. Potter (eds.). *The International Encyclopedia of Communication Research Methods*. Wiley Online Library. https://doi.org/10.1002/9781118901731.iecrm0060

Fitzgerald, J.R. 2007. The FBI's communicated threat assessment database: History, design and implementation. *FBI Enforcement Bulletin*, 72:1-21. https://doi.org/10.1037/e601072007-002

Flowerdew, L. 2004. The argument for using English specialized corpora to understand academic and professional language. In: U. Connor & T.A. Upton (eds.). *Discourse in the professions, perspectives from corpus linguistics*. Amsterdam, Netherlands: John Benjamins. 11-33. https://doi.org/10.1075/scl.16.02flo

Fraser, B. 1998. Threatening revisited. *Forensic Linguistics: International Journal of Speech Language and the Law*, 5(2):159-173. https://doi.org/10.1558/sll.1998.5.2.159

Gibbons, J. 2003. *Forensic linguistics: An introduction to language in the justice system*. Hoboken, NJ: Blackwell.

Golder, B. & Williams, G. 2004. What is 'terrorism'? Problems of legal definition. *UNSW Law Journal*, 27(2):270-295.

Grant, T. 2008. Approaching questions in forensic authorship analysis. In: J. Gibbons & M.T. Turrel (eds.). *Dimensions of forensic linguistics*. Amsterdam, Netherlands: John Benjamins. 215-229. https://doi.org/10.1075/aals.5.15gra

Jacobsen, R.R. 2010. The interpretation of indirect speech acts in relevance theory. *Journal of LIE*, 3:7-23. https://doi.org/10.29302/jolie.2010.3.1

Justia US Law. 2019. California Penal Code, Section 422:11.5 – Criminal threats. https://law.justia.com/codes/california/2019/code-pen/part-1/title-11-5/section-422/ [Accessed 4 November 2020].

Justia US Law. 2021. *The New Jersey Code of Criminal Justice*, Section 2C:12-3 – Terroristic threats. https://law.justia.com/codes/new-jersey/2021/title-2c/section-2c-12-3/ [Accessed 4 November 2020].

Kravchenko, N. 2017a. Illocution of direct speech acts via conventional implicature and semantic presupposition. *Lege Artis: Language Yesterday, Today, Tomorrow*, 2(1):128-168. https://doi.org/10.1515/lart-2017-0004

Kravchenko, N.K. 2017b. Indirect speech acts via conversational implicatures and pragmatic presuppositions. *Cognition, Communication, Discourse*, 14:54-66. https://periodicals.karazin.ua/cognitiondiscourse/article/view/9534 [Accessed 5 November 2020].

Lund, T. 2012. Combining qualitative and quantitative approaches: Some arguments for mixed methods research. *Scandinavian Journal of Educational Research*, 56(2):155-165. https://doi.org/10.1080/00313831.2011.568674

Olsson, J. 2008. *Forensic linguistics: An introduction to language, crime and the law.* 2nd Edition. London: Continuum.

Olsson, J. 2012. *Wordcrime: Solving crime through forensic linguistics.* London: Continuum.

Olsson, J. & Luchjenbroers, J. 2013. *Forensic linguistics.* 3rd Edition. London: Bloomsbury. https://doi.org/10.5040/9781350284845

Patton, M.Q. 1990. *Qualitative evaluation and research method.* London: Sage.

Rapley, T. 2007. *Doing conversation, discourse and document analysis.* London: Sage. https://doi.org/10.4135/9781849208901

Rugala, E.A. & Fitzgerald, J. 2003. Workplace violence: From threat to intervention. *Clinics in Occupational and Environmental Medicine*, 3(4):775-789. https://doi.org/10.1016/S1526-0046(03)00117-1

Russel, J. 2019. Communications after an attack. *Radicalisation Awareness Network.* 28 October. https://home-affairs.ec.europa.eu/system/files_en?file=2019-11/ran_c-n_communications_after_an_attack_lisbon_en.pdf [Accessed 1 June 2021].

Salgueiro, A.B. 2010. Promises, threats and the foundations of speech act theory. *Pragmatics*, 20(2):213-228. https://doi.org/10.1075/prag.20.2.05bla

Sandelowski, M. 1995. Sample size in qualitative research. *Research in Nursing & Health*, 18(2):179-183. https://doi.org/10.1002/nur.4770180211

Saunders, M., Lewis, P. & Thornhill, A. 2012. *Research methods for business students.* 6th Edition. Cape Town: Pearson Education.

Searle, J.R. 1969. *Speech acts: An essay in the philosophy of language.* Cambridge: Cambridge University Press. https://doi.org/10.1017/CBO9781139173438

Searle, J.R. 1975. Indirect speech acts. In: P. Cole & J.L. Morgan (eds.). *Syntax and semantics: Speech acts, Vol. 3.* New York: Academic Press. 59-82. https://doi.org/10.1163/9789004368811_004

Searle, J.R. 1976. A taxonomy of illocutionary acts. In: K. Günderson (ed.). *Language, mind, and knowledge* (Minnesota studies in the philosophy of science, Vol. 7). Minneapolis, MN: University of Minnesota Press. 344-369.

Searle, J.R. 1994. *Speech acts. An essay in the philosophy of language.* Cambridge: Cambridge University Press.

Searle, J.R. 1999. *Mind, language and society: Philosophy in the real world.* Vale, Guernsey: Guernsey Press.

Shuy, R.W. 1993. *Language crimes: The use and abuse of language evidence in the courtroom.* Hoboken, NJ: Blackwell.

Shuy, R.W. 2014. *The language of murder cases: Intentionality, predisposition and voluntariness.* Oxford: Oxford University Press. https://doi.org/10.1093/acprof:oso/9780199354832.001.0001

Storey, K. 1995. The language of threats. *Forensic Linguistics*, 2(1):74-80. Now published as Storey, K. 2013. The language of threats. *International Journal of Speech, Language and the Law*, 2(1):74-80. https://doi.org/10.1558/ijsll.v2i1.74

Teubert, W. & Krishnamurthy, R. 2007. *Corpus linguistics: Critical concepts in linguistics.* Abingdon, Oxfordshire: Routledge.

The Heritage Foundation. 2017. *Terrorism.* http://solutions.heritage.org/defense/terrorism/ [Accessed 20 September 2020].

*The Independent.* 2019. Terrorism. https://www.independent.co.uk/topic/terrorism?CMP=ILC-refresh [Accessed 20 September 2020].

Tiersma, P. 2002. The language and law of product warnings. In: J. Cotterill (ed.). *Language in the legal process.* Houndmills: Palgrave. 54-74. https://doi.org/10.1057/9780230522770_4

Tiersma, P M. & Solan, L.M. 2012. The language of crime. In: L. Solan & P. Tiersma (eds.). *The Oxford handbook on language and law.* Cambridge: Oxford University Press. 340-353. https://doi.org/10.1093/oxfordhb/9780199572120.013.0025

Tognini-Bonelli, E. 2001. *Corpus linguistics at work.* Amsterdam, Netherlands: John Benjamins. https://doi.org/10.1075/scl.6

Torchia, C. & Odula, T. 2015. Kenya: Extremists vow more attacks; president responds. *The Sun Chronicle.* 4 April.

Van den Berg, K. & Surmon, M. 2019. The act of threatening: Applying speech act theory to threat texts. In: M.K. Ralarala, R. Kaschula & G. Heydon (eds.). *New frontiers in forensic linguistics: Themes and perspectives in language and law in Africa and beyond.* Stellenbosch: African Sun Media. 255-278.

Withnall, A. 2015. Listen to Osama bin Laden's chilling warning weeks before 9/11 attack. *The Independent.* 17 August. https://www.independent.co.uk/news/world/americas/osama-bin-laden-issued-chilling-pre-warning-9-11-attack-plan-al-qaeda-audio-tapes-reveal-10459142.html [Accessed 23 June 2019].

Yoshitake, M. 2004. Critique of J.L. Austin's speech act theory: Decentralization of the speaker-centered meaning in communication. *Kyushu Communication Studies,* 2:27-43.

Yule, G. 1996. Pragmatics. *The study of language.* Cambridge: Cambridge University Press. 127-140.

# "EVERYONE IS DOING IT"

## The complex relationship between criminal and anti-criminal networks in Bukavu, Democratic Republic of Congo

*Rosette Sifa Vuninga*

## Introduction

In Bukavu, the capital city of South Kivu province in the eastern region of the Democratic Republic of the Congo (DRC), criminal networks are not new. In the post-Mobutu Sese Seko era, however, these networks have not just increased exponentially, they have also evolved in terms of their modus operandi. The triple alliance between the community, the civil society and the state, however, is at the centre of understanding both the nature and the modus operandi of these networks, their changing dynamics and, particularly, why they persist. This chapter analyses recent trends in crime and anti-crime networks in Bukavu. The chapter argues that *débrouillez-vous* and *auto-prise en charge* – which, respectively, evoke relying on informal economy since the time of Mobutu and relying on oneself (rather than the State's security forces, such as the police and military) in the fight against crime and insecurities since the Congo conflict in the post-Mobutu era – are at the centre of understanding the complex relationship that exists between criminal and anti-criminal networks in Bukavu.

The biggest legacy of President Mobutu in Congo is *débrouillez-vous*, which means, "fend for yourself" (Braun, 2018; Wild-Wood, 2007). This concept has normalised relying on the informal economy in the everyday life of Congolese since the time of Mobutu. It is a concept that simply means 'surviving at all costs'. It reflects, among other things, the corruption and its normalisation in all sectors of the Congolese State, including security (Bayart, 2006). Since the late 1990s, with war and subsequent crises in the Congo, particularly in its eastern region, Congolese have become even more creative in navigating the hard times of the insecurities and related socioeconomic crises. The (informal) economies of insecurities in the eastern Congo have boomed among other war economies in the region, leading to an increase in crime, despite the involvement of the government, civil society and community agents in fighting them (Büscher, 2016; Geenen, 2011; Jackson, 2001). As Hendricks explains:

> …besides the large presence of Police Nationale du Congo (PNC), Forces Armées
> de la République Démocratique de Congo (FARDC, the Congolese Army) and

> the Agence National de Renseignements (ANR, the Congolese agency for intelli-
> gence) officers in the city, a variety of other actors are engaged in policing such as
> UN-peacekeepers, private security company employees, scouts arranging traffic,
> university brigades, street children looking after parked cars and vigilante-type
> organizations. (2018:274-275)

Despite what can be regarded as an effort to reduce insecurities in the eastern Congo and Bukavu in particular, there is clearly a blurry line between criminal activities and surviving (socioeconomically) by all means, *débrouillez-vous*. The popular phrase, 'Everyone is doing it', has been discussed in previous research (Vuninga, 2018; a phrase that captures the widespread public cynicism and increasingly permissive attitudes towards crime in Bukavu and the Congo in general. The phrase points to a widespread acceptance that so much of what people in Bukavu do is either illegal or feeds off the violent conflict in the region and the malfunctioning of the country in general. This, however, shows that the criminal activities in urban spaces of the conflict-ridden region of the Kivu cannot be detached from the socioeconomic and political crises of the Congo since the fall of Mobutu.

## Bukavu and criminal networks since the post-Mobutu conflict

As Verweijen, Thill and Hendricks (2019) argue, since the 1990s, security in the urban areas of the eastern region of the DRC, in particular in the former Kivu region, has been altered by waves of the conflicts in the Great Lakes Region, mainly in Burundi and Rwanda. This crisis and the movement of people related to it is crucial to understanding the conflict in the eastern Congo for over two decades. Research on the conflict in the eastern Congo has not just portrayed youth as the main perpetrators but also as its primary victims (Verweijen et al., 2019). This contrast is based on the fact that youth between the ages of 18 and 35 constitute the majority of those easily recruited into rebel and militia groups; and they are the ones who engage in the most violent activities (such as killing and raping) in the conflict zone of the eastern Congo. The youth are also the most targeted in the violent acts of the conflict (Bentrovato, 2014; Jourdan, 2004). However, whether youth join the rebels (and other armed groups) or the government army fighting against them, research has shown that the youth in the DRC, particularly in the conflict-ridden eastern region, join mostly for socioeconomic, rather than patriotic, reasons (Pankakoski, 2018; Vuninga, 2018).

Although rural areas are the most severely affected by the violence of the eastern Congo conflict, urban areas are not exempt from organised and sometimes armed groups preying on civilians (Verweijen et al., 2019). In cities such as Goma and Bukavu in the North Kivu and South Kivu regions respectively, there has been a rise in gangs as well as anti-gang groups (Hendricks, 2018:2-3). Intellectual and unemployed youth in particular have become more creative in adopting criminal means to overcome their socioeconomic frustrations (Vuninga, 2018). Education is highly valued in the Congo, particularly among the less economically privileged, as it is perceived as a key to socioeconomic mobility (Hartwell, 2016:2-3). However, with the overall state failure, corruption and other factors that shape access to jobs, including ethnicity, class and gender (Mwapu et al., 2016; Deng, 2001), unemployment remains rampant among educated youth, including graduates (Minyangu et al., 2021). Some who count themselves lucky are employed on contract in job sectors that have little to do with their expertise. For example, the majority of those working in relatively unskilled labour (such as gatemen at hotels, in private homes and in offices, as shopkeepers, waiters, cleaners, etc.) are university graduates (Vuninga, 2018). Others are self-employed in the transportation business (cars and motorbike taxis) or run small businesses in marketplaces, their streets, or their homes. Others dedicate their free time to volunteering in community-led organisations (such as churches, NGOs, public health, health centres, etc.) and neighbourhood watch groups while joining or forming networks of criminals.

## Everyday language and crime in Bukavu

The words 'crime' and 'gang' in everyday language in the DRC can mean different things beyond unlawfulness. With regard to crime, in general, this research is barely the first to note that in most – if not all – societies, people tend to distinguish between what is illegal and what is criminal (see, for example, Conklin, 1977; and Wyatt, Van Uhm & Nurse, 2020). The notion of 'illegal' is based on the book of law, the Congolese criminal code, which is only relevant in the courthouse, not in everyday definitions of criminal offence, as people often distinguish between "moral right" and "legal right" (Brandt, 1983:29). While the former is debatable and mainly based on some degree of "entitlement" (Brandt, 1983:29), the latter is fixed, although 'ordinary' people may not consult the law in their everyday life. What blurs the line between the two is the same issue that radically distinguishes them: the informal economy as the means of making a living for most Congolese. People therefore engage in what Lefkowitz (2007: 202) calls a "moral right to civil disobedience" when it suits their needs, like when they use vigilantism to punish criminals. Agents of the law can also choose to apprehend them or to be understanding, depending on their needs. However, agents of order who recourse to law to restrict people from engaging in morally accepted activities from which they make a living are seen as oppressors. For example, it is illegal to sell alcohol in one's home without a licence; to set up a business on the corner of a road; to use unsupervised underage children in street food businesses; to carry a child on one's back while on a motorbike, etc. However, being lawfully apprehended for these acts can be seen as unjust because those engaged in these activities are perceived as doing what they must do to earn a living. In Congo, therefore, what is criminal and what is not is continuously reinvented for socioeconomic and political reasons and context.

A 'gang' is another complex concept in Congolese popular vocabulary. People barely use it to describe a group of organised criminals in the sense in which it refers to gangs in South Africa or America (Achamat, 1993; Pinnock & Douglas-Hamilton, 1997, 1997; Maringira & Masiya, 2018; Rodgers & Jensen, 2009; Vuninga, 2020). As noted by Hendricks (2018:2) in his research in North-Kivu, a gang "does not necessarily refer to criminals, but rather – in both a positive and negative sense – it denotes 'toughness'". On a negative note, 'gangs' or 'gangsters' have characteristics including smoking (weed and cigarette), drinking, and they "do not shy away from anything" (Hendricks, 2018:2). Not to shy away is something that defines a 'gang' in the DRC and evokes an understanding of those with the courage to survive, fend for, defend and protect themselves. For example, groups of women who trade in dangerous war zones or who travel through dangerous and rebel-ridden territory for work or business are called 'gangs'.

The criminal networks of Bukavu are what scholars such as Wyatt et al. refer to as "disorganised" criminal networks to distinguish them from the more organised legendary gangs, such as the Italian Mafia (Wyatt et al., 2020:357-359). They include armed robbers and other groups of criminals that people in Congo often refer to as bandits, a group of thieves, crooks, or *délinquants*. The most important factors that distinguish the groups of criminals operating in Bukavu from typical gangs in places such as the Cape Flat and townships of South Africa include their level of organisation in unity, roles in the form of military titles, loyalty, a well-defined hierarchy among members, as well as territoriality (Valasik & Tita, 2018). Groups of thugs or bandits in Bukavu often come together for a specific operation, almost like mercenary operations. There is often a person, the one with a *coop* (short for '*cooperation*', which mean a deal or a 'hit'), often with financial means or logistics, who puts a team together for a specific operation; they agree on shares or payment; and they part ways after the operation. On most occasions, it is more about the "individual need" of each member rather than a commitment to the group and membership in the sense of loyalty (Hochhaus & Sousa, 1987:74). These groups also barely have names. Occasionally, however, some criminal groups have stuck together and led relatively successful criminal operations in Bukavu, including the Tiya na Se,[1] Wanted, Armée Rouge, and Kaya Men. While all these groups share robbing people of their valuable goods (including cell phones, jewellery, monies, etc.) at night and in quiet streets during the day, and are occasionally engaged in armed robberies, they differ in the amount and type of violence they inflict on their victims.

---

1   "Tiya na se" is Lingala for 'put it down' or 'drop it' because it is the famous phrase they used when robbing their victims of their goods.

Some use intimidation and others physical violence, including beating up their victims or using sharp objects to inflict torture to make them comply with their requests, especially when the victim is physically resistant. They are also territorial in the sense that each is known to operate in a certain neighbourhood.

The most popular of the criminal groups of Bukavu, however, are the Fins d'Heures. The name is French for, 'end of hours' and it refers to their reputation of robbing people in the very late hours of the night. They are (un)popular for their operations in the rich neighbourhoods of Bukavu city centre. Fins d'Heures emerged between 2009 and 2010 and their activities affected many between 2011 and 2015. It is worth noting that they emerged between 2003 and 2013 at the height of the conflict in the eastern Congo, the so-called "unstable decade", which is mostly memorable for the bloody M23 rebel attacks in the Kivu (Nangini et al., 2014:3).

Although considered a gang, it is unclear to many *Bukaviens* (Bukavu inhabitants) whether Fins d'Heures are actually organised groups of criminals or just ordinary people who turn into thieves when an opportunity presents itself. In Bukavu, there are divergent theories about the Fins d'Heures' structure and mode of operation. They are mostly *motards* (motorcycle taxi drivers); and one way of identifying them late at night is that they drive in a group of two or four. They are also gangs of well-educated individuals, with some holding university degrees. Thus, they are known to lure their victims through speaking to them in good French. Generally, they prey on the upper working class, mainly the bosses of NGOs, unlike the other groups mentioned earlier who prey on small businesspeople, including villagers returning to their homes after running their small businesses and other affairs in the city. Although Fins d'Heures frequently use intimidation such as threatening to physically harm or kill their victims, they seldom inflict physical harm. Their strategy mostly consists of snatching valuables from people on the street and speeding off on their motorcycles. They also work in teams, with one luring the victim in need of transportation and then sending a signal to the other *motard* who is often driving behind them to pretend to rob both the *motard* and his client. Regardless of the amount of violence involved, such criminal networks' activities have triggered community responses inspired by the types of crimes and amount of insecurity they have brought about.

## From Nyumba Kumi to Forces Vives and Pomba Solution: community-based approaches to fighting crime in Bukavu

The fight against insecurity in Bukavu has always consisted of mobilising the people around the concept of *auto-prise en charge*, which can be translated as 'taking care of oneself' or 'self-support', or 'standing for oneself' (Thill, 2019:43; Verweijen, 2019). The concept has not only been used in ridding communities of ills such as criminal activities, but it has also been used by the most notorious armed fractions operating in the eastern Congo region to justify their actions, citing that the government forces, or the state in general, is unable to protect them or to deliver in terms of their citizenship rights. For example, the Alliance of Democratic Forces for the Liberation of Congo-Zaire (AFDL), which led the rebellion and succeeded in ousting Mobutu in 1997, was formed in the context of *auto-prise en charge* against Mobutu's dictatorship (on which the socioeconomic crisis in Zaire was also blamed). Other rebel and militia groups, including the Mai Mai, the M23, and the CNDP, to name but a few, were formed for *auto-prise en charge* reasons because of a lack of satisfaction with the post-Mobutu leadership. From 1999, people in urban areas, especially the youth, resorted to *auto-prise en charge*, often as vigilante-inspired means to protect their communities against criminals who increasingly terrorised their neighbourhood. *Nyumba kumi* ('ten houses' in Kiswahili), a neighbourhood watch group based on a ten-house cluster (which is popular in east Africa, mostly in Tanzania, Kenya and Uganda), was initiated in places such as Bagira, Essence and Kadutu – neighbourhoods of Bukavu.

From the early 2000s, the *forces vives* (French for 'vital forces') replaced *nyumba kumi* and other forms of community initiatives in the fight against insecurities in Bukavu. Unlike the *nyumba kumi*, *forces vives* were and remain the most complex community-based anti-crime networks. They are difficult to define; and their proximity to the state security forces, civil society, and political class – both the ruling and the opposition parties – is complex and they are viewed with a high degree of scepticism. This is so much so that, between 2001 and 2004, the *forces vives* were consulted (just like civil society groups) on matters regarding democratic governance in the effort to end the Second Congo War (1998-2003) (Kadima, 2003:46; Namegabe, 2004). According to Namegabe (2004:219), the *forces vives* are "churches and associations". He also defines them as a form of "militarism" within the civil society of the DRC (Namegabe, 2004:219). For Kadima (2003:46), however, civil society groups operate within the umbrella of *forces vives*. His assumption is based on the crucial role played by the *forces vives*, which the civil society was classified under in the Inter-Congolese Dialogue of December 2002 in Pretoria. This dialogue was generally about deciding on power sharing "among Kabila government, the armed groups, the political opposition and the forces vives" (Kadima, 2003:46). *Forces vives* are best understood as "pressure groups" (Demart & Bodeux, 2013:75) and are easily manipulated by the leading government, opposition, and civil society alike, as well as by any structure wanting to access socio-political power, to pass an opinion, or protest against something or someone, ranging from insecurity to corruption and injustices in Congolese government sectors (Kadima, 2003:46; Namegabe, 2004:219-221). However, for ordinary Kivucians, *forces vives* echo the vigilante groups that took both the security of their neighbourhoods and justice against criminals into their own hands, particularly in the first 10 years of President Joseph Kabila's presidency (Thill, 2019:51).

One of the first *forces vives* that shook the city of Bukavu includes the Jeunes Essence Forces Vives (EFV) which, between 2003 and 2010, used violent tactics to suppress youth criminal groups involved in armed robberies in their neighbourhoods. They publicly punished criminals using extreme violence, such as beating them to death and publicly lynching suspects. This method was successful in scaring away criminals in Essence neighbourhoods and inspired other community-based anti-crime groups in nearby places, such as Kadutu and Muhungu. However, their use of extreme violence and regular clashes with the government security forces quickly made EFV unpopular. Their methods were largely condemned by civil society in accordance with human rights. EFV is now Bukavu Forces Vives pour la Paix (which means, 'Bukavu vital forces for peace') and has the status of a not-for-profit organisation. Bukavu Forces Vives pour la Paix does not publicly use violence on criminals. More interestingly, its various offices in Bukavu (where it provides a variety of services ranging from finding stolen goods and restoring them to their owners, to finding criminals who are wanted by the victim they offended), offer all services for a fee.

Other *forces vives* making headlines nowadays in Bukavu include Amka Congo ('Wake up Congo') and its *pomba solution* groups ('*pomba*' in Bukavu Kiswahi's jargon and it means robust, fit, with physical strength) who patrol the city of Bukavu to catch and hand over criminals to the state authorities. Remy Kasindi founded Amka Congo (NGO) in 2015, as part of the office of *Societé Civile* of Bukavu that he works for, with aims including advocating for the development of infrastructure (such as electrical power management and distribution of water and electricity, building roads, etc.). According to Kasindi, Amka Congo amins, among other things, to create means for the Kivu population's "appropriation of their own security", to denounce corruption in private and government sectors, and also to advocate public health[2] in the Kivu region. Today, Amka Congo has branches in Kinshasa, Uviva and Goma, among others.[3] Unlike the early *forces vives*, the *pomba solution* do not take justice into their own hands but

---

2   On Amka Congo, see, for example, https://libregrandlac.com/index.php/article/433/bukavu-:-l-autorite-doit-revoir-la-maniere-de-livraison--de-l-autorisation-de-batir--amka-congo- [Accessed 29 April 2022]; https://www.7sur7.cd/2019/12/18/sud-kivu-le-collectif-amka-congo-exige-le-rapatriement-urgent-de-plus-de-1600-dependants [Accessed 29 April 2022].

3   Follow-up interview with Remy Kasindi, founder and director of Amka Congo Bukavu, 21 January 2022.

rather hand over criminals to the police. Their expertise is based on their fitness and muscles that are needed in physically apprehending thieves. Amka Congo considers itself a *force vive* and its militarism goes beyond apprehending criminals and bringing them to justice.

More recently in Bukavu, groups known as *communautés protectrices* were formed to fight crimes though public health methods. These groups, unlike the common *forces vives*, mostly comprise women of all ages and backgrounds. Their aim is to build communities free of violence, particularly sexual violence.[4] They were initiated by Médecins du Monde, an international NGO dedicated to public health, which works with the Panzi Foundation of the Nobel Prize winner, Dr Denis Mukwege.[5] The *communautés protectrices* work with local hospitals and clinics, churches, school instructors and selected member of civil society to report mostly on sexual violence and related offences. They differ from the early *forces vives* and *pomba solutions* because they work clandestinely as informants. They report to the *communauté sécuritaire*, which includes frontline nurses and doctors who work on physical (including sexual) abuse of victims, and some members of the Congolese police whose contacts are discretely given to the *communautés protectrices*. The latter also work with women's associations such as MAMUSA on sexual offenses, particularly sexual activities with minors. Because they operate like spies, it is not safe for them to take any action, such as administer popular justice or even confront and apprehend an offender in any way. The activities of the *communautés protectrices* and their collaborators, the *communauté sécuritaire*, have helped to produce reliable statistics on crimes in the region, as well as to catch the perpetrators using the information obtained from victims whom they treat.

From the Nyumba Kumi to *communautés protectrices*, it is clear that people of Bukavu have shown their commitment to securing their communities. However, with crimes taking new shapes and changing modus operandi, approaches to fighting them have also upgraded. Among other things, communities have joined hands with the civil society and government forces to ensure not just success but also a degree of human right consideration in the ways they apprehend criminals, some of whom are often also members of the communities. However, from simple patrols to scary criminals to justice mob, then working with the state security forces, one cannot overlook the continuity next to the changes in community-based fight against crime and insecurities

---

4   Justin Mwamba (2021) Sud-Kivu: *autorités et membres des communautés protectrices s'engagent à la prévention des violences sexuelles.* https://actualite.cd/2021/04/10/sud-kivu-autorites-et-membres-des-communautes-protectrices-sengagent-la-prevention-des [Accessed 20 July 2022].

5   Dr Denis Mukwege is known for his medical work in the Kivu region, especially for treating victims of sexual violence since the conflict in the eastern Congo. For more on Dr Mukwege, see, for example, https://www.bbc.com/news/world-africa-54100429 [Accessed 29 April 2022].

in Bukavu. These continuity and changes are linked to the socio-political and economic motivations to be involved in fighting crime, and the civil society that inspires their emergence and methods of operation.

# The NGO-isation of anti-crime networks as "economy of insecurity"

As research proves elsewhere, it is common for community security infrastructures to change over time. In Tanzania, for example, research on *nyumba kumi* and other grassroots security organisations noted both "the continuity and change in the effort of building institutional resilience" (Sambaiga, 2018:49). The history of community security associations in Tanzania is linked to that of their nation as they emerged in the 1960s as part of the TANU's initiative to strengthen its political power at community level. *Nyumba Kumi*, in present-day Tanzania and elsewhere in Kiswahili-speaking east African countries, are not all government supporters. Although still inspired by the ten-cluster house system of the early *nyumba kumi*, there are new groups under new names: they can cover spaces defined beyond ten-house clusters; many of them are apolitical though sometimes critical of political leadership; they have adopted new names for their community security groups; and they have many more features (Sambaiga, 2018). These changes are inspired by several socio-political and economic factors that, in turn, shape the kinds of insecurities and the security measures to be taken, not only at the level of state but at grassroots level.

The two-and-half decades of conflict in the region and its changing dynamics have shaped the security landscape of Bukavu, especially in relation to crimes and how the communities act against them. From the *nyummba kumi* and the *forces vives* to the current *pomba solution* and *communautés protectrices*, there are continuities and novelties in the community-based security infrastructures in Bukavu. The daily increase in mugging, housebreakings and armed robberies led to the formation *of nyumba kumi* in the 1990s. *Forces vives* emerged in the late 1990s, during the rule of the late President Laurent Kabila, as a result of increasing violence in the crimes being committed, as well as the involvement and corruption of the state security forces in some of these crimes (particularly armed robbery and mugging civilians at gunpoint, mostly at night). The *forces vives* were also reacting to the impunity enjoyed by many criminals, which is why they usually took justice into their own hands. These actions made *forces vives* popular to the extent that both the state and civil society competed to control them. It was in that regard that the *forces vives* re-emerged and reorganised themselves as a militant wing of the civil society of the Kivu region that, in turn, transformed them into a political force for 'hire' (or to be (ab)used) by both the leading and opposition parties from the 2006 elections and the following 2011 and 2018 ones. *Forces vives* thus became less about securing their neighbourhoods and more about working with the state security forces, such as the police and military, as well as grabbing leading politicians' attention through many anti-government protests. However, if there is one major influence that led to the formation of new groups, and changes in the modus operandi of community-based anti-crime networks, it was their registration as NGOs or non-profit associations, commonly known in Congo as *asbl* (*association sans but lucratif*).

The emergence of NGOs in the DRC is linked to post-independence and Cold War economic crises, which subjected the DRC, like most African countries, to the infamous Structural Adjustment Program imposed by loans from Western countries. NGOs remarkably emerged on the continent with the HIV/Aids pandemic in the early 1990s (Depelchin, 2005:127-139; Seckinelgin, 2005; Shivji, 2007), as well as because of war and refugee crises from war-torn countries bordering the eastern and western regions of the DRC. These refugees were fleeing the Angolan Civil War (1975-2002) and the conflict in the Great Lakes Region, mainly the civil war in Burundi and Rwanda. To date, NGOs continue to mushroom in the DRC as a result of the continuously degrading socio-political and economic conditions in general, along with the violence of the conflict that continues to haunt its eastern region. Among other things, armed groups (militias, rebels) multiply daily and engage in gross human rights violations to claim political rights, gain access to land, and control resource-rich territories, mostly in rural areas of the Kivu region (Nzongola-Ntalaja, 2002:214-226; Vlassenroot, 2008). This has made NGOs a permanent feature in the DRC and, indeed, one of the most stable and envied 'careers'.

Democratic leadership, human rights awareness, and economic empowerment are among the main aims of the hundreds of NGOs operating in the Congo in general and in Bukavu in particular. Like elsewhere, NGOs in Bukavu are also involved in development projects (agriculture, farming, skills development), public health (raising awareness about disease, pandemics, reproductive health for women, etc.), and empowering the youth and women (Buchely, 2012:72-73), to name but a few. NGOs in eastern Congo also work to assist the victims of the violence of the conflict: sexual violence, orphans, child soldiers' reintegration into society, the *maibobo* (street children) phenomenon, and in fighting other insecurities brought about by criminal activities.

Research shows that, in the post-Cold War, NGOs have changed drastically as they adapt to the global bureaucratic system. More importantly, the changes within NGO stream from their complex relationships with the state, donors (local, but mostly international) and their beneficiaries (Buchely, 2012:77-78; Ullah & Routray, 2007). This automatically leads to unbalanced power relationships between the NGO owners, leaders, workers, and their beneficiaries in the community. What is interesting about

NGOs in the eastern Congo is that they cannot be detached from the economy of violence that justifies their presence and formation and which also sustains them. The community-based anti-crime groups increasingly register as NGOs and work together with the office of civil society. Criminal activities, however, continue to rise, taking ever more sophisticated forms.

The NGO-isation of the community-based anti-crime groups has largely contributed to the "economy of insecurity" in the Kivu region in general and in Bukavu city in particular (Chandler, 2001:690-691; Thill, 2019:50-51). This economy of insecurity is certainly at the centre of understanding the common reason why people, mostly the youth, get involved in either networks of crime or those fighting them. With the exacerbation of unemployment among graduate youth in Bukavu, and with the new rich being NGO clerks, community based anti-crime networks have found their own way to access the *mangeoire*. The latter is French for 'manger', a place or corner in a stable where animal feed is placed. In the Congolese context, *mangeoire* is used to describe the grid and corruption of the political class who capitalise on crime and accumulate wealth at the expense of those they lead and the development of their country. In the Congo, the concept also applies to the weak opposition parties who are perceived as having been founded with the sole aim of getting access to the country's treasury to enrich themselves, "to access to the 'mangeoire'" (Ekambo, 2021:86), rather than to bring about socio-political changes. Community-based, anti-crime groups turning NGOs in Bukavu, along with their complex and indeed disastrous relationships with the state security forces and civil society, have become the means by which the unemployed and often educated youth access the *mangeoire*.

Once they become part of civil society, community protection groups transform the insecurity of their neighbourhoods into a capital generator, a source of income, a job; and just like most local and international NGOs, workers depend on the violent conflict and associated socioeconomic crises in the region; and the community anti-criminal networks-turned-*asbl* depend on criminal networks. It is therefore not surprising that, since the community vigilante groups became NGOs and police collaborators, criminal activities have increased. The change from chasing criminals in the neighbourhood streets to running anti-criminal activities from offices has also created new forms of insecurity. In addition, their affiliations to civil society and the Congolese police have turned community-based anti-criminal networks away from their original and voluntary commitment to rid their communities of crime. They are now more and more committed to "patriotic awakening to save the nation",[6] a cause that mainly benefits the politicians

---

6    See "Bukavu: des jeunes manifestent contre la guerre et la tentative de balkanisation de la RDC", Radio Okapi, last modified on 8 August 2015. http://www.radiookapi.net/actualite/2012/08/11/

and their corrupt security forces who do little to nothing for their communities and who led them to the *auto-prise en charge* in terms of their security in the first place.

## Conclusions

Since the end of the post-Mobutu conflict, community-based anti-crime networks in Bukavu have moved from vigilante-related actions to apprehending criminals in a relatively lawful manner. This progress is linked to their affiliation and/or registration as part of civil society and joining hands with the state security forces in their fight against insecurity in Bukavu. This move shows that the relationship between good governance, economic development and security is appreciated, particularly by the many, mostly educated, and unemployed youth involved in both criminal and anti-criminal networks in Bukavu. It is, however, safe to say that not much good can come from the irregularly and poorly remunerated Congolese police joining hands with civil society and associated anti-crime groups comprising largely educated and unemployed youth. On the one hand, *débrouillez-vous* remains the very essence of the informal economy by which most Congolese make a living and the overall corruption in the private and public sector. On the other hand, *auto-prise en charge* remains at the centre of both the state and civil society mobilisation of people to fight against crime and the insecurity they bring about in their communities. The two combined are central to understanding the complex relationships between criminal and anti-criminal networks in Bukavu in particular and how crime and anti-crime networks feed on and, indeed, sustain each other. The persistence and increase of insecurities related to criminal activities in Bukavu is rooted in the socioeconomic reasons that motivate both criminals and those fighting them. In particular, the NGO-isation of community anti-crime groups has produced another kind of relationship between criminals and those fighting them: mutual dependence and collaboration in exploiting the state of insecurity in the Bukavu. Like the war economies in the region, economies of insecurity blur the line between criminal and non-criminal activities and increase impunity.

## Acknowledgements

The author acknowledges the University of the Western Cape's Centre for Humanities Research for funding their current postdoctoral fellowship. They are also grateful to the Social Science Research Council's African Peacebuilding Network as this chapter draws largely on their 2016 funded Collaborative Research Group fellowship.

---

bukavu-des-jeunes-manifestent-contre-la-guerre-la-tentative-de-balkanisation-de-la-rdc-2. See also Vuninga (2018:8).

# References

Achmat, Z. 1993. "Apostles of civilised vice": 'Immoral practices' and 'unnatural vice' in South African prisons and compounds, 1890-1920. *Social Dynamics*, 19(2):92-110. https://doi.org/10.1080/02533959308458553

Bayart, J.F. 2006. *L'Etat en Afrique: la politique du ventre*. Paris: Fayard.

Bentrovato, D. 2014. Accounting for violence in Eastern Congo: Young people's narratives of war and peace in North and South Kivu. *African Journal on Conflict Resolution*, 14(1):9-35.

Brandt, R.B. 1983. The concept of a moral right and its function. *The Journal of Philosophy*, 80(1):29-45. https://doi.org/10.2307/2026285

Braun, L.N. 2018. 'Débrouillez-Vous': Women's work, transactional sex, and the politics of social networks. *Ethnos*, 83(1):20-38. https://doi.org/10.1080/00141844.2015.1134611

Buchely, L. 2012. The NGO-isation dilemma: International cooperation, grassroots relations, and government action from an accountability perspective: A case study of Colombian migration NGOs and the national system of migration. *Buffalo Public Interest Law Journal*, 31:63-117.

Büscher, K. 2016. Reading urban landscapes of war and peace: The case of Goma, DRC. In: A. Björkdahl & S. Buckley-Zistel (eds.). *Spatializing peace and conflict: Mapping the production of places, sites and scales of violence*. London: Palgrave Macmillan. 79-97. https://doi.org/10.1057/9781137550484_5

Chandler, D. 2001. The road to military humanitarianism: How the human rights NGOs shaped a new humanitarian agenda. *Human Rights Quarterly*, 23(3):678-700. https://doi.org/10.1353/hrq.2001.0031

Conklin, J.E. 1977. *"Illegal but not criminal": Business crime in America*. Englewood Cliffs, NJ: Prentice-Hall.

Demart, S. & Bodeux, L. 2013. Postcolonial stakes of Congolese (DRC) political space: 50 years after independence. *African Diaspora: A Journal of Transnational Africa in a Global World*, 6:72-96. https://doi.org/10.1163/18725457-12341242

Deng, F.M. 2001. Ethnic marginalization as statelessness: Lessons from the Great Lakes region of Africa. In: T. Alexander Aleinikoff & D. Klusmeyer (eds.). *Citizenship today: Global perspectives and practices*. Washington, DC: Carnegie Endowment for International Peace. 183-208. https://doi.org/10.2307/j.ctt6wpkc2.12

Depelchin, J. 2005. *Silences in African history: Between the syndromes of discovery and abolition*. Dar es Salaam: Mkuki na Nyota.

Ekambo, J.C.D. 2021. Multiplicité médiatique et multipartisme en Afrique: symétrie de déficiences. *Les Enjeux de l'Information et de la Communication*, 17(2):83-90. https://doi.org/10.3917/enic.021.0083

Geenen, S. 2011. Relations and regulations in local gold trade networks in South Kivu, Democratic Republic of Congo. *Journal of Eastern African Studies*, 5(3):427-446. https://doi.org/10.1080/17531055.2011.611676

Hartwell, A. 2016. USAID ECCN policy issues brief: Accelerated education for out-of-school children and youth in the DRC.

Hendriks, M. 2018. The politics of everyday policing in Goma: The case of the Anti-gang. *Journal of Eastern African Studies*, 12(2):274-289. https://doi.org/10.1080/17531055.2018.1459976

Hochhaus, C. & Sousa, F. 1987. Why children belong to gangs: A comparison of expectations and reality. *The High School Journal*, 71(2):74-77.

Jackson, S. 2001. Our wealth is being pillaged! War economies and rumours of crime in Kivu. *Politique Africaine*, 84:117-135. https://doi.org/10.3917/polaf.084.0117

Jourdan, L. 2004. Being at war, being young: Violence and youth in North Kivu. In: K. Vlassenroot & T. Raeymakers (eds.). *Conflict and social transformation in eastern DR Congo*. Ghent: Academia Press Scientific Publishers. 157-176.

Mwamba, J. 2021. Sud-Kivu: Autorités et membres des communautés protectrices s'engagent à la prévention des violences sexuelles [South Kivu: Authorities and members of protective communities commit to preventing sexual violence]. Actualite.cd. https://actualite.cd/2021/04/10/sud-kivu-autorites-et-membres-des-communautes-protectrices-sengagent-la-prevention-des [Accessed 20 July 2022].

Kadima, D.K. 2003. Choosing an electoral system: Alternatives for the post-war Democratic Republic of Congo. *Journal of African elections*, 2(1):33-48. https://doi.org/10.20940/JAE/2003/v2i1a3

Lefkowitz, D. 2007. On a moral right to civil disobedience. *Ethics*, 117(2):202-233. https://doi.org/10.1086/510694

Maringira, G. & Masiya, T. 2018. Persistence of youth gang violence in South Africa. *The African Review*, 45:164-179.

Minyangu, M.P., Nguezet, P.M.D., Masirika, S.A., Adeniyi, A., Olayide, O.E. & Kaghoma, C.K. 2021. Understanding gender-based differences in the engagement of the youth in agribusiness in South-Kivu province, Democratic Republic of Congo. *Business Strategy & Development*, 4(1):11-21. https://doi.org/10.1002/bsd2.152

Mwapu, I., Hilhorst, D.J.M., Mashanda, M., Bahananga, M. & Mugenzi, R. 2016. *Women engaging in transactional sex and working in prostitution: Practices and underlying factors of the sex trade in South Kivu, the Democratic Republic of Congo*. Report 10. London: Secure Livelihoods Research Consortium.

Namegabe, P-R. 2004. Le pouvoir traditionnel au Sud-Kivu de 1998-2003: Rôle et perspectives. *L'Afrique des Grands Lacs: Annuaire 2004-2005*. Antwerp: University of Antwerpen. 209-234.

Nangini, C., Jas, M., Fernandes, H.L. & Muggah, R. 2014. Visualizing armed groups: The Democratic Republic of the Congo's M23 in focus. *Stability: International Journal of Security and Development*, 3(1). https://doi.org/10.5334/sta.dd

Nzongola-Ntalaja, Georges. 2002. *The Congo from Leopold to Kabila: a people's history*. New York: Zed Books. https://doi.org/10.5040/9781350223004

Pankakoski, I. 2018. Youth livelihoods and the local conflict in North Kivu: A case study in the eastern Democratic Republic of Congo. Master's thesis. Helsinki: Tampere University.

Pinnock, D. & Douglas-Hamilton, D. 1997. *Gangs, rituals & rites of passage*. Cape Town: African Sun Press with the Institute of Criminology, University of Cape Town.

Rodgers, D. & Jensen, S. 2009. Revolutionaries, barbarians or war machines? Gangs in Nicaragua and South Africa. Violence today: Actually existing barbarism. *Socialist Register*, 45:220-238.

Sambaiga, R.F. 2018. Changing images of *Nyumba Kumi* in Tanzania: Implications for youth engagement in countering violence at community level. *The African Review*, 45(1):49-74.

Seckinelgin, H. 2005. A global disease and its governance: HIV/AIDS in sub-Saharan Africa and the agency of NGOs. *Global Governance: A Review of Multilateralism and International Organizations*, 11(3):351-368. https://doi.org/10.1163/19426720-01103006

Shivji, I.G. 2007. *Silences in NGO discourse: The role and future of NGOs in Africa*. Oxford: Fahamu/Pambazuka.

Thill, M. 2019. *A system of insecurity: Understanding urban violence and crime in Bukavu*. Research report. London: Rift Valley Institute.

Ullah, A.A. & Routray, J.K. 2007. Rural poverty alleviation through NGO interventions in Bangladesh: How far is the achievement? *International Journal of Social Economics*, 34:237-248. https://doi.org/10.1108/03068290710734208

Valasik, M. & Tita, G. 2018. Gangs and space (Chapter 36). In: J.N. Gerben & S.D. Johnson (eds.). *The Oxford handbook of environmental criminology*. London: Oxford University Press. 839-867. https://doi.org/10.1093/oxfordhb/9780190279707.013.25

Verweijen, J., Thill, M. & Hendriks, M. 2019. *Un ordre ambigu: Groupes de jeunes et maintien de l'ordre en milieu urbain dans l'est du Congo*. London: Rift Valley Institute.

Vlassenroot, K., 2008. Armed groups and militias in eastern DR Congo (Report). *Lecture Series on African Security*, 5:1-15. Stockholm: Totalförsvarets forskningsinstitut; Nordiska Afrikainstitutet.

Vuninga, R.S. 2018. "Everyone Is Doing It": The changing dynamics of youth gang activity In Bukavu, Democratic Republic of Congo. *African Peacebuilding Network*. Brooklyn, NJ: Social Science Research Council.

Vuninga, R.S. 2020. Youth gangsters: Negotiating power in intimate relationships among the youth in South Africa. *Politeia*, 39(1):1-16.

Wild-Wood, E. 2007. "Se débrouiller" or the art of serendipity in historical research. *History in Africa*, 34:367-381. https://doi.org/10.1353/hia.2007.0024

Wyatt, T., Van Uhm, D. & Nurse, A. 2020. Differentiating criminal networks in the illegal wildlife trade: Organized, corporate and disorganized crime. *Trends in Organized Crime*, 23(4):350-366. https://doi.org/10.1007/s12117-020-09385-9

# DETERMINING THE AUTHOR(S) OF A DEFAMATION WEBSITE

## Who framed Graeme Joffe?

*Colin Michell*

## Introduction

*'Joffers, my boy'* was heard daily by Johannesburg's commuters on their morning drive to work in the 2000s. Graeme Joffe was a well-known radio personality on *94.7 Highveld's* breakfast show, 'The Rude Awakening' and 'Breakfast Xpress', where he was the sports presenter and commentator. He is probably best remembered for the 'Daily Stupid Sports Joke' (Lowman, 2015). Mr Joffe had been involved in media and sports journalism since completing his journalism degree at South Africa's Rhodes University. Between 1992 and 1999, he was the World Sport Presenter for CNN in Atlanta, USA. On his return to South Africa, he was the presenter for *SuperSport* for two years. During his tenure as a sports journalist and commentator, Mr Joffe became aware of the depth and extent of corruption in the administrative aspects of South African sport. This corruption involved large media houses, The South African Sports Confederation and Olympic Committee (SASCOC), and even reached the upper echelons of government. Once Mr Joffe began to expose the corruption in South African sport, the harassment started. Mr Joffe felt it was his duty to be the voice for all the athletes who were suffering as a consequence of the corruption and maladministration, with a prime example being SASCOC officials enjoying a jet-set lifestyle while athletes had no funding. At first it was simply derogatory tweets on Twitter that called into question Mr Joffe's integrity, but these soon escalated into lawsuits and even potential blackmail (Joffe, 2019). Figure 12.1 shows a tweet to Mr Joffe from one of the suspect authors. The redacted names in the figure are those of two of the three suspect authors.

**FIGURE 12.1**   Threatening tweet to Mr Joffe

In 2013, SASCOC attempted to sue Mr Joffe in his personal capacity for R21 million; and in July 2015, he received a legal threat from a large media company as a result of a column he had written in *SportsFire Daily*. This was the tenth legal threat he had received from this media company in two years. He was also very much alone as an investigative journalist and whistle-blower, with the levels of corruption so deep that nobody would dare support him, as they were all funded by the same media houses (Joffe, 2019).

On 17 April 2015, Mr Joffe was informed by a person he trusted that, as a result of his exposé of irregularities in the disbursement of funds from the National Lottery, his life was in danger if he remained in South Africa. An associate of Mr Joffe hired a private investigator to pursue the veracity of the threats, and it was discovered that Mr Joffe's cell phone had been illegally tapped and his email hacked. He also received abusive threats from within the Department of Sport and Recreation on Twitter; and a case that Mr Joffe had opened at the Sandton Police Station inexplicably disappeared a day after being lodged. This resulted in Mr Joffe having to go into exile in the United States where he was granted asylum status. Prior to this, in November 2014, an anonymous – and now defunct – blog titled 'graemejoffe-exposed' had appeared, using his name and a fake London address. The server for the blog was held in Panama. The blog included eight short sections alluding to personal and professional indiscretions on the part of Mr Joffe (Joffe, 2019). I was then approached by an associate of Mr Joffe, in their personal capacity, to analyse the linguistic content of the blog to determine the possible authorship. Before delving into the analysis of the defamatory blog, the author will present the theoretical underpinnings that informed their methodology.

## Literature review and theoretical underpinnings

In this section, the author will give a concise overview of the literature as it pertains to forensic linguistics and to this particular case, as well as look at the theoretical framework that informed the methodology. They will begin by describing the origins of forensic linguistics as a serious discipline.

### A brief history of forensic linguistics

Even though the term 'forensic linguistics' is a fairly recent development (Coulthard, Grant & Kredens, 2011), the idea that there is a relationship between language and the law has been around since ancient times. Even the Christian Bible has been the subject of linguistic disputes, particularly concerning the authorship of all the New Testament letters of St Paul and the Book of Hebrews. Shakespeare, too, has not been spared the gaze of academic suspicion, as it is believed that he might not have been the sole author of his works, and that Bacon and Marlowe contributed to, or completely wrote, a number of his plays. It has even been intimated that Shakespeare could be a *nom-de-plume* for a group of writers (Holmes, 1994). Yet the term 'forensic linguistics' only really came to prominence in 1968 when a Swedish linguist named Jan Svartvik published *The Evans statements: A case for forensic linguistics* (Svartvik, 1968), wherein he showed that the four statements made by Timothy Evans to the police regarding the murders of his wife and daughters "had a grammatical style measurably different from that of uncontested parts of a statement and thus a new area of forensic expertise was born" (Coulthard & Johnson, 2007:5). Timothy Evans was posthumously pardoned 16 years after being executed for murder in 1950 (Coulthard et al., 2011).

The dawn of the internet revolutionised the field of forensic linguistics. Arguably, the first and most famous example of computers and the internet, in conjunction with language analysis, aided investigators is the Unabomber case. Between 1978 and 1995, Theodore Kaczynski, commonly known as 'the Unabomber', conducted numerous bombing attacks on universities and airlines. He said he would only cease his bombing campaign if his 35 000-word, anti-industrialist manifesto was published in major newspapers. When FBI agents searched Kaczynski's home, they found hundreds of documents authored by Kaczynski, which had never been published. When the documents were analysed alongside the manifesto, it was found that there were several linguistic features and expressions that appeared in both documents; and despite some features being more distinctive than others, the prosecution put forward the argument that "the more common words and phrases being used by Kaczynski became distinctive when used in combination with each other" (Coulthard & Johnson, 2007:162-163). This notion – that each person uses language differently and those differences can be analysed – is the basis of any forensic linguistic analysis, especially when a person is attempting to present themself as someone else or to hide their true identity.

## Online anonymity and cryptolects

A primary factor when investigating online communication within a forensic linguistic context, as discussed by Crystal (2011), is the issue of anonymity. Sociolinguists have always emphasised the importance of contextual factors that motivate or inform what language is used. Factors such as age, gender, class and ethnicity are considered crucial pieces of information, yet the internet is a platform where identities can be hidden, as participants can conceal their identities, so any disclosed information should be treated with suspicion. Even distinctions – such as whether the user is male or female, or a native or non-native user of a language – can be obfuscated. Admittedly, the internet is not the first medium of communication to allow anonymity, but it is the first to allow it on such an unprecedented scale and in so many different media, especially chatrooms, blogs and social networks. This normalisation of anonymity has resulted in an uptick in a number of anti-social behaviours.

> Operating behind a false persona seems to make people less inhibited: they may feel emboldened to talk more and in different ways from their real-world linguistic repertoire. They must also expect to receive messages from others who are likewise less inhibited, and be prepared for negative outcomes. There are obvious inherent risks in talking to someone we do not know, and instances of harassment, insulting or aggressive language, and subterfuge are commonplace. (Crystal, 2011:14)

It could be asked why so much sociolinguistic background is relevant to forensic linguistics. Coulthard et al. (2011:536) explain that sociolinguistic findings can be attributed to certain social variables that can greatly aid in forensic linguistic casework, since the linguist has to ensure that potentially pertinent features are individual, i.e., idiolectal, rather than dialectal, sociolectal, genderlectal, etc. This 'idiolect' is defined by the *Oxford Concise Dictionary of Linguistics* (Matthews, 1997:169) as "the speech or 'dialect' of an individual", which differs from 'dialect', which is defined as "any distinct variety of a language, especially one spoken in a specific part of a country or other geographical area" (Matthews, 1997:96). The idiolect is a central theme permeating authorship attribution that takes the view that "every native speaker has their own distinct and individual version of the language they speak and write, their own *idiolect* and the assumption that this *idiolect* will manifest itself through distinctive and idiosyncratic choices in texts" (Coulthard, 2004:431).

## Stylistic analysis of text

To tease out the writer's idiolect from a text, it is necessary to do a stylistic analysis, explained by McMenamin (2010) as the study of style in a language. He further divides this into two sections, namely literary stylistics and linguistic stylistics. Literary stylistics concerns itself with the adherence or non-adherence to grammar rules and appropriateness; and linguistic stylistics is the analysis of observed style markers used by groups and individuals. McMenamin (2002) states that successful authorship identification in the analysis of style of written language hinges on the two principles of inherent variability in language: (1) no two writers of a language write in exactly the same way; and (2) no individual writer writes the same way all the time. The results of stylistic analysis may be used for: (1) determination of resemblance of questioned writings to a canon of known writings; (2) elimination or identification of one or more suspect authors; and lastly (3) determination that the data can result in neither elimination nor identification. That these linguistic features are present in unique combinations in the repertoire of every language user means that underlying patterns of use can be empirically established to make identification or exclusion of authorship possible. Hubbard (1995:57) elaborates further as he describes these features as being "more like subconscious, automatic habits that develop and become typical of different individuals", much like idiosyncratic paralinguistic features and body language. The reasons a writer chooses one linguistic form over another is the result of individual preference or habit and the task to be performed. Therefore, a writer makes choices from a variety of alternatives found within a large common stock of linguistic forms (McMenamin, 2002).

However, there are times when a writer has to consider consciously which forms to use, since communicatively competent users are able to change their style of writing, depending on the situation, as they are aware that language is context sensitive (Hubbard, 1995).

## Language variation

A salient feature of both dialect and idiolect is linguistic variation, where language usage changes over time or according to differing sociolinguistic contexts. Olsson (2008) applies variation directly to a forensic context when he talks about 'intra-author variation' and 'inter-author variation'. Intra-author variation refers to the ways in which an author's text differs from another text written by the same author, whereas inter-author variation refers to the ways texts vary between different authors. Olsson (2008:34) discusses eight different causes of intra-author variation, which have relevance when selecting texts for analysis, namely: (1) genre; (2) text type (3) fiction vs non-fiction; (4) private vs public texts; (5) time lapse; (6) disguise; (7) changes in circumstance, and (8) sociometric parameters. However, in the case under review, the only cause of variation that could have any bearing is time lapse since the website content was written over an eight-month period: if some time has passed between posts, and there has been a change in circumstances, this may be reflected in the language used. The defamatory website used language that is closer to spoken language than to what would be considered normal written language, as is the case with a great deal of online language use (Crystal, 2007). As a broad generalisation, spoken language is characterised by shorter clauses and a lower ratio of lexical to grammatical words, whereas written language uses longer clauses and has a higher lexical density (Coulthard, 2005). Writing style is generally informed by the language appropriate for certain genres, periods and contexts; and, just like spoken style, writing style also shares the social context connection. Writers and speakers tend to use recurrent choices, quite often a subconscious habit of choosing one form over another. Although McMenamin (2002) was not referring directly to the language of digital communication, it is possible to attach his notion of recurrent choices to the language of blogs, tweets, Facebook updates, etc., for example, 'you' / 'u' / 'ya' (Crystal, 2007), where all three forms are considered correct, and are acceptable, depending on the addressee. It is the variation within the norm that is of interest to this case. McMenamin (2002:110) talks of two types of choices: "variation within the norm and deviation from the norm". Variation within the norm means choices that conform to the norms of prescriptive grammar, or which are considered correct. Deviation from the norm refers to choices that would be considered grammatically incorrect. "The norm itself must be defined in order for it to be used as the standard for identifying variation within it or deviation from it" (McMenamin, 2002:110). He further asserts that prescriptive norms are especially helpful in authorship studies, as they can be the basis for describing variation. Which forms speakers and writers of a community use can be counted vis-à-vis possible alternate forms, i.e., how often certain forms are used and in which specific linguistic and social circumstances (McMenamin, 2002:116). These variations are often the source of the chosen style markers needed to attribute (or not attribute) authorship.

## Style markers

Exactly what constitutes a reliable style marker and how to identify it, especially when one is dealing with a relatively short text, is still a matter of debate (Grant & Baker, 2001). Style markers can be categorised as character-based, word-based, sentence-based, document-based, structural, or syntactic. A few examples of style markers include: function word usage (common adverbs, auxiliary verbs, conjunctions, prepositions and pronouns); word collocations; sentence length, and punctuation. However, Baayen et al. (2000) point out that style markers may still be sensitive to differences in genre and topic, especially when the text corpus is small. Grant and Baker (2001) discuss the characteristics of a reliable style marker and how it can be identified without falling into the trap of overgeneralisation. Since authorship attribution is a classification problem, it leads to the conundrum of: "What stylistic features can discriminate between these texts by different authors?" (Grant & Baker, 2001:68). The style markers in which the author is most interested for this study are punctuation and spelling. Both are useful when analysing online communication, as it is a medium that encourages creative usage of spelling and punctuation (Chaski, 2001) A few ways to analyse the use and non-use of punctuation marks are to count the frequency of use within a text, look at where the punctuation marks are used and whether the author has any idiosyncratic uses of punctuation marks. However, Chaski (2005:5) adds to this by stating that punctuation "has only really been successful when combined on its own with an understanding of its syntactic role in a text." Olsson (2008) describes using punctuation as a style marker as being particularly useful when dealing with short texts, as it is highly probable that the number of punctuation devices will be greater than the number of any single word; and they are likely to occur in sufficient quantities to be counted.

In modern texts, particularly those in digitally mediated communication, with its creative uses of punctuation (Crystal, 2011), there is "a great deal of optionality in how an author chooses to use these grammatical characters" (Grieve, 2005:19). Crystal (2011) describes how, in online communication, dashes are used to show a change in direction of thought, dots are used to express incompleteness, and commas are used to show pauses in rhythm. Moreover, when dealing with online communication, it is necessary to move beyond the traditional set of punctuation marks (full stops, commas, question marks, etc.) to include symbols such as #, @ and carets (^), as well as emoticons, such as smilies (☺), which may perform punctuation duty (Crystal, 2011).

Both spelling and punctuation have been used as style markers in high-profile authorship attribution cases. In the legal dispute between Facebook founder, Mark Zuckerberg, and Paul Ceglia over Ceglia's claim to part ownership of Facebook in July 2011, Professor Gerald McMenamin was asked to analyse known Zuckerberg emails against questioned emails, purportedly from Zuckerberg to Ceglia. McMenamin's report showed that he had analysed 11 style markers and, of those 11, three were spelling and two were punctuation, namely apostrophes and suspension points (ellipses). In the questioned Zuckerberg texts, there appears to be a number of errors regarding apostrophes: doesnt, parents (meaning parents'), sites (site's = contraction for 'site is') and sites (site's = possession), whereas in the known Zuckerberg texts, all contractions and possessives are used correctly. The second punctuation style marker that was analysed was suspension points. In the questioned text, there is one example of suspension points and the points are spaced (" ... I've been tweaking the search engine today") whereas, in the known Zuckerberg texts, there are three examples of suspension points, and they are not spaced (1) ("online as quickly as I can..."), (2) ("So let me know..."), (3) ("boxes ... there") (McMenamin, 2011).

## Aspects of a qualitative analysis

Given the nature of this authorship attribution case, where the author is examining a relatively short text, and there is the possibility of more than one author, a qualitative method was chosen for the analysis. A qualitative study looks at what forms are used and how and why they are used (Johnstone, 2000). However, qualitative analysis within forensic linguistics has been criticised for not being sufficiently scientific. Chaski (2005:2) argues that "[w]ithout the databases to ground the significance of stylistic features, the examiner's intuition about the significance of stylistic features can lead to methodological subjectivity and bias." McMenamin (2002:129) concedes that a qualitative analysis on its own will not achieve an "absolute conclusion about any kind of indirect evidence, like a set of known and questioned writing". Despite that, a qualitative assessment is still relevant for the following three reasons: (1) a qualitative analysis is the first step in order to discover, describe and categorise relevant linguistic features within a text; (2) qualitative evidence is far more demonstrable in a court of law than quantitative evidence, particularly if it precedes that quantitative evidence; and (3) the non-mathematical nature of qualitative analysis "will appeal to the structured sense of probability held by judges and juries" (McMenamin, 2002:129).

Qualitative data can be collected and evaluated using numerous different methods and it does not have to be numerical; and even if it is numerical, it is not always necessary or possible to conduct a statistical evaluation (Olsson, 2008). This is particularly true when analysing texts from online communication where the frequency of features may be too small, as could be seen from McMenamin's work on the Zuckerberg/Ceglia case discussed earlier, which was criticised by Chaski for being 'unscientific'. Furthermore, as expressed by McMenamin, (2002:131), there is an argument that says that "while linguistic data frequently present countable variables, sometimes the linguistic significance of an identified variable is not captured by counting, or a variable is linguistically significant, but it does not occur regularly enough to be meaningfully counted." To give the qualitative analysis less of a subjective feel, the author made use of the Scientific Working Group for Forensic Document Examination (SWGDOC, 2022) scale. McMenamin (2002:124) states that "conclusions regarding authorship are stated in terms of identification or exclusion on a five-, seven-, nine-point continuum" scale, which has been accepted by the American Society for Testing and Materials (ASTM); alternatively, one could employ a similar scale developed by the Scientific Working Group for Forensic Document Examination (McMenamin, 2002:124; SWGDOC, 2022) to present conclusions regarding resemblance between known and questioned documents. Table 12.1 breaks down the descriptors and presents the criteria needed to draw a conclusion. It is a nine-point scale, where nine would result in a positive identification if all criteria were met. Bands six, seven and eight also positively identify the questioned text but allow for some variance, as would be expected when analysing texts. The assigning of a band five would indicate that it was not possible to reach a conclusion due to inconclusive or insufficient data. Bands two, three and four effectively eliminate the suspected author due to too many inconsistencies, even though the 'suspect' authors' writing shares some features with those in the disputed text; and band one is a definite elimination. The author will be reaching their conclusions regarding the similarities between the defamatory blog and the known writings using this particular band scale.

**TABLE 12.1**  Criteria for conclusions on authorship questions (SWGDOC)

| | Resemblance<br>Questioned vs Known | Criteria | Consistency<br>Questioned v Questioned |
|---|---|---|---|
| 9 | Identification<br>(did write) | • Substantial significant similarities in the range of variation.<br>• No significant dissimilarities.<br>• No limitations present: non-occurrence of variables, dissimilarities, quantity of writing. | Definite<br>(one writer) |
| 8 | Highly Probable<br>(did write) | • Substantial significant similarities in the range of variation.<br>• No significant dissimilarities.<br>• Limitations are present: non-occurrence of variables, dissimilarities, quantity of writing. | Highly Probable<br>(one writer) |
| 7 | Probable<br>(did write) | 1. Some significant similarities in the range of variation.<br>2. No significant dissimilarities.<br>3. Limitations are present: non-occurrence of variables, dissimilarities, individualising characteristics, quantity of writing. | Probable<br>(one writer) |
| 6 | Indications<br>(did write) | • Few significant similarities in the range of variation.<br>• No significant dissimilarities.<br>• Limitations may be present: non-occurrence of variables, dissimilarities, individualising characteristics, quantity of writing. | Indications<br>(one writer) |
| 5 | No Conclusion<br>(inconclusive) | • Insufficient significant similarities in the range of variation.<br>• Insufficient significant dissimilarities in range of variation.<br>• Limitations may be present: non-occurrence of variables, individualising characteristics, quantity of writing.<br>• There may be similarities and dissimilarities. | No Conclusion<br>(inconclusive) |
| 4 | Indications<br>(did not write) | 1. Few significant dissimilarities in the range of variation.<br>2. Limitations may be present: non-occurrence of variables, individualising characteristics, quantity of writing.<br>3. There may be similarities. | Indications<br>(more than one writer) |
| 3 | Probable<br>(did not write) | 1. Some significant dissimilarities in the range of variation.<br>2. Limitations may be present, associated with: non-occurrence of variables, individualising characteristics, quantity of writing.<br>3. There may be similarities. | Probable<br>(more than one writer) |

| | Resemblance Questioned vs Known | Criteria | Consistency Questioned v Questioned |
|---|---|---|---|
| 2 | Highly Probable (did not write) | 1. Substantial significant dissimilarities in range of variation. <br> 2. Limitations are present: non-occurrence of variables, individualising characteristics, quantity of writing. <br> 3. There may be similarities. | Highly Probable (more than one writer) |
| 1 | Elimination (did not write) | 1. Substantial significant dissimilarities in range of variation. <br> 2. No limitations present: individualising characteristics, quantity of writing. <br> 3. There may be non-occurring variables. <br> 4. There may be similarities. | Definite (more than one writer) |

# Method

This section describes the practical procedures followed in the qualitative analysis. It starts with how the features were identified and then categorised, then moves on to discuss the descriptors used to describe the degree of possibility that can be attributed to each of the suspect authors. The now defunct website, 'graemejoffe-exposed.com', had a linguistic content of 2 670 words, and was divided into nine distinct sections written between November 2014 and July 2015. Mr Joffe named three potential authors of the blog, and I was tasked to ascertain whether one or more of those suspected authors could have written the blog entries. All three of the potential authors had attacked Mr Joffe online and were associated with a large media house that produces sport magazines. Even though Mr Joffe names the three potential authors in his book, *Sport: Greed and Betrayal: Wanted for Crimes against Journalism* (2019), I have chosen to refer to them in this article as Suspect Author 1, Suspect Author 2, and Suspect Author 3. To obtain known writings from the three suspected authors, I mined their public and open Twitter accounts and was able to obtain the following data:

- Suspect Author 1 (3 252 words)
- Suspect Author 2 (2 549 words)
- Suspect Author 3 (2 776 words)

My task was to analyse the internal linguistic structure of the website vis-à-vis the known Twitter writings of the three suspected authors with the aim of identifying or excluding the possible authors of the website.

Before doing any comparative analysis, it is important to deconstruct the defamatory website in question.

## Overview of the website

The website consisted of 2 670 words divided into the following nine subsections:

- Text 1: Is this the end for Joffers my boy?
- Text 2: Who has naughty Joffers been meeting with? | Graeme Joffe
- Text 3: Hello everyone, my name is Graeme Joffe and i've got a gambling addiction | Graeme Joffe
- Text 4: Where is Graemeatticus Joffertis | Graeme Joffe
- Text 5: Who is Graeme Joffe's "Deep throat"? | Graeme Joffe
- Text 6: Who is picking up Graeme Joffe's bills | Graeme Joffe
- Text 7: Amateur Joffe Embarrassed on Twitter | Graeme Joffe
- Text 8: Even High Court Judge Slams Joffe
- Text 9: THE TRUTH
- Text 10: Hamba Kahle

Table 12.2 is an overview of the website regarding the word count, number of sentences, average sentence length, and average word length for each of the sections of the website. Text 2: *Who has naughty Joffers been meeting with? | Graeme Joffe* has not been included as it is only 14 words.

**TABLE 12.2**  Quantitative overview

|  | Txt 1 | Txt 3 | Txt 4 | Txt 5 | Txt 6 | Txt 7 | Txt 8 | Txt 9 | Txt 10 |
|---|---|---|---|---|---|---|---|---|---|
| Word count | 427 | 273 | 143 | 119 | 191 | 242 | 295 | 654 | 291 |
| Sentences | 19 | 10 | 8 | 7 | 9 | 15 | 12 | 29 | 12 |
| Average sentence length | 22.47 | 27.3 | 18.87 | 17 | 21.22 | 16.13 | 24.58 | 22.55 | 24.25 |
| Average word length | 4.39 | 4.46 | 4.53 | 4.78 | 4.58 | 4.57 | 4.59 | 5 | 4.62 |

One feature of this particular case is the possibility that of more than one author, and the observable variations regarding average sentence length point to that possibility. This, together with the fact that that there are different styles of writing within the different subsections, along with the relatively low word count, convinced me to focus my analysis on the stylistic aspects rather than doing a stylometric analysis.

I analysed the linguistic features used within the questioned website against the linguistic features found in the three Twitter accounts to see if any of the linguistic features used by the three potential authors matched the linguistic features exhibited on the website. To perform this task, the author did the following: (1) they mined the known writing for features (style markers) that appeared to be idiosyncratic; and (2) they looked for similar style markers in the three sets of Twitter feeds. Table 12.3 shows the different style markers and an example of each.

**TABLE 12.3**   Chosen style markers

| Style marker | Example |
| --- | --- |
| Multiple exclamation marks | This is absolute gold !!!! |
| Multiple question marks | What do I do now???? |
| Double quotation marks | "Joffers my booooooooiiii" |
| Brackets | (Drunk in love) |
| Hyphens | Demi-celebrity |
| Dashes | Fated adventures – Township TV |
| Capitalisation | PUBLIC SERVICE ANNOUNCEMENT |
| Capitalisation+exclamation marks | THAT IS A FACT!!! |
| Word+no space+elliptical dots | Real name – Colin Webster.......... |
| Word+space+elliptical dots | Last minute .... Is this an Omen |

## Stylistic analysis

In this section, the author will show examples of the chosen style markers from the defamatory website and corresponding examples from three potential authors' known writing. Table 12.4 to Table 12.12 show examples of these.

**TABLE 12.4**   Multiple exclamation marks

| Website | Suspect 1 | Suspect 2 | Suspect 3 |
| --- | --- | --- | --- |
| THAT IS A FACT!!!!! <br><br> that his attornies have most likely told him he's on the road to a big klap!!!! <br><br> What can be more embarrassing than being called out by one of your own!!!! <br><br> How much does it cost to retain the services of legal firm Norton Rose Fulbright. Quite a lot!!!! | This is absolute gold!!!! <br><br> If its not a worldie it's not a goal! Courtinho!!!! <br><br> HENDERSON ARE YOU MAD!!!!! WORLDIE!!!! <br><br> The Mother City breeds them champs!!! <br><br> A car just blew up outside my Cape Town office!!!!!!! <br><br> BOOOOOOO-OOOOKKKKKEEEEE!!!! <br><br> Get in Courtinho!!! | None | Sorry - I remembered wrong (age, you know) - it's the other way - roar is US!!! <br><br> Yes. Like the fact that our geriatrics will finally retire. Hopefully!! <br><br> This time you are doubling up in another way :-)- good luck!!! <br><br> Just tuned in to watch Sykes score a great try for the Kings!!! Yoh, Yoh, and another by Acker!! |

**TABLE 12.5**  Multiple question marks

| Website | Suspect 1 | Suspect 2 | Suspect 3 |
|---|---|---|---|
| What do I do now????? | None | None | Hmmm ... how remote can it be with you lurking in the shadows???<br>How did Ledecky do that??!?? |

**TABLE 12.6**  Quotation marks

| Website | Suspect 1 | Suspect 2 | Suspect 3 |
|---|---|---|---|
| "Joffers my booooooooiiiiii"<br>"hit the nail on the head"<br>"It was a dark and stormy night................"<br>"good old days"<br>"services"<br>"confidential"<br>"plagiarising sports stories and including made up quotes".<br>"made up stories, twisting facts and using other journalist's quotes in his own articles was regarded as poor journalism".<br>himself the "Thuli Madonsela" of SA sport<br>"friends"<br>"Deepthroat"? | "On the run"<br>"Move along, nothing to see here"<br>"running like an epileptic giraffe". | None | So, an anagram of "diaspora fund" is "pounds afraid" ... hmmm "dollar kakstorm" would have been more apt?<br>... "Jump faaar!!"<br>Anagrams for "diaspora legacy" ... "payola disgrace", "cagier payloads" and "social paygrade".<br>"I really am clean"; "So pls don't put me on trial" |

**TABLE 12.7**  Use of brackets

| Website | Suspect 1 | Suspect 2 | Suspect 3 |
|---|---|---|---|
| (THIS IS A WELL KNOWN FACT IN THE INDUSTRY)<br>(The Rude Awakening, Breakfast Xpress) | (forced on meyer)<br>(Drunk in love)<br>(or inconsistency thereof)<br>(who were simply doing their job) | (at least until the first whistle goes in said semi)<br>2 massive (legal tackles) and<br>(2 col wing & 1 Zim-born prop) | Sorry - I remembered wrong (age, you know) - it's the other way - roar is US!!!<br>SA is sporting - gave him a head start (and probably no load-shedding)<br>The fans should sue both organisations (if they can)<br>(sorry - good luck)<br>For about R2400 (maybe more these days) smokers |

**TABLE 12.8** Use of hyphens

| Website | Suspect 1 | Suspect 2 | Suspect 3 |
|---|---|---|---|
| demi-celebrity<br>ill-fated adventures<br>high-life he<br>hand-outs<br>Joffe's co-ownership<br>Joffers-My-Boy<br>taking handouts from | sounds ominously Mugabe-esque<br>Ever-improving combo | one-off.<br>semi-final<br>goal-kicking ritual (2 col wing & 1 Zim-born prop)<br>Top 2 try-scorers in Bok set-up & Zim-born<br>@RugbyChampship play-offs | Everybody was kung fu-fighting?<br>the Lima Has-Beens Games<br>leopard-crawling!!!<br>(and probably no loadshedding)<br>Star Wars wasn't a docu-drama!!<br>hard-working |

**TABLE 12.9** Use of dashes (dashes appear as hyphens on Twitter)

| Website | Suspect 1 | Suspect 2 | Suspect 3 |
|---|---|---|---|
| fated adventures – Township TV<br>His sources are well placed – obviously disgruntled<br>real name – Colin Webster.....<br>are doing a service – you are dupes<br>ANNOUNCEMENT – After living the Sandton | LEWIS - DOWN-TOWN (OFFICIAL MUSI...: http://you-tu.be/JGhoLcsr8GA - This is<br>(who were simply doing their job) here - http://dai-lym.ai/1L8gs8g<br>the BET Awards - http://bet.us/1BQwToO<br>Mealamu - 175 Super Rugby matches | MOM - 26 carries<br>White Buffalo once called - 2 his dismay - baby Joseph<br>The power of the individual - Serge could do<br>The @LionsRugbyUnion - officially the team I have most enjoyed watching this season - and that includes | Ag, shame - one of those hardship tours!<br>Sorry - I remembered wrong (age, you know) - it's the other way - roar is US!!!<br>Ahhh - so that's what happened - the Boks and Ikeys got their fixtures mixed up! |

**TABLE 12.10** Capitalisation

| Website | Suspect 1 | Suspect 2 | Suspect 3 |
|---|---|---|---|
| THIS IS A WELL KNOWN FACT IN THE INDUSTRY<br>THAT IS A FACT!!!!!<br>THERE IS NO PLACE IN JOURNALISM FOR GRAEME JOFFE!!!!<br>PUBLIC SERVICE ANNOUNCEMENT<br>GRAHAMSTOWN<br>IS THIS THE END FOR JOFFERS MY BOY!!!!<br>PUBLIC WARNING | MACKLEMORE & RYAN LEWIS - DOWNTOWN (OFFICIAL MUSI...:<br>HENDERSON ARE YOU MAD!!!!! WORLDIE!!!!<br>BOOOOOOOOOOOOKKKK-KKEEEEE!!!! | None | None |

**TABLE 12.11**   Capitalisation+exclamation marks

| Website | Suspect 1 | Suspect 2 | Suspect 3 |
|---|---|---|---|
| THAT IS A FACT!!!!!<br><br>THERE IS NO PLACE IN JOURNALISM FOR GRAEME JOFFE!!!! | HENDERSON ARE YOU MAD!!!!! WORLDIE!!!!<br><br>BOOOOOOOOOOOOKKKKK-KEEEEE!!!! | None | None |

**TABLE 12.12**   Word+no space+elliptical dots

| Website | Suspect 1 | Suspect 2 | Suspect 3 |
|---|---|---|---|
| real name – Colin Webster.....<br>*Hello Graeme.....*<br>"It was a dark and stormy night................"<br>"hit the nail on the head" confirming what we all already knew........................ | Read why I say this, here...<br>Chelsea and they're at home.<br>...against teams that kick international gig in a consultant capacity...<br>Steven Gerrard he hates the blue shite too... | in 2015...revolt | None |

# Discussion

It should be noted that, even though the language of blogs and the language used on Twitter are both examples of online digital communication, they are slightly different genres, and the writing styles can be different. Each tweet can be a maximum of 140 characters, whereas blogs are composed of full paragraphs. Despite these differences, the writing styles of the analysed texts shared similar features and were, for the most part, spontaneous, unedited, and conversational in style. All the chosen style markers are commonly found in Tweets and blogs, where the non-standard use of punctuation is common and deliberate. Table 12.13 here shows the chosen style markers and how often they occurred.

**TABLE 12.13**   Quantitative occurrence of style markers

| Feature | Website | Suspect 1 | Suspect 2 | Suspect 3 |
|---|---|---|---|---|
| Multiple exclamation marks | 14 | 19 | 0 | 37 |
| Multiple question marks | 1 | 0 | 0 | 7 |
| Double quotation marks | 11 | 3 | 0 | 4 |
| Brackets | 2 | 5 | 3 | 5 |
| Hyphens | 7 | 2 | 11 | 12 |
| Dashes | 6 | 6 | 9 | 28 |
| Capitalisation | 7 | 3 | 0 | 0 |
| Capitalisation+exclamation marks | 3 | 3 | 0 | 0 |
| Word+no space+elliptical dots | 4 | 4 | 1 | 1 |
| Word+space+elliptical dots | 0 | 0 | 0 | 31 |

## Conclusions

Even though all three potential authors used most of the style markers, two stand out for closer scrutiny, namely Capitalisation+exclamation marks and Word+no space+elliptical dots. These two constructions are quite unusual, and the fact that Suspect 1 used both indicates the possibility of him being one of the authors of the defamatory blog. Regarding the SWGDOC scale, the author would rate Suspect 1 at level 7 – probable as the main author, as he or she meets the criteria for that band score: (1) some significant similarities in range of variation; and (2) no significant dissimilarities. There is still a fair amount of difference in writing styles within the original defamatory blog, suggesting the possibility of multiple authorship; and this prevents awarding a full band 9 on SWGDOC. Even though the evidence points most strongly to Suspect 1 being the main author of the defamatory blog, the stylistic differences in the different blog entries do point to the possibility that other authors may have had some input.

## References


Baayen, H., Tweedie, FJ., Neijt, AH., Halteren, H. & Van Krebbers, L. 2000. Back to the cave of shadows: Stylistic fingerprints in authorship attribution. The ALLC/ACH 2000 Conference. University of Glasgow. Unpublished paper.

Chaski, C.E. 2001. Empirical evaluations of language-based author identification techniques. *Forensic Linguistics*, 8(1):1-65. https://doi.org/10.1558/sll.2001.8.1.1

Chaski, C.E. 2005. Who's at the keyboard? Authorship attribution in digital evidence investigations. *International Journal of Digital Evidence*, 4(1):1-13.

Coulthard, M. 2004. Author identification, idiolect, and linguistic uniqueness. *Applied Linguistics*, 25(4):431-447. https://doi.org/10.1093/applin/25.4.431

Coulthard, M. 2005. Some forensic applications of descriptive linguistics. *Veredas: Revista de Estudos Linguísticos*, 9(1-2):9-28. https://www.ufjf.br/revistaveredas/files/2009/12/artigo016.pdf [Accessed 10 December 2022].

Coulthard, M. 2010. In my opinion. In: M. Coulthard & A. Johnson (eds.). *The Routledge handbook of forensic linguistics*. New York: Routledge. 508-522.

Coulthard, M., Grant, T. & Kredens, K. 2011. Forensic linguistics. In: R. Wodak, B. Johnstone & P.E. Kerswill (eds.). *The SAGE handbook of sociolinguistics*. London: Sage. 529-544. https://doi.org/10.4135/9781446200957.n36

Coulthard, M. & Johnson, A. 2007. *An introduction to forensic linguistics: Language in evidence*. London: Routledge. https://doi.org/10.4324/9780203969717

Coulthard, M. & Johnson, A. (eds.). 2010. *The Routledge handbook of forensic linguistics*. New York: Routledge. https://doi.org/10.4324/9780203855607

Crystal, D. 2007. *Language and the internet*. Cambridge: Cambridge University Press.

Crystal, D. 2011. *Internet linguistics: A student guide*. New York: Routledge. https://doi.org/10.4324/9780203830901

Grant, T.D. & Baker, K. 2001. Identifying reliable, valid markers of authorship: A response to Chaski. *International Journal of Speech Language and the Law*, 8(1):66-79.

Grieve, J.W. 2005. Quantitative authorship attribution: A history and an evaluation of techniques. Master's thesis. Burnaby, Canada: Simon Fraser University.

Holmes, D. 1994. Authorship attribution. *Computers and Humanities*, 28:87-106. https://doi.org/10.1007/BF01830689

Hubbard, E.H. 1995. Linguistic fingerprinting? A case study in forensic stylometrics. *South African Journal of Linguistics: supplement*, 26:55-72. https://doi.org/10.1080/1011806 3.1995.9724005

Joffe, G. 2019. *Sport: GREED & BETRAYAL: Wanted for crimes against journalism.* Independently Published.

Johnstone, B. 2000. *Qualitative methods in sociolinguistics.* New York: Oxford University Press.

Lowman, S. 2015. Graeme Joffe shuts up shop, sings to US officials – here's why. *News24 / Business*, 31 July. https://www.news24.com/Fin24/graeme-joffe-shuts-up-shop-sings-to-us-officials-heres-why-20150731 [Accessed 10 December 2022].

Matthews, P.H. 1997. *Oxford concise dictionary of linguistics.* Oxford: Oxford University Press.

McMenamin, G. 2002. *Forensic linguistics: Advances in forensic stylistics.* Boca Raton: CRC Press. https://doi.org/10.1201/9781420041170

McMenamin, G.R. 2010. Forensic stylistics: Theory and practice of forensic stylistics. In: M. Coulthard & A. Johnson (eds.). *Routledge handbook of forensic linguistics.* New York: Routledge. 487-507.

McMenamin, G.R. 2011. Style Markers in QUESTIONED vis-à-vis KNOWN – *Zuckerberg Ceglia v Zuckerberg*, Case 1: 10-cv-00569-RJA-LGF, United States District Court Western District of New York.

Olsson, J. 2008. *Forensic linguistics: An introduction to language, crime and the law.* 2nd Edition. London: Continuum.

Svartvik, J. 1968. *The Evans statements: A case for forensic linguistics.* Vol. 20 of Gothenburg Studies in English. Gothenburg, Sweden: University of Göteborg.

SWGDOC (Scientific Working Group for Forensic Document Examination). 2022. SWGDOC E01-13: SWGDOC Standard for Examination of Handwritten Items. https://www.swgdoc.org/documents/SWGDOC%20Standard%20for%20Examination%20 of%20Handwritten%20Items.pdf [Accessed 13 December 2022].

# ABOUT THE CONTRIBUTORS

**Roger W. Shuy**, Distinguished Research Professor of Linguistics, Emeritus, Georgetown University (USA), founded and headed Georgetown's sociolinguistics PhD programme until he retired in 1996. He was one of the co-founders of The American Association of Applied Linguistics and the annual conference on *New Ways of Analyzing Variation.* In 2009, he was elected Fellow of the Linguistic Society of America; and in 2017, he was awarded that organisation's Lifetime Service Award. Based on his consulting and testimony in some 500 law cases, he has published 15 books about linguistics and law. He also founded and served as series editor of Oxford University Press's scholarship series, Language and Law.

**Wellman Kondowe** is a Senior Lecturer in Linguistics at Mzuzu University (Malawi) and the current Head of the Department of Language, Cultural, and Creative Studies. He is a holder of a master's degree and a PhD in Applied Linguistics, both obtained from Central China Normal University, where he graduated in 2014 and 2020 respectively. He holds a bachelor's degree in education from the University of Malawi (2009). His research interest is in forensic linguistics and applied language studies. He has published extensively in different international journals. Some of his important publications include 'Towards the principle of believability: A new sociopragmatic model in forensic settings' and 'A study of intentional insincerity in Malawian criminal justice: Witnesses' discursive strategies'. Both appear in *Language and the law: Global perspectives in forensic linguistics from Africa and beyond* (2002), edited by M.K. Ralarara, R.H. Kaschula and G. Heydon (Stellenbosch: African Sun Media). He is currently co-editing a volume on multilingualism, to be published by Routledge (Taylor & Francis).

**George Mtanga** studied English and African Languages and Linguistics in the Department of Language, Cultural and Creative Studies at Mzuzu University (Malawi) under the supervision of Dr Wellman Kondowe. As a junior (early-career) researcher, he has developed a growing interest in forensic linguistics, an interest inspired by the influential earlier works of scholars such as Roger Shuy and Peter Tiersma, who provided a marked departure from traditional linguistics. George Mtanga's chapter in this book is his first academic publication.

**Paul Svongoro** is an Andrew W. Mellon Postdoctoral Research Fellow at the University of the Western Cape (South Africa) and a Senior Lecturer at Africa University (Zimbabwe). His research interests are in the broad area of applied language studies, including forensic linguistics, corpus-based translation studies, academic literacy, and professional communication. He has completed several language-related consultancy projects and has published widely in journals accredited to the Department of Higher Education in South Africa. The journals include *Per Linguam, Communitas, Southern African Linguistics and Applied Language Studies* (SALALS), *The South African Journal of African Languages* (SAJAL) and the *Journal of Literary Studies.*

**Débora de Carvalho Figueiredo** holds a graduate degree in Law (1990), an MA (1996) and a PhD (2000) in Applied Linguistics. She is currently an Associate Professor of English at the Federal University of Santa Catarina (Brazil). She has published in the journals *Language and Law/Linguagem e Direito* (2014, 2017) and *Critical Discourse Studies* (2020); and in the books *Systemic functional linguistics and critical discourse analysis* (London: Continuum, 2004), *Language in the legal process* (London: Palgrave, 2002), and *Genre in a changing world* (Fort Collins: The WAC Clearinghouse/Parlor Press, 2009). Her research interests include issues of gender, power, class and identity in media and legal discourse.

**Ana Luiza Soares Barcelos** holds a bachelor's degree in Linguistics and English Language Literature from the Federal University of Santa Catarina (UFSC) and a Specialist Certificate in Penal Law and Criminology from Complexo de Ensino Renato Saraiva.

**Luiza Ferreira da Costa** has a teaching and bachelor's degree in English from the Federal University of Santa Catarina (2020), and a *lato sensu* Postgraduate Certificate in Criminal Law and Criminology from Faculdade CERS (2022). Currently, Luiza is conducting a critical analysis of judicial discourse for her master's work at the Graduate Program in English at the Federal University of Santa Catarina, with completion scheduled for 2024. She is also a member of NUGAL – Núcleo de Estudos de Gênero Através da Linguagem (Nucleus for Gender Studies through Language).

**Ndikaru wa Teresia** is a well-known activist for environmental and human rights' issues in Kenya. He has made a remarkable contribution to the rights of the oppressed people in Thika. He is a Senior Lecturer in the Department of Criminology and Legal Studies, and the Catholic Chaplain at The Technical University of Kenya, Nairobi. He obtained his BA Degree from Pontifical University of Urbaniana, Rome, Italy; a master's degree in Disaster Management from the University of Nairobi, and a PhD in Criminology from Kenyatta University. Dr Ndikaru is a prolific writer with several books to his name. He is widely published in reputable international, peer-reviewed journals.

**Zakeera Docrat** is an Andrew W. Mellon Foundation Postdoctoral Research Fellow in forensic/legal linguistics at the University of the Western Cape (UWC). Dr Docrat holds the following degrees: BA, BA Honours (*cum laude*), LLB, MA (*cum laude*) and PhD. In June 2021, Dr Docrat published her first book, titled *A handbook on legal languages and the quest for linguistic equality in South Africa and beyond.* She is an award-winning researcher who has published widely and presented at national and international conferences. Dr Docrat is Vice-Chairperson of the Indigenous Languages Action Forum (ILAF).

**Patricia Muraguri** is an Assistant Lecturer at Mbeya University of Science and Technology (Tanzania) and a PhD candidate at Moi University (Kenya). She holds a BEd (Hons) in Linguistics and Literature from Kenyatta University (Kenya), and an MA in Linguistics from the University of Dar es Salaam. Her interests include forensic linguistics, discourse analysis, sociolinguistics, and morphology. She is a member of the Language Association of Eastern Africa (LAEA).

**Emmanuel Satia** is a Commonwealth Scholar and a Lecturer in the Department of Literature, Linguistics, Foreign Languages and Film Studies, Moi University (Kenya). He holds a Diploma in Education (English and Swahili), a BA (Hons) in Linguistics and Literature, an MA in Linguistics and African Languages from the University of Nairobi (Kenya), and a PhD in Forensic Linguistics (Moi University/University of Leeds). His interests include forensic linguistics, corpus linguistics, discourse analysis and sociolinguistics. He serves as a member of the Editorial Board of *The University of Nairobi Journal of Language and Linguistics*, and of the journal *MwangawaLugha* of Moi University's Department of Kiswahili and other African Languages. He is also a co-founder of the Association of English Language Educators and Researchers (ASELER), of the relaunched Language Association of Eastern Africa (LAEA), and a member of the African Association of Forensic and Legal Linguistics (AAFLL).

**Boke Joyce Wambura** is a Lecturer at Tom Mboya University (Kenya). She holds a PhD in Linguistics from the University of Leeds (UK), an MA in Linguistics and a BEd (Hons) in Linguistics and Literature, both from Egerton University (Kenya). Her main areas of interest include language and gender, discourse analysis and female genital mutilation (FGM) studies. She is a member of the British Association of Applied Linguistics (BAAL), and a founding member of the Language Association of Eastern Africa (LAEA) and the Association of English Language Educators and Researchers (ASELER), Kenya.

**Sisanda Nkoala**, a Senior Lecturer in the Media Studies Department at the Cape Peninsula University of Technology, also serves as the Language and Transformation Coordinator for the Faculty of Informatics and Design at the institution. Her PhD in Rhetoric Studies from the University of Cape Town focuses on television news reports on crime and the South African criminal justice system. Before joining academia, she was a journalist and won an award for her work on missing children and the 2015/2016 #RhodesMustFall protests.

**Gilbert Francis Odhiambo** is a teacher of English language. He has a master's degree in Applied Linguistics from The Technical University of Kenya. The title of his dissertation is 'Terrorism threat notes: A corpus-based linguistic analysis of selected texts'. His research interest is in forensic linguistics.

**Daniel Ochieng Orwenjo** is an Associate Professor of Applied Linguistics and Director of the Centre for Language and Communication Studies of The Technical University of Kenya. He holds a Doctor of Philosophy degree (*magna cum laude*) from the University of Frankfurt, Germany. His main research interests revolve around the nexus between linguistics and other disciplines by, on the one hand, focusing on the application of linguistic knowledge in solving real life problems in other disciplines such as education, law, anthropology, sociology and psychology, and on using knowledge in these disciplines to solve linguistic problems.

**Rosette Sifa Vuninga** is an Andrew W. Mellon Postdoctoral Fellow at the University of the Western Cape's Centre for Humanities Research in Cape Town, South Africa. She is also a Doctoral Fellow of the 2020 African Peacebuilding Network (APN) of the Social Sciences Research Council (SSRC) and a member of the 2016 APN's Collaborative Research Group. Her PhD project focuses on ways in which ethnic and regional identities are experienced among the Congolese people of Cape Town. Vuninga's research is in the field of migration and explores issues related to transborder politics of identity and belonging, as well as gender politics in migrant networks. Research interests also include networks of violence, with a particular interest on aspects of gender, class and identity. Her publications include peer-reviewed journal articles, book chapters, a book review and working papers.

**Colin Michell** is a Lecturer in the General Studies Department at the Higher Colleges of Technology in the United Arab Emirates. He has a master's degree in Linguistics with a specialisation in forensic linguistics. He has consulted on several high-profile cases of disputed authorship in South Africa. Through the University of Exeter, he is currently in the final stages of a doctorate in education in which he is exploring the dangers of right-wing radicalisation as it applies to an educational setting. His academic interests include researching extremism, authorship attribution, plagiarism detection, TESOL, critical discourse analysis, critical testing, and sociolinguistics.

# INDEX

## N

# U

UNCRPD. *See* Convention on the Rights of Persons with Disabilities *under* United
    Nations
UNDP. *See* Development Programme *under* United Nations
UNPRPD. *See* Partnership on the Rights of Persons with Disabilities Project *under*
    United Nations
United Nations
    Convention on the Rights of Persons with Disabilities (UNCRPD)  56, 58, 60, 64, 65, 66
    Development Programme (UNDP)  60
    Partnership on the Rights of Persons with Disabilities Project (UNPRPD)  60

# V

victimhood, perceived  137-155, 216, 224
victimisation  226
    hierarchy of in the usage of terms  6, 148-152
    reporting of  54, 88, 180, 186, 189, 190, 191, 192, 194-196, 230
victims
    assistance of  55, 64, 229, 232
    death of  162, 227
    and language  x, 5, 79-87, 157, 227
    legitimate  124
violence against women  75, 78, 81, 92, 157, 159, 165, 167, 168, 169
    and children  6-7, 179-199
    *See also* female genital mutilation; marital rape

# W

warnings  15, 17-18, 20, 21, 22, 27, 28, 104, 174, 204, 205, 208, 214, 215-216, 217-218, 252
written opinions  6, 137-155